Howard Townsend, M.D.
of Albany,
1823-1867.

Historic Homes and Institutions

AND

Genealogical and Family History

OF

NEW YORK

BY

WILLIAM S. PELLETREAU, A. M.

Member of Long Island Historical Society; Author of "Old New York Houses,"
"Early Long Island Wills," "Records of Southampton, Long Island,"
"History of Smithtown, Long Island," etc , etc

"It is a thing of no small importance to possess the relics of our ancestors, to practice the same sacred rites, and to be buried by their side."—CICERO

ILLUSTRATED

Volume III

CLEARFIELD

Originally published
New York, 1907

Reprinted for Clearfield Company by
Genealogical Publishing Company
Baltimore, Maryland, 1998, 2011

ISBN, Volume III: 978-0-8063-4782-0
Four-volume set ISBN: 978-0-8063-4779-0

Made in the United States of America

Genealogical and Family History

THEODORE S. ROOSEVELT.

The eyes of the nation never turned with more anxious questioning to one man than to Theodore Roosevelt; they soon came to rest upon him with good will, confidence and trust. Under the administration of President McKinley the country had enjoyed over four years of marked growth, advancement and progress Through his kindly nature, his great diplomacy and powers of statescraft he had done more than any other individual to bring the whole country into harmony and unity, and had given it prestige among the great world powers. The marvelous hold which he had upon the affections of the people, east and west, north and south, was manifest in the universal grief which reached its culmination in the five minutes of absolute silence which prevailed throughout the land in every avenue of life as the hour for his burial arrived

And the people turned to their new ruler anxiously and yet with faith in their hearts, for he had proved his bravery on 'he San Juan hills, had manifested the purity and strength of his purpose in public office and in his earnest and purposeful way had shown himself to be the peer of some of the most gifted men of the nation He is, however, the youngest chief executive that has presided over the destinies of the United States, but since he has handled the reins of government he has shown a wonderful insight into public affairs of every description. The man of war has become the man of peace; the man of action has become the man of thought, his diplomacy has elicited the highest commendation; and while his great strength of purpose has in no wise diminished, he has directed it in different channels, having marked influence upon the public good.

President Roosevelt springs from one of the old and distinguished families of German origin. This family was one of considerable importance in Holland, as shown by the coat of armor, indicating the origin of the family. Arms, argent on a mount

Roosevelt.

vert, a rose bush with three roses ppr.; crest, three ostrich feathers per pale, gules and argent; motto, Qui plantavit curabit (the one who planted it will care for it). This is the same in substance as that borne on the arms of the State of Connecticut, viz., Qui transtulit sustinet (he who transplanted sustains).

Claes Martinzen Van Roosevelt, meaning Nicholas the son of Martin, of the Rosefield, who emigrated to America from Holland in 1654, was the first of the name in this country. His descendants intermarried with the Schuylers, Bogaerts, Provosts, Van Schaicks, De Peysters, Latrobes, Hoffmans, Barclays, Van Courtlandts, Lispenards, etc. The family early obtained an extensive tract of land in New York city, extending from Chatham street to the East river, lying between Pearl, Roosevelt and Catharine streets, or, as it was originally called, Ruger's old farm. Hence in this way and by its commercial enterprises it has become affluent. The family has been represented in Colonial and State affairs through every generation down to the present period, and owing to the achievements of the present representative of the family the name is as familiar to every schoolboy throughout the country as is that of Washington or Grant.

The wife of Claes Martinzen Van Roosevelt was Jannetje Samuels or Thomas, probably the latter.

Nicholas Roosevelt, fourth child of Claes and Jannetje Roosevelt, was baptized October 2, 1658, and married December 26, 1682, Heytje Jans, and who was an Alderman of New York, 1698 to 1701. He removed to Esopus, and died July 30, 1742.

Johannes Roosevelt, eldest child of Nicholas and Heytje (Jans) Roosevelt, was baptized February 27, 1689. He was assistant Alderman of New York from 1717 till 1727 and Alderman from 1730 until 1733 He married Heltje Sjverts. This name is also spelled Hyla Suerts in the Dutch records of New York. She was the daughter of Olphert Suerts, who married Margrieji Cloppers, born May 30, 1708, a daughter of Cornelius Jansen Cloppers.

Jacobus Roosevelt, fifth child of Johannes, was born August 14, 1724. He married Annetje Bogart, and his second wife was Elenora Thompson. The sixth of their seven children was Jacobus Roosevelt, who was born October 25, 1759, and died August 13, 1840. He was known as James I. Roosevelt, and was commissary during the war of the Revolution, giving his services gratuitously. "Getting supplies" for the Continental army became so impressed on his mind as to enter into his every-day transactions, and long after the war, whenever he went to market, as was the custom of the head of the family in those days, taking a servant along to carry the basket, he always referred to it as going for "supplies " He married Mary Van Schaick.

Cornelius Van Schaick Roosevelt, youngest child of Jacobus (2), was born January 30, 1794. From his father and grandfather he inherited a large fortune, and this he augmented by various successful financial ventures, becoming one of the richest men in New York. For many years he was engaged in the importation of hardware and plate glass. He was one of those who founded the Chemical Bank on the single principle of honesty, and that institution has never failed to pay its obligations in gold, and during the Civil war redeemed its notes at one time at $280 in greenbacks. He introduced in business the principle of giving no notes. Mr. Roosevelt married Margaret Barnhill, of Pennsylvania and of Scotch-Irish ancestry Her grandfather was Thomas Potts, a member of the Continental Congress. The issue of this marriage was: Weir, C. V. S., Jr , James A , Robert and Theodore (1st).

Theodore Roosevelt (1), youngest child of Cornelius Van Schaick Roosevelt and Margaret (Barnhill) Roosevelt, his wife, was born in New York city, September 29, 1831, and died there February 9, 1878. He joined the firm of Roosevelt & Company, glass importers, then located at No. 2 Maiden Lane, and continued in that business till 1876, when he established a banking house in partnership with his son at No. 32 Pine street. Mr Roosevelt was among the pioneers in the development of what was known as the up-town district of Manhattan island. He built an elegant residence on West Fifty-seventh street, and there he passed the last hours of his life.

At the time of his death Mr. Roosevelt was one of the three state commissioners of public charities, a position for which he was admirably fitted by his experience and his peculiar devotion to philanthropic enterprises. He was vice-president of the Union League Club and a member of the Century, St. Nicholas and various kindred organizations. When Arthur was supposed to be on the point of giving up the position of collector of the port of New York, attention was turned upon Mr. Roosevelt as a gentleman conspicuously fitted for it, and one who, it was thought, would discharge its functions to the advantage of the community and his own honor At first an opposition was made on account of his participation in an importing business from which some believed he had not entirely alienated himself He was tendered the position by President Hayes, but the senate, for the above-named reasons, failed to confirm the appointment

Mr. Roosevelt's charitable enterprises were so numerous and varied in character that it is difficult to refer to them all, but perhaps no more useful institution owes to him a share of its paternity than the Orthopaedic Hospital in Fifty-ninth street, near Ninth avenue, New York. Knowing that prompt and skilled treatment would in many instances spare the victims of accident or disease from becoming deformed, he had lent his best exertions to establish an institution where such permanent treatment would be readily accessible. The Newsboys' Lodging House is also deeply indebted to him for its success From its inception he paid special attention to the development of its resources and the perfection of its managment. The up-town branch of the establishment devolved entirely upon him for a support which was liberally accorded. He also greatly enlisted himself in the Young Men's Christian Association, and aided by his counsel and his purse in developing its usefulness. In fact, during a business career which absorbed a great part of his time and thought for the amelioration of his fellow creatures' conditions, he was evolving plans for having charity more widely distributed and turned to the best advantage. When the scheme of uniting all benevolent organizations for the purpose of mutual assistance and general co-operation was proposed, Mr. Roosevelt warmly encouraged the movement. He took part in organizing the Bureau of United Charities, which he believed would subserve a great object, but was forced with his associates to give over his design by the disinclination of some charitable institutions to make their methods and resources public.

He married Martha, daughter of James and Martha Oswald Bulloch, of Roswell, Georgia. Her maternal great-grandfather was Daniel Stewart, who joined the Revolutionary army when a boy and was captured by the British, but escaped from a prison ship and afterward served as captain under Sumter and Marion. Martha Bulloch's paternal grandfather was James Bulloch, who was a captain of the Georgia troops in the Revolution and an original member of the Society of the Cincinnati. James Bulloch's father was Archibald Bulloch, first Revolutionary governor of Georgia, who married Mary de Vaux, whose paternal grandfather, a Huguenot, fled from France after the Revocation of the Edict of Nantes. Her maternal grandfather was Edward Bellinger, one of the Carolina landgraves. Archibald Bulloch's father was James Bulloch, who came from Scotland about 1715 and settled in Georgia, was a member of the Provincial Congress, and held positions of honor and trust. He was a blood relative of the Douglasses, Bartons and other prominent families. Their children were: Anna, wife of Captain W. S. Cowles, of the United States navy; Theodore; Elliott; and Corinne, the wife of Douglas Robinson, Jr. Mrs. Roosevelt died February

15, 1884 She was a member of the Rev. Dr. Hall's church, and took a deep interest in many charities, including the Orthopaedic Hospital, of which her husband was one of the founders

Theodore Roosevelt, the leading subject of this sketch, was born in New York city, October 27, 1858, and was graduated at Harvard with the class of 1880. Among the early New York families to establish a summer home at Oyster Bay, Long Island, was that of Cornelius Van Schaick Roosevelt, the grandfather of the President The place where he resided was known as Tranquillity, and to him it was all that the name implied—rest, peace and quietness His son, Theodore Roosevelt, Sr , became very much attached to the place and spent the long summer and autumn months at this most delightful resort. Thus it happened that the early childhood of young Theodore was spent amid these surroundings. It was said that "he was a mere wisp of a boy, pale and puny, without health or strength; but he had a will, and determined to overcome his lack of physical vigor " The boys in the neighborhood knew him as the wiry, earnest, determined little fellow, perfectly fearless and ready to encounter any difficulty or danger that would add to his bodily health and strength He "rode and swam and climbed and jumped;" his "yacht" was a rowboat in which he could exercise his muscles and toughen every limb, and this "toughening" process was continued years after on his western ranch

Memories of his childhood days at Oyster Bay clung to him long after he left home to prepare for his great life work, and not long after his graduation in 1880 he purchased one hundred acres, mostly woodland, to which he gave the name of "Sagamore Hill"—a name at the time having no particular significance, but, associated with his subsequent achievements, it is fitly named.

Politics seemed to have a fascination for Colonel Roosevelt from an early age, but before entering the field he called on his Uncle Robert and said: "Uncle Bob, I want your advice. Shall I run for the Assembly?" "I can't say," replied his uncle. "Here is Colonel Charles Hutchinson, of Utica, who may answer the question." "Take it," said Hutchinson; "there's an opening for young men of independent fortune and good education in public life. You ought to make the experiment." Young Roosevelt "made the experiment" and succeeded, as he has in every subsequent "experiment" of his life. The word "fail" is not a part of his vocabulary. He literally "batters down" all opposition as he did on the famous field of San Juan, and then quietly surveys the situation and sums up the cost preparatory to a second onslaught if necessary.

A writer in one of the New York dailies gives his impressions of the young man as he saw him at a State convention some time after his first election to the Assembly:

"Mr. Theodore Roosevelt in the convention seemed to be a light-footed, agile, nervous, yet prompt boy, with light brown, yet slightly curling hair, blue eyes and an eye-glass, and ready to rise and speak with a clear, sharp, boyish voice, a manner more of the undergraduate than the finished orator, but unmistakable, candid, untrifling and withal kind and chivalric. He has a slight flush of the countenance and resolute expression of the head, well adapted to start sympathy and possibly enthusiasm I was a little reminded of Blanche Roosevelt, the singer. He applauded Warner Miller with his hands when the latter was applauded in rising to make a counter nomination George Bliss applauded Roosevelt with his feet but did not applaud Miller. Roosevelt sometimes turned and conferred with Robert McCord behind him. He set the conciliatory, yet manly tone in much which characterized the whole convention, and I never saw a State convention anywhere in the Union, though I have seen them from Massachusetts to Michigan and South Carolina, equal in modesty, intelligence and appearance to this."

Mr Roosevelt was elected to the Assembly as a Republican

He led the minority during the session of 1882, was active in reform measures, and on his re-election in 1883 was largely instrumental in carrying out the State civil-service-reform law and an act for regulating primary elections. As chairman of the committee on cities in 1884 he succeeded in abolishing the fees of the county clerk and register and in providing for their payment by salaries; curtailing abuses in the sheriff's and surrogate's offices; and securing the passage of a bill that deprived aldermen of the power to confirm appointments to office, and centered in the mayor the responsibility of administering municipal affairs He was chairman of the New York delegation to the National Republican Convention in 1884, and an unsuccessful candidate for Mayor of New York in 1886. He was nominated as an independent but was endorsed by the Republicans. In May, 1889, President Harrison appointed him Civil Service Commissioner, and he served as president of the board until May, 1895. He succeeded in changing the whole system of public appointments and in establishing important reforms. He re signed in May, 1895, to accept the position of president of the New York Board of Police Commissioners, and with characteristic energy and vigor he began the work of reform by the application of civil-service principles in appointments to and promotions on the force He rigidly enforced the excise law and succeeded in closing the saloons on Sunday, and in purifying the city of many corrupting influences which then existed

Colonel Roosevelt's life on his ranch on the borders of the Little Missouri river in the far West, with all of its exciting adventures, has been given in his Hunting Trips of a Ranchman. He went out as a "tenderfoot," but he was soon able to give the cowboy and the ranchman points that they little dreamed of.

Colonel Roosevelt is as modest as he is brave, and his most

intimate friends could never succeed in drawing from him any incident of his life the description of which necessitated any reference to himself as the hero. The following incident would probably never have found its way into print but for the fact that the local editor considered the joke on the "profession" too good to be suppressed: It appears that the colonel, while stopping at a hotel in a border town, was approached by a typical western "tough," who with accustomed Western politeness invited the "tenderfoot" to take a drink The invitation was politely declined with thanks It was repeated, and this time *pressed* by the "tough" with his finger on the trigger of his gun Suddenly he felt something between his eyes and the ball struck wide of the mark and entered the ceiling above He fell backward and went to sleep. When he awoke he was not certain whether he had been struck with a cannon ball or the heels of a mule; he concluded, however, that it was not always safe to meddle with a "tenderfoot."

Colonel Roosevelt first became known to the general public outside of his own state when he accepted the position of assistant secretary of the navy in 1897. Shortly after he assumed the duties of office he asked for an appropriation of eight hundred thousand dollars for ammunition for practical target shooting in the navy, and a few months later for another appropriation of five hundred thousand dollars for the same purpose. The results at Manila and Santiago justified what was considered at the time reckless extravagance. His connection with the Spanish war which followed is best told in the language of Colonel Watterson in his History of the Spanish-American war He says:

"It is the nature of Americans to welcome bold experiments and to applaud success There was no volunteer body of the war that received as much attention and invited as much interest as the regiment of cavalry known as Roosevelt's Rough Riders. That was its popular name, although Lieutenant-Colonel Roosevelt was but second in command. His was the resolute spirit that prompted its organization and fixed public interest upon it.

"The Hon. Theodore Roosevelt was assistant secretary of the navy at the opening of the war, one of those characteristic personalities in the public and private life of the United States that represent the vigor of democracy without regard to difference of opinion. Of the old Dutch stock of New York's oldest settlers, he was born to great wealth and with determined character Carefully educated in universities, he made his entrance into politics early, with vigorous ideals and practical methods. Greeted with the epithet of the 'dude politician,' he received the epithet with the good nature that an athletic, courageous and good-natured man would naturally exhibit He was soon a representative in national conventions, was the forlorn hope of his party for the mayoralty of New York, was appointed president of the Civil Service Commission, was police commissioner of New York and became assistant secretary of the navy in 1897 Recognizing then the probabilities of the war with Spain, he began to encourage the system of state naval reserves, and made many addresses in which he upheld the manful necessity of war to compel peace and secure justice. The good condition of the navy at the outbreak of war was largely due to his labor and enthusiasm When war was inevitable, he resigned his position as assistant secretary and asked for a commission to organize a regiment of cavalry, of which Dr Wood was to be commissioned colonel Great was the public surprise His friends remonstrated with him and urged that he was jeopardizing his career The authorities suggested that he would be invaluable in the navy department. 'The navy department,' he answered, 'is in good order. I have done all I can here There are other men who can carry it on as well as I; but I should be false to my ideals, false to the views I have openly expressed, if I were to remain here while fighting is going on after urging other men to risk their lives for their country.' He declined a colonel's commission and asked it for his friend, Dr. Wood. There was his answer in this self-reliant courage of American manhood. Mr. Roosevelt had written admirable historical works, exciting stories of adventure in hunting 'big game' while he was leading the life of a ranchman in the far west He was at once at the beginning and end of the American type, rich, intelligent, thoughtful, cultured, and had 'sand.'"

Referring to Colonel Roosevelt's participation in the battle of San Juan, Hon. Henry B. Russell in "The Story of the Two Wars" said: "A little before four o'clock occurred the second

Theodore Roosevelt

thrilling episode of the day. Under the brow of the little hill a council of war was held, the question being whether they should push on and take the main hill where the Spanish blockhouses were. Colonel Roosevelt volunteered to head the charge. It seemed a mad rush A foreign officer standing near the position when the men started out to make the charge was heard to say: 'Men, for heaven's sake don't go up that hill. It will be impossible for human beings to take that position. You can't stand the fire ' But with a terrific yell they rushed up to the enemy's works, and the Spanish, whose courage had fled after the first charge, retired, and when night came they had been driven back upon the city"

Colonel Watterson in describing the charge said:

"After a moment's pause for formation, the volunteers with Lieutenant-Colonel Roosevelt marching in front of the line, made a dash for the block-house, the men raising the terrible yell of the western Indians as they went A murderous fire poured from the block-house. Lieutenant-Colonel Roosevelt turned and waving his sword called on his command to follow him up the hill. The Spaniards poured a steady fire and for a second the volunteer fighters hesitated under the shock of it At that critical moment the Tenth Cavalry on the valley road to our left and the First Cavalry in the rear that had been ordered against the wings of the enemy had made their attacks and charged up the slopes with the intrepidity of disciplined veterans. The sound of the guns was echoed by cheers from the Rough Riders, who dashed against the block-house with cyclonic force At the sight of such impetuous daring the enemy burst from the fort and ran to the cover of the woods behind, leaving seventeen dead on the ground as they fled. Then they gave way on both wings and three thousand Spaniards were in full flight before nine hundred and fifty Americans that had fought against enormous odds and disadvantages No pursuit was possible, and our victorious troops camped on the ground and held it"

The most authentic as well as the most graphic account of the famous charge of Colonel Roosevelt is that given by himself in his volume on "The Rough Riders." He says:

"The infantry got nearer and nearer the crest of the hill At last we could see the Spaniards running from the rifle pits as the Americans came on in their final rush Then I stopped my men for fear they would injure their comrades, and called to them to charge the next line of trenches on the hills in our front, from which we had been undergoing a good deal of punishment. Thinking that the men would all come, I jumped over the wire fence in front of us and started at the double; but, as a matter of fact, the troopers were so excited, both with shooting and being shot, and shouting and cheering, that they did not

hear, or did not heed me; and after running about a hundred
yards I found I had only five men along with me. Bullets were
ripping the grass all around us and one of the men, Clay Green,
was mortally wounded; another, Winslow Clark, a Harvard man,
was shot first in the leg and then through the body. * * *
There was no use going with the remaining three men, and I
bade them stay where they were while I went back and brought
up the rest of the brigade. This was a decidedly cool request,
for there was really no possible point in letting them stay there
while I went back; but at the moment it seemed perfectly natural
to me, and apparently so to them, for they cheerfully nodded
and sat down on the grass, firing back at the line of trenches
from which the Spaniards were shooting at them. Meanwhile
I ran back, jumped over the wire fence, and went over the crest
of the hill, filled with anger against the troopers, and especially
those of my own regiment, for not having accompanied me
They, of course, were quite innocent of wrong doing; and even
while I taunted them bitterly for not having followed me, it
was all I could do not to smile at the look of injury and surprise
that came over their faces, while they cried out, 'We didn't hear
you; we didn't see you go, colonel; lead on now, we'll sure
follow you.' I wanted the other regiments to come too, so I
ran down to where General Sumner was and asked him if I
might make the charge, and he told me to go and that he would
see that the men followed By this time everybody had his
attention attracted, and when I leaped over the fence again,
with Major Jenkins beside me, the men of the various regiments
which were already on the hill came with a rush, and we started
across the wide valley which lay between us and the Spanish
intrenchments. * * * Long before we got near them the
Spaniards ran, save a few here and there, who either surrendered or were shot down * * * Lieutenant Davis' first
sergeant, Clarence Gould, killed a Spanish soldier with his revolver just as the Spaniard was aiming at one of my Rough
Riders. At about the same time I also shot one. I was with
Henry Bardshar, running up at the double, and two Spaniards
leaped from the trenches and fired at us, not ten yards away
As they turned to run I closed in and fired twice, missing the
first and killing the second. My revolver was from the sunken
battleship Maine, and had been given me by my brother-in-law,
Captain W S. Cowles, of the navy. At the time I did not know
of Gould's exploit, and supposed my feat to be unique; and al-

though Gould had killed his Spaniard in the trenches not very far from me, I never learned of it until weeks after.

"There was a very great confusion at the time, the different regiments being completely intermingled—white regulars, colored regulars and Rough Riders General Sumner had kept a considerable force in reserve on Kettle Hill, under Major Jackson of the Third Cavalry. We were still under a heavy fire, and I got together a mixed lot of men and pushed on from the trenches and ranch houses which we had just taken, driving the Spaniards through a line of palm-trees and over the crest of a chain of hills. When we reached these crests we found ourselves overlooking Santiago.

"While I was re-forming the troops on the chain of hills, one of General Sherman's aides, Captain Robert Howze—as dashing and gallant an officer as there was in the whole gallant cavalry division, by the way—came up with orders to me to halt where I was, not advancing further, but to hold the hill at all hazards.

"I now had under me all the fragments of the six cavalry regiments which were at the extreme front, being the highest officer left there, and I was in immediate command of them for the remainder of the afternoon and that night * * * The Spaniards who had been holding the trenches and the line of hills had fallen back upon their supports, and we were under a very heavy fire both from rifles and great guns. Our artillery made one or two efforts to come into action on the firing line of the infantry, but the black powder rendered each attempt fruitless. The Spanish guns used smokeless powder, so that it was difficult to place them As night came on the firing gradually died away. Before this happened, however, Captains Morton and Boughton, of the Third Cavalry, came over to tell me that a rumor had reached them to the effect that there had been some talk of retiring, and that they wished to protest in the strongest manner. I had been watching them both, as they handled their troops with the cool confidence of the veteran regular officer, and had been congratulating myself that they were off toward the right flank; for as long as they were there I knew I was perfectly safe in that direction I had heard no rumor about retiring, and I cordially agreed with them that it would be far worse than a blunder to abandon our position.

"Soon after dark General Wheeler, who in the afternoon had resumed command of the cavalry division, came to the front A very few words with General Wheeler reassured us about retiring He had been through too much heavy fighting in the Civil war to regard the present fight as very serious, and he told us not to be under any apprehension, for he had sent word that there was no need whatever of retiring, and was sure we would stay where we were until the chance came to advance He was second in command, and to him more than to any other one man was due the prompt abandonment of the proposal to fall back—a proposal which, if adopted, would have meant shame and disaster. Shortly afterward General Wheeler sent us orders to intrench * * * We finished digging the trench soon after midnight, and then the worn-out men lay down in rows on their rifles and dropped heavily to sleep. * * * Before any one had time to awake from the cold, however, we were all awakened by the Spaniards, whose skirmishers suddenly opened fire upon us. * * * At the alarm everybody jumped to his feet, and the stiff, shivering, haggard men, their eyes only half opened, all clutched their rifles and ran forward to the trench on the crest of the hill

"The sputtering shots died away and we went to sleep again. But in another hour dawn broke and the Spaniards opened fire in good earnest. * * * In this fight our regiment had numbered four hundred and ninety men, as, in addition to the killed and wounded of the first fight, some had to go to the hospital for sickness and some had been left behind with the baggage or were detailed on other duty. Eighty-nine were killed and wounded, the heaviest loss suffered by any regiment in the cavalry division The Spaniards made a stiff fight, standing firm until we charged home. They fought much more stubbornly than at Las Guasimas. We ought to have expected this, for they have always done well in holding intrenchments On this day they showed themselves to be brave foes, worthy of honor for their gallantry

"In the attack on the San Juan hills our forces numbered about 6,600 There were about 4,500 Spaniards against us Our total loss in killed and wounded was 1,071. Of the cavalry division there were, all told, some 2,300 officers and men, of whom 375 were killed and wounded. In the division over a fourth of the officers were killed or wounded, their loss being relatively half as great again as that of the enlisted men—which was as it should be I think we suffered more heavily than the Spaniards did in killed and wounded, though we also captured some scores of prisoners It would have been very extraordinary if the reverse was the case, for we did the charging; and to carry earthworks on foot with dismounted cavalry, when the earthworks are held by unbroken infantry, armed with the best modern rifles, is a serious task "

The city surrendered on the 17th of July, and soon after this the men, being relieved from the constant strain and excitement, began to feel the effects of the climate. Colonel Roosevelt says:

"Every officer other than myself, except one, was down with sickness at one time or another Very few of the men, indeed, retained their strength and energy, and though the percentage actually on the sick list never got over twenty, there were less than fifty per cent who were fit for any kind of work. Yellow fever also broke out in the rear, chiefly among the Cubans. It never became epidemic, but it caused a perfect panic among some of our own doctors and especially in the minds of one or two generals and of the home authorities. * * * The Washington authorities seemed determined that we should stay in Cuba They unfortunately knew nothing of the country, nor the circumstances of the army Several suggestions were made, and among others it was proposed that we should go up the mountains and make our camps there. * * * The soil along the sides of the mountains was deep and soft, while the rains were heavy We could, with much difficulty, have got our regiments up the mountains; but not half the men would have got up there with their belongings; and once there it would have been an impossibility to feed them About the last of July General Shafter called a conference in the palace of all the division and brigade commanders * * * It was deemed best to make some record of our opinion in the shape of a letter or report which would show that to keep the army in Santiago meant its absolute and objectless ruin, and that it should at once be recalled. At first there was naturally some hesitation on the part of the regular officers to take the initiative, for their entire future career might be sacrificed; so I wrote a letter to General Shafter, reading over the rough draft to the various generals and adopting their corrections. Before I had finished making these corrections it was determined that we should send a circular letter on behalf of all of us to General Shafter, and when I returned from presenting him mine I found this circular letter already prepared and we all of us signed it. Both letters were made public. The result was immediate. Within three days the army was ordered to be ready to sail for home This letter was known as the famous 'Round Robin.' "

Colonel Roosevelt with his Rough Riders was encamped at Montauk Point, Long Island, and in the following autumn, peace having been formally declared, he bade farewell to his men, every one of whom was devoted to him, and returned to his home at Oyster Bay.

On September 27, 1898, Colonel Roosevelt was nominated for governor of New York state He conducted his own campaign, visiting every important town in the state. His brilliant military record gave him great prestige, and he was enthusiastically received wherever he went. He carried the state by a plurality of 18,079. As governor he encouraged honest legislation and carried through every reform measure to which he had pledged himself. He carefully scrutinized every bill and withheld his signature from all that had the least taint of irregularity, regardless of party obligations. No man ever had a more difficult task to carry forward the work of reform which he had planned than did Governor Roosevelt at this time. The political pressure brought to bear upon him by the leading men in his own party was very great, but he remained firm and true to his own convictions, even at the risk of losing the influence of those on whom he relied for support. Above all, he put in office as high-minded and able a set of public officials as the state has ever had since its foundation It was his wish to be elected for a second term that he might complete the work he had begun, but circumstances beyond his control and that of his friends changed all his future plans

Governor Roosevelt was a delegate to the Republican convention held at Philadelphia in the summer of 1900. The renomination of President McKinley was a foregone conclusion.

Two or three candidates were brought forward for the vice-presidency, but from the very beginning a pressure was brought to bear by those who sought to defeat his aspirations for a second term as governor to force on him the nomination for vice-president. They failed, however, to accomplish their object, and Governor Roosevelt compelled the New York delegation to definitely abandon its efforts to put him forward, and at the same time he introduced the name of Lieutenant-Governor Woodruff, hoping thereby to secure his nomination, but the delegates simply refused to consider any other candidate and insisted on the governor's nomination in order to save the electoral vote of half a dozen western states and thereby assure a majority in Congress. Under these circumstances Governor Roosevelt felt that he was in duty bound to accept, and he was nominated for vice-president, amid the greatest excitement and enthusiasm, the East and the West, the North and the South rallying around him and pledging him their earnest support.

The presidential campaign of 1900 was the most remarkable of all ever held in this country, and from the beginning to the end Governor Roosevelt fought the battle almost single-handed and alone He represented honest money, honest principles and a defense of President McKinley's administration; while his opponent, William J Bryan, clung to his "16 to 1" silver policy, on which he had been defeated four years previously, and exposed the "expansion" policy of the administration Colonel Roosevelt traveled from one end of the country to the other, even invading the home territory of his opponent, speaking several times a day from the train platform, in the open air on improvised platforms and in public halls, and wherever the people could gather to hear him. With one or two exceptions he met with a hearty reception wherever he went—even in "the enemy's country." The result was one of the grandest victories ever achieved by the Republican party and Governor Roosevelt was duly inaugurated vice-president of the United States on the 4th of March, 1901. In his inaugural address he said:

"The history of free government is in a large part the history of those representing legislative bodies in which, from the earliest times, free government has found its loftiest expression. They must ever hold a peculiar and exalted position in the record which tells how the great nations of the world have endeavored to achieve and preserve orderly freedom. No man can render to his fellows greater service than is rendered by him who with fearlessness and honesty, with sanity and disinterestedness, does his life work as a member of such a body Especially is this the case when the legislature in which the service is rendered is a vital part in the governmental machinery of one of those world powers to whose hands, in the course of the ages, is entrusted a leading part in shaping the destinies of mankind. For weal or for woe, for good or for evil, this is true of our own mightly nation Great privileges and great powers are ours, and heavy are the responsibilities that go with these privileges and these powers. Accordingly, as we do well or ill, so shall mankind in the future be raised or cast down.

"We belong to a young nation, already of giant strength, yet whose present strength is but a forecast of the power that is to come We stand supreme in a continent, in a hemisphere. East and west we look across the two great oceans toward the larger world life in which, whether we will or not, we must take an ever increasing share; and as, keen-eyed, we gaze into the coming years duties new and old rise thick and fast to confront us from within and from without There is every reason why we should face these duties with a sober appreciation alike of their importance and of their difficulty But there is also every reason for facing them with high-hearted resolution and with eager and confident faith in our capacity to do them aright.

"A great work lies ready to the hand of this generation; it should count itself happy indeed that to it is given the privilege of doing such a work A leading part therein must be taken by this, the august and powerful legislative body over which I have been called to preside Most deeply I appreciate the privilege of my position, for high indeed is the honor of presiding over the American senate at the outset of the twentieth century."

On Friday, September 6, 1901, the startling news was flashed over the wire that President McKinley, while visiting the Pan-American Exposition, had been shot by a Polish anarchist named Czolgosz. Vice-President Roosevelt hastened to Buffalo as quickly as possible, reaching there the following day. He was completely overwhelmed by the news, but on arriving at the house of Dr. Milburn, where the President had been taken and where he had been stopping with his family for some days previously, he was overjoyed to learn from the attending surgeons that the wound was not necessarily fatal and that there were hopes of his recovery. He remained in Buffalo for a few days, until the danger point seemed past. He then went on a hunting trip in the Adirondacks. Soon after this a change for the worse took place in the President's condition, and as soon as it was found that death was inevitable, messengers were sent to the vice-president, who traveled day and night, reaching Buffalo some hours after the President's death He was driven at once to the house of his friend, Mr. Ansley Wilcox. As soon as he entered Mr Roosevelt was told that it had been planned for him to take the oath of office at once This agreement had been reached at a meeting of the cabinet held during the forenoon at the Milburn residence. The new President refused to recognize it as an agreement, and he declared he was not ready to take the oath yet. He was here more for the purpose of paying his respects to William McKinley than of qualifying as William McKinley's successor.

"But, Mr. President," he was expostulated with, "everything is in readiness Don't you think it would be far better to do as the cabinet has decided?"

"No," retorted the President; "it would be far worse. I intend to pay my respects at William McKinley's bier as a private citizen and offer my condolence to the members of the family as such. Then I will return and take the oath."

In the face of such an emphatic stand by the new chief executive all arguments availed nothing and President Roosevelt had his own way. He left the Milburn house about half past two o'clock and entered his carriage alone. When he found that he was being escorted by a squad of mounted policemen he stood up and shouted: "Get back! I want no escort. I will have no escort I am now on a mission as a private citizen." He then drove swiftly to the Milburn house and after paying his respects to the dead President returned to the Wilcox house to take the oath, reaching there shortly after three o'clock. All the members of the cabinet and a number of others were assembled there Among these was Judge Hazel, who was to administer the oath

"President Roosevelt," said Mr. Root, "I have been requested by all the members of the cabinet of the late President who are here in the city of Buffalo, being all except two, to request that for reasons of weight affecting the administration of government, you should proceed without delay to take the constitutional oath of office."

A silence fell upon the group. It lasted but a minute and then Mr. Roosevelt spoke: "Mr Secretary, I shall take the oath at once, agreeable to the request of the members of the cabinet, and in this hour of trouble and national bereavement I wish to state that it shall be my aim to continue absolutely unbroken the policy of President McKinley, for the peace and prosperity and honor of our beloved country." He then took the oath and Vice-President Theodore Roosevelt became the twenty-sixth President of the United States. His course is so clearly marked that all recognize his policy, and although the youngest who ever occupied the presidential chair, he has the confidence and support of leading men throughout the nation.

It is difficult to conceive how any one so thoroughly absorbed in public affairs could find time to devote to literary work, and yet Colonel Roosevelt has achieved a world-wide reputation as an author, and his works have become standard on the subjects

Theodore Roosevelt Library

he has treated. Among the best known are: "History of the Naval War of 1812" (1882) and "Hunting Trips of a Ranchman" (1883). As a biographer he has won fame as the author of the "Life of Thomas Benton" (1886); and "Life of Gouverneur Morris" (1888). He has also published "History of the City of New York" (1890); "Essays on Practical Politics" (1898); and has collaborated with Captain A. S. Mahan in writing the "Imperial History of the British Navy"; he is also joint author with Henry Cabot Lodge of "Hero Tales from American History." The most important of his works, however, are the volumes bearing the collective title "'The Winning of the West" These have for their subject the acquisition by the United States of the territory west of the Alleghanies, and in their intrinsic merit and their importance as contributions to history they rank with the works of Parkman. His books have been characterized as "marked by felicity, vigor and clearness of expression, with descriptive power"

As a man of letters it may be said as more completely true of Mr Roosevelt than any other writer, whose books are as numerous and widely read as his are, that he has merely adopted literary expression with the aim of placing before the public facts and ideas which he sincerely believes to be worthy of consideration and preservation His presentation of facts, however, is useful and stimulating rather than merely entertaining, while his ideas represent an eloquent appeal for a general and wholesome examination of the truths which he so fervently believes and so ardently advocates In other words, Mr. Roosevelt is in no sense a professional author. The books he has written simply represent one phase of a very active career. On the title page of "Ranch Life and Hunting Trail" we find cited that passage from Browning ending with the words—

How good is man's life, the mere living.

which speaks more eloquently and is more characteristic of Mr. Roosevelt as a man, and, therefore, necessarily as an author, than all that litterateurs have written and all that poets have sung about the beauties of rhetoric and the philosophy of style.

Mr. Roosevelt's first published work was his history of "The Naval War of 1812," which bears the date of 1882, and it is a singular coincidence that his most recent production, written just as his term as vice-president of the United States was to be brought to a fateful close, should be a contribution to an English work on the same subject, "The Royal Navy," Vol VI, by Laird Clowes. A comparison of these works offers an excellent opportunity to observe the mental development of the man in a most important field of historical study and observation One was written at the age of twenty-three; the other at forty-two. It is not from the fact that we find the patriotism less intense, or the presence of any taint of Anglomania in the later work, but because the man has learned to think for himself, has freed himself entirely from the anti-British prejudices which for years have inspired the makers of many American school books; and he has from a fuller knowledge been able to appreciate the merits of the enemy and to point out the reasons for his misfortunes in a clear, almost scientific manner and without undue laudation of American enterprise and courage Moreover, it is not singular that his historical works, particularly "The Winning of the West," should have a vitality which few histories possess. It is because he has lived with and knows intimately the trapper, the hunter, the frontiersman of today, that he has been enabled to reproduce the distant predecessors of these men and their surroundings with marvelous intimacy

In the last nineteen years Mr Roosevelt has written over a dozen books, which are included in many departments—history, biography, travel, observation and politico-ethical discussion. At the same time he has occupied successively various positions in public life upon which he has left the stamp of his individuality and the results of his tireless energy What these offices were and what he did in them have taken their place in our state, municipal and national history, and are now more or less familiar to every one But the more one becomes familiar with Mr. Roosevelt's public achievements the more must one marvel that he could have produced the books that he did, which, from the point of view of mere mechanical and mental labor, would have been considered more than adequate to establish the literary reputation of a professional writer.

To attempt a character sketch of Colonel Roosevelt is a most difficult undertaking. He can be judged only by his acts. His motive is always apparent, for he is incapable of duplicity. His utterances both public and private are clear, distinct and unequivocal. Whether his opinions are right or wrong they are honestly held and are stated with simplicity and directness. He is emphatically a man of action, and his writings deal with matters of observation rather than thought; he is no theorist, but intensely practical. With determination and undaunted courage he combines tenacity of purpose. If he ever experienced the sensation of fear it is known only to himself. He has the instinct of a soldier, and in emergencies does not stop to consider whether or not the odds are against him, but obeys orders with decision and accepts the consequences. He is as generous as he is brave; bears no malice; and after inflicting punishment on an adversary he would instantly seek to alleviate the pain he has caused. With the heart of a lion in danger, he is moved to pity at the sight of suffering, and without a moment's hesitation would befriend a fallen adversary. His qualities and achievements have made him a popular hero, and in a democratic society like ours there is no distinction which he may not hope to attain

Colonel Roosevelt married, first, Miss Alice Hathaway Lee; second, Miss Edith Kermit Caron, and his children are Alice, Theodore, Jr, Kermit, Ethel, Archibald and Quintin. The children rough it at their country home, Sagamore Hill, as did their father, enjoying the utmost freedom, apparently unconscious

Theodore Roosevelts Home, Oyster Bay

of the honors that have been showered upon the father by a grateful and appreciative constituency. The veteran war horse "Texas" that carried him through the Santiago campaign munches his oats and hay in the stable in peace and quietness, glad no doubt that his campaigning days are over and that for the remainder of his life he can enjoy the cool breezes of Oyster Bay in summer and a warm, comfortable stall in winter.

The entrance to Sagamore Hill is up a winding road through a thickly wooded country for some distance until a "private road" turning sharply to the left is reached, which leads up to the home of the president. The view on reaching the crest of the hill is a most beautiful one, although partly obscured on the west and south sides of the house by the dense growth of forest trees From the east and south sides a fine view of the bay is presented A lawn of several acres slopes down to the wall of forest trees, and the other side, which is nearly level, is devoted to farming purposes The character of the exterior of the dwelling is known as the Queen Anne style of architecture It is a substantial edifice, the first story being of brick, the second and third stories of frame. A wide piazza extends around two sides, from which a beautiful view of the surrounding country is obtained The entrance to the house is through a vine-covered port-cochere The wide hall, simply furnished, contains numerous trophies of the colonel's life in the far west. The large library looks like the workshop of an active brain worker A portrait of the father which hangs on the wall looks benignly down on the son, who, with unceasing energy and tireless industry, works out the great problems of life, stimulating in others a desire to be something and do something for their fellow men.

Mr. Roosevelt was elected to the presidency in November, 1904, by a popular plurality of 2,542,062 The most conspicuous and useful act was his mediation between Russia and Japan, which had as its result the restoration of peace under the provisions of the Treaty of Portsmouth

RIKER FAMILY

Abraham Rycken, or de Rycke (the name is written in both forms in the early records) was the progenitor of the present Riker families in New York, New Jersey and other states, his descendants in the third generation having assumed the present form of the name. He emigrated about 1638, in which year he received an allotment of land from Governor Kieft, for which he afterwards took out a patent dated August 8, 1640, the land being situated at the Wallabout In 1642 Ryker was in New Amsterdam, where he lived many years upon a place of his own on the Heeren Gracht, now Broad street In 1656 he made a voyage to the Delaware river for the express purpose of purchasing beaver skins, then a leading article of traffic. In 1654 he obtained a grant of land at the Poor Bowery, to which he removed after adding to his domain the island known as Riker's Island. Having attained to more than three score years and ten, he died in 1689, leaving his farm by will to his son Abraham

He married Grietie, daughter of Hendrick Harmensen, one of the first settlers on Long Island and probably the first stock raiser and pioneer farmer, having located at what has since been known as the Poor Bowery, to which he established his claim as early as 1638, thus giving the Rikers the precedence as the pioneer settlers of Long Island.

Abraham Riker by his wife Grietie had children: 1 Ryck Abramsen, who adopted the name of Lent 2. Jacob, born 1640, died in infancy 3 Jacob (2), born 1643 4 Hendrick, born 1646. died young. 5 Mary, born 1649, married Sebout H Krankhevt, afterwards of the manor of Cortlandt. 6 John, born 1654, married 1691, Sarah Schonten Their son Abraham, born 1695, settled in Essex county, New Jersey. 7. Aletta, born 1653, married Capt John Harmensen, also of the manor of Cortlandt 8. Abraham (2), born 1655. 9 Hendrick, born 1662, adopted the name of Lent The parents were members of the Dutch church, and most of their children were baptized in the church at Fort Amsterdam.

Abraham Riker (2), eighth child of Abraham (1) and Grietie (Harmensen) Riker, was born at New Amsterdam

(Island of Manhattan) in 1655 He was taken in early childhood to the farm which his father purchased in the town of Newtown He was a man of superior intelligence and a capable farmer He inherited the paternal estate and added considerably to the extent of his grounds, his most important purchase being that of a third of the Tudor patent, November 2, 1688 This was a patent obtained by John Tudor, March 18, 1686, which he sold two years after to Riker and two other parties.

Abraham Riker died in 1746. He settled his estate on his sons Abraham and Andrew, November 10, 1733. His death in his ninety-first year was most singular Deprived of sight for some years, it was his custom to sit on the lawn under a pear tree, the sprouts and roots of which yet remain There sitting, August 20, 1746, he suddenly recovered the use of his eyes, looked upon his family, among them being grandchildren whom he never saw before, after which he walked back to his favorite seat under the pear tree and immediately expired.

He married Grietie, daughter of John Gerrits Van Buytenhuysen, of New York, by his intermarriage with Tryntie, daughter of John Van Luyt, of Holland She died November 15, 1732 Their children were: 1. Catharine 2 Margaret, married, first, Peter Braisted; second, Thomas Lynch; third, Anthony Duane, father of Hon James Duane, afterwards mayor of New York. 3. Mary, married Haseult Van Keuren, of Kingston. 4. Abraham 5. John 6. Hendrick. 7 Andrew. 8. Jacob.

Andrew Riker, seventh child of Abraham (2) and Grietie (Buytenhuysen) Riker, was born at the homestead, Bowery Bay, in 1669 He inherited the homestead property, and became a man of means and influence. In 1756 detachment of the King's regulars were quartered at Newtown, and Andrew Riker's house was the abode of the French officers for a considerable period.

He married, November 13, 1733, Jane, widow of Captain Dennis Lawrence, and daughter of John Berrien, Esq, son of Cornelius Jansen Berrien, a French Huguenot, who settled in Flatbush in 1669, and there married Jannetje, daughter of Jan Stryker, who held offices in the town government and was a deacon in the Dutch church.

Andrew Riker died February 12, 1763, in his sixty-fourth year; his widow died September 26, 1775, in her seventy-third year Their children were: 1 Margaret, died unmarried,

GENEALOGICAL AND FAMILY HISTORY

April 3, 1760   2 John Berrien. 3 Abraham. 4. Samuel. 5. Ruth, married Major Jonathan Lawrence

Samuel Riker, fourth child of Andrew and Jane Riker, was born April 8, 1743. After receiving a fair education and holding a clerkship some years in a New York mercantile house, he tired of city life and returned to the old homestead, which he subsequently purchased. He was among the first to espouse the cause of the colonists in their struggle for independence. On December 10, 1774, at a meeting of freeholders at Newtown, a series of spirited resolutions passed a few days previous by their neighbors at Jamaica were read by one of the gentlemen and unanimously responded to, after which a committee of correspondence was appointed, which consisted of the following: Jacob Blackwell, Richard Alsop, Daniel Rapelje, Esq, Philip Edsall, Thomas Lawrence, Daniel Lawrence, Jonathan Lawrence, Samuel Moore, William Firman, William Howard, Jeremias Remsen, Jun., Samuel Riker, John Albertis, Abraham Brinkerhoff, James Way, Samuel Morrill and Jonathan Coe.

The Newtown Troop of Light Horse, consisting of forty-four men, was commanded by Captain Richard Lawrence, and afterwards by his brother, Captain Daniel Lawrence. Samuel Riker was second lieutenant; Jonathan Coe, cornet; Peter Rapelje, quartermaster. After the resignation of Captain Lawrence, Riker and Coe were promoted.

Captain Abraham Riker, of the New York Continental Line, who the previous fall was at the storming of Quebec, recruited a company, which was attached to the regiment of Colonel Reitzman, which formed a part of the brigade of Major General Lord Stirling. Lieutenant Samuel Riker was active in guarding the outposts of the American army until compelled to flee before the approach of the British troops He escaped with others after the battle of Long Island, and subsequently returned with the intention of rejoining the army, but was discovered and captured by the British. He returned home after the war and was elected to various public positions, among these that of supervisor. He was in the State Assembly in 1784, and the last public act of his life was to represent his district in congress in 1808-9, having also on a previous occasion held a seat in that national body.

He died May 19, 1823 He married, January 17, 1769, Anna Lawrence, born November 27, 1749, daughter of Joseph Lawrence, son of John (3), son of Captain John (2), born about 1650, son of Major Thomas Lawrence, a descendant of Sir Robert Laurens

Samuel Riker, by his wife, Anna (Lawrence) Riker, had children: 1. Joseph Lawrence, born March 26, 1770; adopted a seafaring life, and died at the island of Jamaica, July 20, 1796. 2. Andrew, born September 21, 1771 (see record of J. L. Riker's wife). 3. Richard, born September 9, 1773. 4 Abraham, born May 24, 1776. 5 Patience L., born May 10, 1778; married John Lawrence. 6. Samuel, born March 3, 1780. 7. Jane Margaret, born April 4, 1782; married first John Tom; second, Dr. William James Macneven. 8. Anna Elvira, born May 1, 1785; married Dr. Dow Ditmars. 9. John Lawrence, born April 9, 1787.

Richard Riker, third child of Samuel and Anna (Lawrence) Riker, was born at Newtown, September 9, 1773. He was educated chiefly under Rev. Dr. Witherspoon, president of Nassau Hall, New Jersey. He entered the office of the elder Jones, and was admitted to the bar in 1795. In 1802 he was appointed district attorney of New York, which he held for ten years, and in 1815 he was made recorder of the city, which he retained with short intermissions till 1837, having discharged the arduous and responsible duties of such offices for nearly thirty years. For ten years (1802-12) he was district attorney of New York, and for twenty years, was recorder of New York. His polished manner and social prominence won for him the title of the "American Chesterfield" from Fanny Kemble, and it clung to him through life. He was a warm friend of Alexander Hamilton, although an ardent Democrat. He served De Witt Clinton as second in his duel with John Swartwout's brother Robert. History of Hudson county, says:

Mr. Riker died in the seventieth year of his age, September 26, 1842. To the celebrated law firm which he founded, his sons D. Phoenix and John H. Riker were admitted in 1826 and in 1840 respectively, and their cousin Henry L., son of John L., in 1842.

Mr. Riker married, in March, 1807, Janette, daughter of Daniel Phoenix, Esq., treasurer of the city of New York. Their children were Daniel Phoenix, Anna E., Elizabeth P., Janette, John H. and Rebecca P.

John Lawrence Riker (1), brother of Richard Riker, and youngest child of Samuel and Anna (Lawrence) Riker, was born April 9, 1787. He was educated at Erasmus Hall in Flatbush, and began his legal studies in the office of his brother Richard. On attaining his majority he established the law business on his own account, and soon entered upon a successful practice that continued until his death. He resided in New York until 1825, when he purchased the old homestead at Bowery Bay, where he spent the remainder of his days. He rode daily to Fulton ferry on horseback, leaving his horse on the Brooklyn side and returning in the evening. At the breaking out of the war of 1812-15 he volunteered, and was commissioned captain of the Ninety-seventh Regiment of Infantry, August 11, 1812.

He married, first, Maria Smith; second, Lavinia Smith, daughters of Sylvanus Smith, of North Hempstead, Long Island. Sylvanus was the son of Sylvanus Smith (1), son of John, and grandson or great-grandson of John Smith, the ancestor.

John Lawrence Riker (2), fifth child of John Lawrence (1) and first child of Lavinia (Smith) Riker, was born at the homestead, Bowery Bay, November 23, 1830. After completing his studies he came to New York, and first entered the house of Lawrence & Hicks, and later that of Benjamin H Field, dealer in drugs, dyes, chemicals, etc His promotion was rapid, and he became a partner in 1854, which continued until December 31, 1860, when he retired to form a copartnership with his brother, Daniel S., in the same line of business, on January 1, 1861, just previous to the breaking out of the Civil war. The new firm soon acquired a reputation for upright business methods and square dealings, which has been maintained to the present time While other members of the family have formed the firm from time to time, the name of J. L. & D. S. Riker remains the same. While other business interests of late years absorbed much of the time of Mr. Riker, he remained the senior member of the firm until 1903, although the principal management of the business devolved upon his son, John J. His business operations have brought him in close touch with large financial institutions, and he has frequently been called on to assist in the management of these, having accepted the vice-presidency of some, and a directorship in several others, notably the Bank of New York, Second National Bank, Metropolitan Trust Company, Chamber of Commerce, Atlantic Marine Insurance Company, Continental Insurance Company (fire), Laflin & Rand Powder Company, and many manufacturing companies. He is a member of the St. Nicholas Society, the Society of Colonial Wars, Sons of the Revolution, a trustee and vice-president of the Holland Society, and a member of the various social clubs, Union League, Metropolitan St. Nicholas, etc. He has served as vestryman, and now as senior warden, in the Church of the Incarnation (Episcopal), for more than a quarter of a century. He married Mary, daughter of John C. Jackson and their children were: 1 John Jackson Riker. 2. Henry Laurens Riker, born June 20, 1860; died, unmarried, August 13, 1900 He was a member of the Down Town Club, New York Athletic Club, Sons of the Revolution and St. Nicholas. He was graduated at Columbia College, class of '80, and entered the counting room of his father's firm His tastes were more literary and musical, and he spent much of his time in helping and aiding the poor and humble, and was much beloved by them and his friends. 3. Margaret Moore Riker, married J. Amory Haskell, December 9, 1901 (see record). 4. Lavinia, married James Remsen Strong, June 1, 1902 5. Samuel Riker, Jr , married Frances Mortimer Townsend, November 18, 1896. 6. Silvanus, twin brother of Samuel; died in infancy 7. Martha Jackson Riker, married James Howe Proctor, April 28, 1897 8. Charles Lawrence Riker, married Selina Schroeder, October 16, 1900. 9. Mary Jackson Riker, married, April 29, 1903, Henry Ingersoll Riker, son of Daniel S. and Joanna (Field) Riker.

Major John Jackson Riker, eldest child of John Lawrence and Mary (Jackson) Riker, was born at Newtown, April 6, 1858. After completing his studies he entered his father's firm in a subordinate capacity, mastered all the details of the business, and qualified himself for the important position which he has filled for many years as managing partner of the business.

He joined the famous Seventh Regiment, N. G. S. N Y., May 26, 1878, and in August, 1879, was appointed aide-de-camp, with the rank of lieutenant, on the staff of General William G. Ward, commanding First Brigade On April 1, 1880, he was promoted senior aide, with rank of captain, and on May 19, 1880, he was made brigade inspector of rifle practice, with rank of major, and on October 27, 1882, was made brigade inspector. He resigned October 25, 1883. He was elected major of the Twelfth Regiment June 9, 1884, and after bringing it up to a high state of efficiency he resigned, June 14, 1889. Major Riker has been for many years an active worker in the Society of the Sons of the Revolution He represented the society during the Washington centennial, April 23, 1889, as their marshal Through collateral descent from Surgeon John Berrien Riker, of the fourth New Jersey line, he is a member of the New Jersey Society of the Cincinnati. He is a member and former secretary of the St. Nicholas Club, and is a member of the Society of Colonial Wars. He was a school trustee of the Twenty-first ward for some years. He married Edith, daughter of Samuel Blackwell Bartow, of New York city, a grandson of Colonel Jacob Blackwell, of the Revolution

Samuel Riker, sixth child of John Lawrence and second child of his second wife, Lavinia (Smith) Riker, was born at the homestead at Bowery Bay, April 10, 1832. After completing his general education he read law in the office of J. H. & H. L. Riker, and was admitted to the bar in May, 1853, and at once admitted to partnership in the law firm, which then consisted of his father, brother and cousin, John H. Riker; the first two died in 1861, and the latter retired in 1884

Mr. Riker took up a special line of practice—the law of real property, the investigation of titles to lands, drawing of wills, marriage settlements, trust deeds, etc. He came into general prominence in 1859 in connection with his construction of the will of William Jay (a son of the eminent John Jay), who had drawn his own will. This will involved some intricate and novel points of law, but through the efforts of Mr. Riker, an understanding was arrived at without resort to litigation. Mr. Riker never advised a client to carry a matter into court when it could be avoided. During his long term of practice of nearly forty years, Mr. Riker not only occupied a leading position at the New York bar, but he was recognized as an authority on the special line he had chosen. Besides his list of well known individual clients and estates, Mr. Riker has acted for large and well known institutions. He was attorney and counsel for the Sailors' Snug Harbor for upwards of thirty years, preparing all instruments relating to their large landed estate in the city of New York and on Staten Island. He acted as executor of the wills of Sarah Burr and her sisters, and distributed several millions of dollars among a large number of charitable institutions in New York city. He retired from active practice in 1893, and with him the old Riker law firm, which had been in existence for nearly a century, ended.

Mr Riker married in 1865, Mary Anna, daughter of Jacob P and Mary R. Stryker, of Newtown.

William James Riker, youngest son of John Lawrence (1) and Lavinia (Smith) Riker, was born at Bowery Bay, in the town of Newtown. He received his knowledge of the elementary branches at the private schools of Astoria and was graduated at Flushing Institute in 1858 Not long after he entered the house of Benjamin H. Field in the same line of business which he has since followed. He remained there until 1861, and then joined his brothers in the same business, becoming a partner in the firm in 1866 He joined the Twenty-Second Regiment, N G S. N Y., at its inception, but owing to pressing matters that called him abroad he severed his connection with the regiment. He is a member of several societies and clubs, in some of which he takes an active interest. Among these are the St. Nicholas Society, the Metropolitan Museum of Art, American Geographical Society, American Museum of Natural History, New York Yacht Club, New York Athletic Club, Down Town

Association, etc. He is a trustee in the Bank for Savings in New York, the oldest institution of the kind in the city.

He married, in 1865, Charlotte Lawrence, daughter of Dr. J. P. Stryker, son of Garret Stryker; and Anne Polhemus, a direct descendant of Rev. Johannus Theodorus Polhemus, a minister of the Reformed Church of Holland, who came to New Amsterdam in 1654 and became the pastor of the Flatbush church The descendants through this line include some of the oldest and most distinguished families on Long Island The issue of the above marriage is: 1. Andrew Lawrence Riker, born October 22, 1868. He is an electrical engineer. He married Edith Whiting, daughter of James R. and grand-daughter of Judge James R. Whiting. They have: Edith Whiting, Charlotte Lawrence and Andrew Lawrence Riker. 2. Jennie Riker, died November 30, 1886.

PAYNE FAMILY.

John Howard Payne was born in New York city, June 9, 1792. He was destined for a business career, but early showed a predilection for literature and the stage. He edited some trifling publications while still in his teens—publications now interesting only as curiosities—and in 1809 made his first professional career as an actor in the old Park Theatre, New York, taking the part of Norval in Douglass' tragedy of that name, a part which used to be the starting point in the career of every budding Roscius. The play has long been relegated to the bookshelf and is never now acted, but in the early part of the past century it was a prime favorite. Payne's success in the part was most flattering and after playing it in many American cities he repeated it in Drury Lane Theatre, London, with equal commendation from the critics and the public. That success determined his career and for some twenty years thereafter he was associated with the stage as actor, manager and playwright General James Grant Wilson writes: "While living in London and Paris, where he was intimate with Washington Irving, Payne wrote a host of dramas, chiefly adaptations from the French. In one of these, 'Clari; or The Maid of Milan,' occurs his deathless song of 'Home, Sweet Home,' which made the fortunes of all concerned, except the always unfortunate author. By it alone Payne will be remembered after his multitude of poems and dramas have been forgotten, which, indeed, has almost happened already His tragedy of 'Brutus,' produced in 1818, with Edmund Kean in the principal part, is his only dramatic composition that still holds possession of the stage, with the single exception of 'Charles the Second,' the leading character in which was a favorite with Charles Kemble." In 1832 the wanderer returned to America, as poor as when he left it, and pursued his theatrical career with varying fortunes, generally brief bits of success mingled with long periods of misfortune and poverty. Home he had none throughout his career since the death of his mother when he was a lad of thirteen years, and it was destined that he should die in exile from his native land. In 1841 he was appointed consul at Tunis and there he resided until his death, in 1852. His body was interred in a little cemetery on the shores of the Mediterranean until 1883, when it was removed to Oak Hill cemetery, Washington, and so poor Payne was home at last. His career was a sad one; poverty and he were close acquaintances; he "fattened on trouble and starvation," as he said himself, and he often in later years told a story of the bitterness he once felt on hearing his famous song sung one night in London when he himself was unable to raise the price of a night's lodging and had to find a home in the streets He made plenty of money but had no idea of how to keep it, and a hit, when it was made, only carried him and his friends--partners in his joys and often strangers to his sorrows—through for a few days, and then the weary round of misery was faced again. The penalties of genius were never better illustrated than in the sad career of this gifted singer. The genealogy of the Payne family has been made a theme of special study by Mr. Henry Whittemore, and, as much misunderstanding exists concerning the poet's ancestors and even concerning his birthplace, we give the record in full:

Thomas Paine, the progenitor of the family from which John Howard Payne descended, was the son of Thomas, supposed to have come from Kent, England, and presumably identical with Thomas Payne of Yarmouth, the first deputy from that place to the Old Colony Court at Plymouth in June, 1639.

Thomas Paine (2), son of Thomas (1), came to New England when a lad of ten years of age, and settled in Eastham before 1653, as he was constable there at that date. He was admitted freeman, 1658. He represented Eastham at the Colony Court 1671-2-3, 1676-78-80-81, and in 1690. He removed to Boston before 1695. He was a man of more than ordinary education, and was a very fine penman. He died at Eastham, August 16, 1706. He married Mary Snow, daughter of Hon. Nicholas Snow, who came in the Anne to Plymouth in 1623, and in 1654 removed to Eastham, Massachusetts. He married Constance Hopkins, daughter of Stephen Hopkins, of Plymouth, fourteenth signer of the "Mayflower Compact."

The children of Thomas and Mary (Snow) Paine were: Mary, Samuel, Thomas, Eleazer, Elisha, John, born March 14, 1660-1, Nicholas, James, Joseph, Dorcas.

Deacon John Paine, sixth child of Thomas (2) and Mary (Snow) Paine, was born in Eastham, Massachusetts, March 14, 1660-1. He was admitted freeman June, 1696. He was elected clerk of the town 1706 and re-elected until 1729 He was treasurer from 1709 to 1736, and Representative to the General Court at Boston 1703-9-14-16-18-24-5. He was of a literary turn of mind and some of his spare moments were devoted to literary pursuits. Scraps of prose and poetry written by him are still in the hands of his descendants. He died October 26, 1731.

He married first Bennet Freeman, daughter of Major John and Mercy (Prence) Freeman, born March, 1671. She was "a pleasant companion, a most loving and obedient wife, a tender and compassionate mother and a good Christian." By her he had John, Mary, William, born June 6, 1695; Benjamin, Sarah, Elizabeth, Theophilus, Joseph, Nathaniel, Rebecca, Mercy, Benjamin again.

He married, second, Alice Mayo, and had by her Hannah, James, Thomas, Alice, Hannah.

Lieut. William Paine, third child of Deacon John and Bennet (Freeman) Paine, was born at Eastham, June 6, 1695. He was a Representative to the Provincial Legislature from Eastham 1731-32-35-38-39-40-43-44. He was appointed one of His Majesty's Justices in 1738. He took part with the Colonial forces in the capture of Louisburg as lieutenant in Capt. Elisha Doane's company, Col. Gorham's Seventh Massachusetts Regiment, and died in service in 1746.

His first wife was Sarah Bacon, of Barnstable, whom he married in 1727. He married, second, June 14, 1741, Elizabeth Myrick, a widow, the daughter of Rev. Samuel Osborn, pastor of the South Church in Eastham, and sister of Dr. John Osborn, the distinguished physician and poetical writer of Middletown, Connecticut. By his first wife he had Sarah, Ruth, Josiah, Jedediah He had one child by his second wife, William, born 1746.

William Paine, or Payne (2), son of Lieut William and Elizabeth (Myrick, nee Osborn) Paine, was born in 1746, the year his father died in the Colonial service His mother remarried and he was placed in the family of Rev. Joseph Crocker, pastor of the South Congregational Church of Eastham. He commenced the study of medicine under Dr. Joseph Warren, who fell at Bunker Hill. He was interrupted in his studies by the events which immediately preceded the Revolution, and opened an English Grammar School in Boston, but on account of the occupation of that city by the British he gave it up and became a tutor in a private family Writing to a friend of his experience at that time, he says: He was obliged to be in his school "from the first entrance of light till nine in the evening." While on a visit to Barnstable he married Lucy Taylor, who died shortly after the marriage. He went to New London, Connecticut, and there engaged in a mercantile adventure to the West Indies. On his return he formed the acquaintance of Miss Sarah Isaacs, of East Hampton, Long Island, who was on a visit there, and soon after married her Her father was a convert from the Jewish faith, who came from Hamburg, Germany, previous to the Revolution and settled at East Hampton. He was a man of education and wealth, but difficulties in his own country and the Revolution in his adopted country induced heavy losses and left him comparatively poor. His wife, a Miss Hedges, was the daughter of a lady whose maiden name was Talmage. His uncle Talmage was the Earl of Dysart, a British nobleman.

William Paine, or, as he wrote his name, "Payne," settled in East Hampton after his marriage, about 1780, and became one of the teachers of the academy there. His wife, who was a woman of remarkable beauty, fine education and many excellent traits of character, assisted her husband in teaching. Payne continued there for about ten years. Several of his children were born there, and this was really the only home he ever possessed He removed to New York in 1790, where he taught school for some years In 1793 he resided at No. 5 Dey street, and he also

Payne Home.

resided and taught school on Little Queen street. In 1799 he was invited by some influential men in Boston to open a school there, which became quite noted. He returned to New York about 1809 and taught school on Common near Grand street. He died March 7, 1812.

In the cemetery at East Hampton is the grave marked by a stone of Andrew Isaacs, the father of William Payne's wife, Sarah (Isaacs) Payne, on which is inscribed: "Behold an Israelite in Whom is No Guile."

William Payne by his wife Sarah (Isaacs) Payne had issue:

1. Lucy Taylor, born 1781, at East Hampton, married, in 1816, Dr. John Cheever Osborne, of New York; died in Brooklyn, 1865, left no issue.

2. William Osborne, born at East Hampton, August 4, 1783, died March 24, 1804.

3. Sarah Isaacs, born at East Hampton, July 11, 1785, died in New York, October 14, 1808.

4. Eloise Richards, born at East Hampton, March 12, 1787, died at Leicester, Massachusetts, July, 1819.

5. Anna Beren Leagers, born at East Hampton, April 9, 1789, died at Newport, Rhode Island, October 11, 1789.

6. John Howard, the poet, born in New York city, at 33 Pearl street, June 9, 1791, died at Tunis, Africa, April 9, 1852

7. Eliza Maria, born in New York city, September 19, 1795, died there May 25, 1797.

8. Thatcher Taylor, born in New York city, August 14, 1796, married in New York, 1833, Mrs. Anna Elizabeth Bailey, died in Brooklyn, December 27, 1863.

9. Elizabeth Mary, born in Boston, Massachusetts, died there aged about two years.

WILLIAM CULLEN BRYANT.

Stephen Bryant is the first of the name mentioned in the New England records. The date and place of his birth are not given. The "History of North Bridgewater, Massachusetts," states that he was in Plymouth Colony as early as 1632. His name is entered on the list of 1643 among those able to bear arms, which he probably did He was admitted a freeman of the colony in 1653, and was chosen constable of Duxbury, June 6, 1654, and was constable at Plymouth, January 1, 1663. He married Abigail, daughter of John Shaw, of Plymouth, and had children: Abigail, John, Mary, Stephen, Sarah, Lydia, Elizabeth.

Stephen Bryant (2), son of Stephen (1) and Abigail (Shaw) Bryant, was born at Plymouth, February 2, 1658 He married Mehitabel ———— and had Stephen (3), David, William, Hannah, Ichabod, Timothy.

Ichabod Bryant, fifth child of Stephen (2) and Mehitabel (————) Bryant, was born at Middleboro, Massachusetts, July 5, 1699; died August 2, 1759. He married Ruth Staples, who died March 27, 1777 They had Philip, Nathan, Seth, Job, Gamalius, Phebe, Ruth, Sarah, Anna, Prudence

Dr. Philip Bryant (1), eldest child of Ichabod and Ruth (Staples) Bryant, was born in Middleboro, Massachusetts, December, 1732. He lived some time with his father at Titicut (Teightaqued), a parish formed of part of Middleboro and part of South Bridgewater, and then removed to North Bridgewater. He studied medicine with Dr. Abiel Howard, of West Bridgewater. He continued to practice medicine with much success. He married in 1757, Selena, daughter of Dr Abial Howard She died June 25, 1777. He married second, Hannah, daughter of Benjamin Richards He died December 19, 1816, aged eighty. His children were all by his first wife. These were Oliver, born March 5, 1758, Ruth, Daniel, Bezaleel, Philip, Jr, Cyrus, Anna, Selena, Charity

Dr. Philip Bryant (2), son of Dr. Philip (1) and Selena (Howard) Bryant, was born at West Bridgewater, Massachusetts, August 12, 1767 He was a physician and settled at Cumington, Massachusetts.

Dr Bryant married in 1792, Sarah Snell, daughter of Ebenezer and Sarah (Packard) Snell, born at North Bridgewater, Massachusetts, April 6, 1766. Their children were 1 Anson, born April 16, 1793, married Adeline Plummer. 2. William Cullen, born November 3, 1794, married Frances Fairchild 3. Cyrus, born July 12, 1798 4. Sarah Snell, born July 24, 1802. 5. Arthur, born November 28, 1803, married Henrietta R Plummer

William Cullen Bryant, second child of Dr. Philip (2) and Sarah (Snell) Bryant, was born in Cumington, Massachusetts, November 3, 1794. He made metrical translations from the Latin before he was ten years old His father superintended his education His "Embargo," a political satire, and the "Spanish Revolution" were published in his fourteenth year, and again in 1809. Entering Williams College in 1810 he remained two years, taking high rank in literary studies. He chose the legal profession and was admitted to the bar in 1815, and commenced practice in Plainfield, Massachusetts, removing thence to Great Barrington : but though he rose to distinction in the courts, his tastes inclined him to literature. "Thanatopsis" was written in his eighteenth year. He wrote several prose articles for the North American Review in 1818. In 1821 he delivered before the Phi Beta Kappa Society of Harvard University a poem on "The Ages," and a volume containing several of his poems, published at Cambridge, at once stamped him as a genuine poet He was married while living at Great Barrington, and there wrote some of his finest poems.

He moved to New York in 1825 and edited the *New York Review,* which was soon after merged into the *United States Review,* for which he wrote poems and criticisms. In 1826 he became one of the editors of the *Evening Post.* This he subsequently, upon obtaining its exclusive control, changed from a Federal to a Democratic print, favoring free trade

In 1832-45-49-57 he traveled in Europe, his observations forming material for his books entitled "Letters of a Traveler," "Letters From Spain and Other Countries." In 1849 he extended his journey into Egypt and Syria. From 1827 to 1834, with Sands & Verplank, he edited "The Talisman," an annual, and contributed "Medfield" and the "Skelerton Cave" to the "Tales of the Glauber Spa." In 1832 a complete edition of his poems appeared in New York, and Washington Irving, then in England, caused it to be reprinted there with a laudatory preface, securing him a European reputation. Before going abroad in 1832 he associated William Legget with himself in the management of *The Post,* and he continued his connection with the paper up to the time of his death He made his first purchase of property in Roslyn in 1845, soon after removing there.

Of all the American poets, probably none was more beloved than Bryant, and when he had attained his eightieth year, the suggestion was made by a few of his admiring friends that a suitable tribute of respect to his genius was due to him, and after consultation it was decided that a commemorative vase of appropriate original design and choice workmanship, would be the best form of intended tribute, especially since Mr. Bryant did not need any material aid, and moreover, the sculptor and painter and engraver conspicuously paid their respects to him A committee of twenty-five gentlemen of New York and Brook-

Cedarmere, Home of Wm. Cullen Bryant.

lyn took the matter into their charge, and associated with them prominent citizens of other parts of the country from Boston to San Francisco The committee waited upon Mr. Bryant at his home upon the eightieth anniversary of his birthday, November 3, 1874, and after an address by Mr Jonathan Sturgess, the written testimonial of respect with its large list of signers was presented, and Mr Bryant made an appropriate and memorable reply. The occasion was remarkable from the representative character of the company that met together, and from the interest of the interview.

Arrangements were made at once for competitive designs and the field of competition was thrown open to the whole craft of silversmiths. The design of Mr. Whitehouse, of the firm of Tiffany & Company, was accepted unanimously, alike from its beauty and fitness and the public were encouraged to study their merits by friendly comments from the committee, and by articles in the newspapers and illustrations in the magazines.

In stating his conception of the design to the committee, Mr. James H. Whitehead the artist said: "When the Bryant testimonial was first mentioned to me, my thoughts at once flew to the country—to the crossing of the boughs of trees, to the plants and flowers, and to a general contemplation of nature; and these, together with a certain Homeric influence, produced in my mind the germ of the design—the form of a Greek vase, with the most beautiful American flowers growing round and entwining themselves gracefully about it, each breathing its own particular glory as it grew."

The vase is entirely covered with a fretwork formed of apple branches and their blossoms, or a delicate basket work from the apple tree, which so well expressed Mr. Bryant's poetry in its fragrant bloom and its wholesome fruit. Beneath this fretwork, and forming the finer lines of the fret, are the primrose and the amaranth, which out of the lips of their loveliness speak their lessons of inspiration and of immortality. The body of the vase which is thus formed and enriched, bears expressive and elaborate medallions of the poet and of the main aspects of his life and works. The most prominent of these medallions is a portrait bust of the poet. Above his head is the lyre which represents his art, and below is the printing press in its primitive form, which suggests his career of journalism, while more prominent still, further below, is the elaborate and beautiful design of the water-fowl which so presents God over nature in the charming and exalting poem of that name. On the opposite side of the vase there is a carefully designed and executed study of Poetry contemplating Nature—two female figures, which balance wisely the somewhat severely masculine character of the other designs, and give their womanly grace to the honor of the poet whose life and works so well harmonize in respect for woman, and for the home, marriage, and religion, that give her the best defense and power. Between these two principal medallions there are on each side two groups illustratting scenes in the poet's life, making four groups in all. The first group presents him in company with his father, who points to Homer as a model in poetic composition:

"For he is grave who taught my youth
The art of verse, and in the bud of life
Offered me to the muses."

The next group presents him as the student of nature such as he appears in "Thanatopsis" or "A Forest Hymn."

The third design illustrates his life as journalist, and the fourth represents him in his good old age as translator of the Iliad and the Odyssey. The lower part of the bowl bears ornamentation from the characteristic products of American agriculture—cotton and Indian corn. The neck is encircled with primrose and ivy in token of youth and old age, while the "fringed genitian" suggests the grave thought from its blue petals:

> "I would thus when I shall see
> The hour of death draw near to me,
> Hope blossoming within my heart,
> May look to heaven as 1 depart."

KING FAMILY.

* "John Alsop King, Jr., second son of Governor John Alsop King and Mary Ray, his wife, was born at Jamaica, Long Island, July 14, 1817. His early years were passed at Jamaica, where he was educated at the Union Hall Academy, the classical school of Dr. Louis E. A. Eigenbrodt. At the early age of fifteen he entered Harvard College in the sophomore class, and was graduated with much credit. For a short time afterward he was a clerk in the house of Ebenezer Stevens, but, disliking the business, he took up the study of law, and was admitted to the bar of New York and practiced his profession for several years

"After his marriage, in 1839, he went to Europe and spent some years in travel there, and subsequently made frequent visits there. His last journey extended to Egypt, where he and his family remained for a winter.

"In 1854 he bought a beautiful point of land on Long Island Sound, part of the Hewlet Point property, where he built his fine mansion and made his home there for the remainder of his life. His tastes led him to become a member of the agricultural societies of Queens county, and he took an active part in their proceedings, as well as a deep interest in all the affairs of the neighborhood, both political and religious. Here, as elsewhere, his genial disposition and courteous manners won for him the esteem of those with whom he was brought in contact.

"The Republican party of that day was guided by the principles which he had inherited, and he became interested in promoting them. His first public appointment was as presidential elector in 1872; this was followed by an election to the state

---

* Extract from a paper read by the Very Rev Eugene A Hoffman before the New York Historical Society, February 5, 1901

senate, in which he served during the years 1874-1875. He was a zealous supporter and defender of the Erie canal, and of the constitutional amendments which brought about many reforms in the state government. With the aid of the members of the first district, he succeeded in securing the repeal of the infamous act of 1868, by which, unknown to the owners, the salt meadow water fronts of Staten and Long Islands had been sold for a trifling sum to a land company. For his services in securing the passage of the act establishing the Court of Arbitration he received a vote of thanks from the New York Chamber of Commerce. In the year 1876 he was nominated in his district for the office of representative in the national congress, but was defeated, as he was also in 1880, the district being strongly Democratic.

"In 1881 Mr. King was appointed, by Governor Cornell, the commissioner for the state of New York, to receive and extend the courtesies and hospitalities of the state to the delegation from France and the other foreign guests invited by the United States to take part at Yorktown in the centennial celebration Both duties were faithfully performed

"From that time, though still interested in the welfare of his party, he was no longer prominent in politics, but devoted himself to other pursuits for which he had long felt a deep concern. These were chiefly in connection with the church in which he was brought up, and which was that of his affections, the Protestant Episcopal church His desire to promote its interests and to do good in his generation was shown by his connecting himself with Zion church at Little Neck, Long Island, of which he was for many years a warden, and afterwards by his materially aiding in building the Church of All Saints at Great Neck, of which he was every year elected a warden up to the close of his life He was a delegate to the diocesan convention of New York, from Grace church, Jamaica, from 1850 to 1866, and, after the division of the diocese of New York, a delegate to the Long Island diocesan convention, from Zion church, Little Neck, from 1863 to 1887, and from All Saints' church, Great Neck, from 1888 to the date of his death. During all these years he was a member of important committees of the diocesan conventions and was always present at their meetings, except when absent from the country. He was a trustee of the Fund for Aged and Infirm Clergymen from the year 1869, and a trustee of the General Theological Seminary from the year 1872. Both these offices, as well as those of member of the board of

John Alsop King Homestead at Great Neck.

managers of the Domestic and Foreign Missionary Society, and trustee of King Hall, Washington, D. C, founded and largely endowed by himself, for the higher education of the colored race, he held up to the time of his death He was a deputy to the Federal Council on every occasion from its formation in 1871, and a deputy to eight successive Triennial General Conventions of the church. He was also a lay member of the Cathedral Chapter of Long Island, and, following the example of his ancestors, he was a liberal benefactor of Grace church, Jamaica. He and his wife were greatly interested in the New York Asylum for the Blind, of which he was a manager, and it has been truly said that in all his efforts to promote benevolent objects, his wife and daughters were ever ready to join with him

"Mr King became a member of the New York Historical Society in 1881. In 1887 he was elected its eighteenth president, and, devoting himself to its interests, was annually re-elected to the same office. He delivered the address at the eighty-third anniversary of the founding of the society, November 15, 1887, the subject of his address being 'The Framing of the Federal Constitution and the Causes Leading Thereto.' This address was published by the society. At a meeting held June 5, 1900, Mr. King presented and read a memorial of Robert Schell, late treasurer of the society.

"He was very seldom missing from the presidential chair at the monthly meetings of the society, and was a frequent visitor to the library, looking over, with Mr. Kilby, the librarian, the latest additions to the books and manuscripts. The last time he presided was at the meeting on October 2nd. Mr. King's elder brother, Dr. Charles Ray King, was then the oldest member of the society

"Our late president was deeply interested in procuring a new building for the society, and it was under his inspiration that ten full city lots, in the block between Seventy-sixth and Seventy-seventh streets, west of the park, were purchased as a site for the purpose. He had intended, early in the year, to call a meeting of the society, to take steps for raising the money to build at least a part of it.

"This is but an imperfect summary of the many good deeds of our friend's busy and well-spent life. It reveals a man of marked manliness of character, with a singularly sweet and loving disposition Holding decided views, conscientiously maintained, on questions which came before him, they were not put forward without a due regard for those who differed from him. Notwithstanding the multiplicity of works in which he engaged, they were always accompanied by such modesty and reticence that few, even of his intimate friends, were aware of the energy and punctuality with which he devoted himself to the duties which he voluntarily assumed for the good of others. Of all the boards and committees of which he was a member he was never absent from a meeting unless prevented by other imperative duties. For twenty years it has been my privilege to sit beside him in the board of managers of our Missionary Society. In all that time I have been a constant observer of the careful and conscientious manner in which he discharged its important responsibilities In addition to all these public duties, how many days and hours he devoted to personal acts of kindness will never be known until that day when their recipients will rise up and call him blessed. His heart and his hand were always open to every appeal of suffering and want.

"Such was the honorable and noble life of our late president—devoted to the good of others, free in every stage of it from the reproach of weakness or of personal ends, marked throughout by high aims conscientiously carried out, by an enlightened love of goodness, and by the unhesitating devotion of the individual, his faculties and his possessions to the service of God and his fellow men.

"In private life he was what we are accustomed to describe as a gentleman of the old school As the first bishop of Long Island has truthfully recorded: 'Manners with him was a phase of morals Courage and politeness were, in his view, only other names for benevolence in small things. He not only believed in saying what is true and doing what is right, but in saying and doing it with kindly regard to the feelings and circumstances of others His gracious affability was more than a sentiment, because it stood for the dignity of a principle.'

"Lastly, I do not hesitate to hold up his life as a pattern of an humble, sincere and devout Christian man. Accepting with his whole heart the fundamental truths of the Christian faith as set forth in the ancient creeds, illustrating them in his daily walk and conversation, his constant aim was, as the Lord requires, 'to do justly, to love mercy, and to walk humbly with his God.'

"And so when the end came, it was in keeping with his life As every Christian should desire to die—surrounded by his children, with mental abilities unabated, receiving from a beloved pastor the last *viaticum*—he calmly fell asleep and was gathered unto his fathers, having the testimony of a good conscience, in the communion of the Catholic church, in the confidence of a certain faith, in the comfort of a reasonable, religious, and only hope, in favor with his God, and in perfect charity with the world.

"His funeral services were held in St. Thomas' church, which, though the weather was very stormy, was filled with the representatives of the various institutions for which he had labored, and a large number of the leading men of the city. His body was laid in the grave by the side of his ancestors and kindred, under the shadow of the old church at Jamaica, Long Island, in sure and certain hope of the resurrection and the life of the world to come There we left it, with the words on our lips and in our hearts: 'Blessed are the dead who die in the Lord; even so saith the Spirit, for they rest from their labors.' "

Mr. King married, February 21, 1839, Mary Colden Rhinelander, only daughter of Philip and Mary Colden Hoffman Rhinelander. of New York, son of William Rhinelander, Jr., son of William Rhinelander (1), son of Philip Jacob Rhinelander, the ancestor of the Rhinelander family. Their children were: 1 Mary Rhinelander. 2. Cornelia Ray, died early 3. Alice, married Gherardi Davis. 4. Frederic, died in childhood 5. Ellen King

Miss May Rhinelander King, who occupies the beautiful homestead at Great Neck, is now the only representative of this branch of the King family residing on Long Island.

JAMES S. T STRANAHAN.

True men are the crown jewels of the republic The very names of the distinguished dead are a continual inspiration and an abiding lesson. The name Garibaldi thrills the sons of Italy; the enthusiasm of the liberty-loving Swiss is aroused by the mention of Hofer; Wallace and Bruce are names which inspire every Scot; and in our own land a feeling of veneration and honor is felt as those of Washington and Lincoln are uttered.

This is not only true of those who have advanced the spirit of liberty, but of the men who have broadened the realms of thought; who have opened the fields of knowledge and contributed in any measure to the progress of the world, their efforts redounding to the benefit of their fellow men along the lines of material, intellectual, æsthetic or moral development. The work which they perform is a more enduring monument than any which might be erected of stone or bronze, for it wins the enduring love of a grateful people, and the story of their lives is handed down to posterity, and their names are honored throughout time When the years have become a part of a long vanished past, history throws around the great men of earth an idealization,—in other words, only the resplendent virtues are emphasized; but even in the light of the present, the strong, practical judgment of the day acknowledges the value of the service which James S T. Stranahan rendered to his fellow men, and the city of Brooklyn largely stands as the visible evidence of a life whose far-reaching influence has affected for good so many of his fellow men

One of the strongest forces in the psychic world is the association of ideas, and to a student of history the city of Brooklyn cannot be mentioned without bringing to mind James S. T. Stranahan, who left the impress of his forceful individuality upon almost every line of progress and improvement that has led to the substantial growth and advancement of the city. His life's span covered nine decades—years of purpose well directed, plans carefully formed—an era of splendid achievement.

His life record began on the 25th of April, 1808, at the old family homestead in Madison county, New York, near Peterboro, his parents being Samuel and Lynda (Josselyn) Stranahan. He traced his lineage to Scotch-Irish ancestry, of Presbyterian faith—men of strong, rugged, determined character, and women of virtue, diligence and culture. The first of the name of whom record is left was James Stranahan, who was born in the north of Ireland, in 1699. The orthography of the name has undergone many changes, having been in the following forms: Stranahan, Strachan and Strahan. The name, however, is derived from the parish of Strachan, Kincardineshire, Scotland. James Stranahan, the grandfather of him whose name forms the caption of this review, crossed the Atlantic to the new world in 1725, locating in Scituate, Rhode Island, where he became a prosperous farmer. He afterward removed to Plainfield, Connecticut, where he died in 1792, at the advanced age of ninety-three years His namesake and eldest son served as a Revolutionary soldier in the war which brought independence to the nation, and lived and died in Plainfield, Connecticut.

James S T Stranahan lost his father when eight years of age, and his happy boyhood days were soon transformed into a period of labor, for his stepfather needed his assistance in the development of the farm and the care of the stock. However, when the work of the farm was ended for the season he entered the district schools, and there acquired his early education, which was later supplemented by several terms of study in an academy From the age of seventeen he depended entirely upon his own resources. After completing his academical work he engaged in teaching school, with the intention of later fitting himself for the profession of civil engineer; but the occupation of trading with the Indians in the northwest seemed to offer greater inducements, and in 1829 he visited the upper lake region. He made several trips into the wilderness, and these, together with the advice of General Lewis Cass, then governor of the territory of Michigan, led him to abandon that plan, and he returned to his home.

The elemental strength of his character was first clearly demonstrated by his work in building the town of Florence, New York. From his boyhood he had known Gerrit Smith, the eminent capitalist and philanthropist, who in 1832 made him a proposition according to the terms of which he was to go to Oneida county, New York, where Mr. Smith owned large tracts of land, and found a manufacturing town He was then a young man of only twenty-four years, but the work was successfully accomplished, and the village of Florence, New York, was transformed into a thriving little city of between two and three thousand His active identification with things political began during the period of his residence in Florence, for in 1838 he was elected to the state legislature on the Whig ticket, in a Democratic district.

A broader field of labor soon engaged the attention and energies of Mr Stranahan, who in 1840 removed to Newark, New Jersey, and became an active factor in railroad building. In 1844 he came to Brooklyn, and from that time until his death he was a most potent factor in the commercial life, the political interests and the general upbuilding of the city. He found it a municipality with but fifty thousand inhabitants. He went to the city a comparative stranger For some decades prior to his death he was known as "the first citizen of Brooklyn." Therein is found an expression of the high regard in which he was uniformly held It is also an indication of the part which he played in its public affairs, the title being a free-will offering of a grateful people, who recognized his merit, his ability and the wonderful work which he had accomplished for Brooklyn.

The public, however, is a discriminating factor, and not at once did Mr Stranahan gain his exalted position in public opinion. His first official service was as alderman, to which position he was elected in 1848 and in 1850 he was nominated for mayor, but his party was in the minority and he was defeated. His personal attributes at that time were not so well known as they were in later years, and thus he could not overcome the party strength of his opponent. However, his nomination served the purpose of bringing him before the public, and in 1854, when the country was intensely excited over the slavery question, he became a candidate for congress, and, although he was a strong anti-slavery man and the district was Democratic, he was triumphantly elected. In 1857, when the Metropolitan Police Commission was organized, he was appointed a commissioner, and he was one of the most active members of the board during the struggle between the new forces and the old New York municipal police force of New York, Brooklyn and Staten Island, who revolted under the new leadership of Fernando Wood, then mayor. Mr. Stranahan had joined the ranks of the new Republican party on its organization, and in 1864 he was a presidential elector on the Lincoln and Johnson ticket. In 1860, and again in 1864, he had been sent as a delegate to the Republican national convention, and at both times supported the Illinois statesman, Lincoln, for the presidency. During the Civil war he was president of the War Fund Committee, an organization formed of over one hundred leading men of Brooklyn, whose patriotic sentiment gave rise to the *Brooklyn Union,* a paper which was in full accord with the governmental policy, and upheld the hands of the president in every possible way. Its purpose was to encourage enlistments and to further the efforts of the government in prosecuting the war. Mr. Stranahan had an unshaken confidence in the ultimate triumph of the Union cause, and his splendid executive ability and unfaltering determination were of incalculable benefit in promoting the efficiency of the committee. His labors, too, were the potent element in carrying forward a work in which this commission was associated with the Woman's Relief Association, of which Mrs. Stranahan was president. This work was the establishment of a great sanitary fair, which has become historical and which was the means of raising four hundred thousand dollars to carry on the work of the sanitary commission in connection with the war. Mr. Stranahan never sought public office for himself except in the few instances mentioned, and then his nomination came as a tribute to his ability In 1888, however, he was an elector for Benjamin Harrison, and being the oldest member of the electoral college, was honored by being appointed the messenger to carry the electoral vote from the state of New York to Washington.

It is almost impossible to give in a brief biographical sketch an accurate record of the great work which Mr. Stranahan did in connection with the upbuilding of Brooklyn. His name is a familiar one in the city on account of his labors in behalf of the park system. Under the legislative act of 1860 he became president of the Brooklyn Park Commission, and he remained in office for twenty-two years, a period in which the growth of the city made demands for a park system that, under his guidance, was developed and carried forward to splendid completion. Prospect Park is an everlasting monument to him. He was also the originator of the splendid system of boulevards, the Ocean Parkway and the Eastern Parkway, which has provided in Brooklyn a connection of the city with the sea in a system of drives unsurpassed by any in the world. The concourse on Coney Island also resulted from his instrumentality. The element which made Mr. Stranahan's work different from that of all others was that he could forsee possibilities. It was this which led to the development of Coney Island, for to him it seemed that the natural boundary of Brooklyn on the southwest was the Atlantic ocean, and he took steps to secure the rare advantage of an attractive highway from the city to the sea. It seems that every work with which he was connected proved of the greatest value to the city.

The enterprises which he managed were gigantic in volume and far-reaching in effect. For more than forty years he was a director of the Union Ferry Company, and under his guidance were developed the great Atlantic docks. Brooklyn had no warehouse on its water front and the region which is now the Atlantic docks was shallow water at the edge of the bay when he came to the city. He foresaw the possibilities for commerce by establishing docks at this point, and he labored with a courage and patience that has scarcely been equaled in the history of material improvement in the world. It was twenty-six years from the time he advanced his plans for the dock system before the Atlantic Dock Company made a dividend to its stockholders, and yet today its shipping returns are greater than those of almost any other port of the world. Only to the civil engineer is the scope of this wonderful undertaking familiar. One who has not studied the science cannot conceive of the amplitude of this work. Mr. Stranahan was also connected with the Brooklyn Bridge Company from its organization, and was one of the first subscribers to its stock; he was a member of the board of directors of the New York Bridge Company, and he served continuously as trustee from the time the work came under the control of the two cities until June 8, 1885. At the meeting of the trustees on that date he occupied the chair as president of the board, and at that time his term expired. He also served continuously as a member of the executive committee, and upon nearly all of the important committees appointed during construction. He foresaw the immense volume of traffic that would be conducted over this mammoth span, and insisted that the original plans should be altered to insure to the giant structure strength sufficient to enable it to carry a train of Pullman cars. Mr. Stranahan consulted with Commodore Vanderbilt, who agreed with him in the opinion that the time would arrive when solid Pullman trains would run in and out of Brooklyn from and to far western points.

The following speech, delivered by Mr. Stranahan, May 8, 1883, at the annual banquet of the Chamber of Commerce of the city of New York, in response to the following toast, "The Great Bridge, the Engineering Triumph of the Nineteenth Century; Its Originators and Directors, for Their Patience, Fidelity and Zeal Deserve Everlasting Gratitude; Its Constructors Achieve Immortal Fame and Its Complete Success," is reproduced for three reasons—because it is historic, because it is a literary gem, illustrative of Mr Stranahan's convincing style of oratory, and because it contains his views in regard to the union of the two cities:

Mr. President and Gentlemen:
I cannot, in responding to the toast which you have just read, do less, and will not attempt more, than to make a brief reference to the East river bridge.

That bridge, so long the object of public thought, and not infrequently the target of newspaper criticism, now substantially finished and destined in a short time to be opened for general use, needs no eulogy from my lips. There it stands, its own orator, and there for generations it will stand, its own historian. It will for ages be one of the attractions and one of the wonders of this great metropolitan center. Its fame will be world-wide; and the foreign traveler who seeks these shores will feast his eyes and gratify his curiosity in gazing upon a structure that now has no parallel in any of the products of human art.

The past history of the bridge is so lost in the reality of the present that the briefest reference thereto will suffice for the occasion I hardly need say that the construction of this work has, at all times, been under the supervision of men of acknowledged integrity; and that, for the past eight years, the mayors and comptrollers of the two cities have been members of the board of trustees. I know of no public work that has been conducted with greater economy or a stricter regard for the general good. Though the trustees have often been sharply criticised by the loose talker and the newspaper scribbler, they have steadily and persistently pursued their work, confident that time and the result would be their best vindication.

High honor should be awarded to the chief engineers, the elder and the younger Roebling, the former of whom lost his life, and the latter his health, in a work second to no other of its kind in any age The skill and painstaking labor of the assistant engineers, having the immediate charge of the work, have attracted the attention and won the admiration of every intelligent visitor to the bridge.

The original estimate was that the bridge would cost $7,000,000, and the land on which it rests has cost $3,800,000, making an aggregate cost of $10,800,000. The actual cost, including the land taken, is about $15,000,000. This estimate, however, did not contemplate such a structure as the one that now exists. The height of the bridge was increased in obedience to the order of the general government, and its width and strength by the direction of the trustees. The bridge, as actually constructed, will support the freight and passenger trains of the trunk railways of the country It has two carriage roads, instead of one, as at first intended The original plan was that the approaches to the bridge should be simple iron trestle-work, for which the trustees thought it expedient to substitute massive arches of brick and granite. The cables and suspended structure are composed of steel, instead of iron. In a word, the bridge, as it now is, if it has cost more than the original estimate, is not the bridge that was contemplated in that estimate It is higher, wider and composed of stronger material It furnishes an elevated highway between the two cities that is wider than Broadway These changes, in the way of improvement, abundantly explain the increase of cost They were needed to make the bridge what it should be

I feel confident that, on the opening of the bridge, the opinion of the general public will confer with that of a distinguished member of the chamber, who, after a walk with me over the structure, exclaimed, as we came near the New York side: "Well, I had no idea of the magnitude of this work It is indeed, grand in its conception, and, if possible, grander still in the courage of its execution " The bridge told its own story to that gentleman; and that story it will repeat in the ears of millions. To stand upon it, and see it, and see all that it reveals to the eye, is to admire. All sense of danger and all ideas of weakness at once disappear. The marvel is that human power, even when availing itself of natural laws, could produce such a result.

I do not know, Mr. Chairman, whether you have heard it or not; yet I may as well say that the people of Brooklyn have an idea in regard to this bridge which is quite sure to reveal itself at no distant period. Brooklyn, as you are aware, is by the East river isolated from the main land. The people of that city hope that the bridge will remove that isolation, and put them in direct railway communication not only with New York city, but with all parts of the country. This will greatly serve their convenience and promote their prosperity. New York will certainly not object, and will not be the loser. If a bridge over the Harlem river connects New York with the main land, why should not a bridge over the East river perform a similar service in behalf of Brooklyn and Long Island? Brooklyn believes in utilizing the bridge to this end; and fortunately the end can be gained without any serious disturbance of existing conditions in the city of New York.

The Second avenue railway has, between the Harlem river and Twenty-third street, sufficient width for four tracks, and, between this street and the New York terminus of the bridge, for three tracks; and it is withal so strongly built as to make it entirely possible to utilize it to the full extent of giving to Brooklyn and the system of railroads on Long Island an outlet through the Hudson river and New Haven roads to all parts of the country. This view contemplates no public or private concessions on the part of the city of New York It rests simply upon that business theory which so strongly marks the great trunk lines of the country, and to which the Hudson river and New Haven roads are no strangers. Though Brooklyn does not expect to rival the commercial grandeur of the greater city, she does expect in this way to be put in rapid and easy connection with the outside world, and, by her extended water front, by her capabilities of indefinite territorial expansion, and by her numerous attractions as a place of residence, to maintain, at the least, her past record in the growth of population and wealth.

Mr. Chairman, Brooklyn has another idea, and has long had it, the accomplishment of which she hopes will be facilitated by this bridge. The Thames flows through the heart of London, and the Seine through the heart of Paris; but in neither case have you two cities It is London on both sides of the

Thames, and Paris on both sides of the Seine. The corporate unity is not dissevered by either river. Numerous bridges make the connection between the two sides in both cities; and it is best for both that it should be so. The population on neither side would be advantaged by being split up into two municipalities Here, however, we have our New York city and our Brooklyn, with the East river rolling between them. They are distant cities, in immediate contiguity with each other, and separated by a water highway. Is this distinctness of municipality any advantage to either? 1 think not. Would the consolidation of these two cities into one municipal corporation be any harm to either? I think not. The people are the same people, have the same manners and customs, and have common commercial and social interests; and one municipal government would serve them quite as well as two, and at far less cost I know of no reason why this distinctness should be continued other than the fact that it exists; and I confess I see no good reason why it should exist at all I may be mistaken, but I think that the public sentiment of Brooklyn would cordially welcome a consolidation of the two cities under the title of New York The East river bridge, now superadded to the ferry system, will, as Brooklyn hopes, so facilitate their mutual intercourse that both, without any special courtship on either side, will alike ask the legislature of the state to enact the ceremony of a municipal marriage; and if this shall be done, then I venture to predict that each will be so happy and so well content with the other that neither will ever seek a divorce.

I have thus, Mr. Chairman, briefly responded to the toast upon which I have been asked to speak; and, as I close, I cannot forbear to express the solid satisfaction which the trustees, who have for years given an unpaid service to the construction of the East river bridge, now feel, not only in view of its completion, but also of the character of the result attained. They will pass away; generations will come and go; but the monument will live Centuries will roll away; and the bridge, though it may grow old in years, and in the far distant future be studied and used as the product of a by-gone age, will still retain its strength The cables will not snap, and the towers will not fall. The anchorages will be true to their trust. The massive arches will not collapse. The steel and granite will not rot. Fire will not burn the bridge Freight trains and Pullman cars will not break it The winds will not shake it. Time and toil will not fatigue it Its youth and age will be alike periods of vigor.

That bridge, Mr Chairman, was built to stand; and stand it will—so long that we may well call it immortal.

Mr. Stranahan's work in another regard largely brought about the union of Brooklyn and New York. Long before the consummation of the project, he was one of the strongest advocates; in fact, he was the first man to put forth the idea. He viewed the question from the standpoint of a statesman, and worked upon the subject with the ability and skill of a diplomat. He realized that the completion of the Brooklyn bridge was a step toward the ultimate success of this condition. He realized that the cost of maintaining one central city government would be much less than two, and the work in all the departments might be far more effective, and he lived to see the consummation of his hopes.

Mr. Stranahan was twice married. In early manhood he wedded Marianne Fitch, who was born in Westmoreland, Oneida county, New York, and was a daughter of Ebenezer R. Fitch. For three years, from 1837 until 1840, they resided in Florence, New York, and during their four years' residence in Newark, New Jersey, their two children were born Mrs. Stranahan died in Manchester, Vermont, in August, 1866, after twenty-two years' residence in Brooklyn. Mr. Stranahan afterward married Miss Clara C Harrison, a native of Massachusetts Before her marriage she was one of the leaders in educational circles in Brooklyn, and for a number of years was principal of a private seminary for the higher education of young ladies, which had an enrollment of two hundred pupils, and fourteen teachers and professors in its various departments. She is a graduate of Mrs. Emma Willard's far-famed seminary, of Troy, New York. She took a very active part in the great sanitary fair as a member of the committee on art, and of the committee on the postoffice and *Drum Beat,* the latter a paper issued daily during the continuance of the fair, and of which Dr. Storrs was editor. From the postoffice many hundred letters of greatly varied character were distributed. A volume of autograph letters, chiefly from statesmen conspicuous at that time, were collected and bound through her agency, and brought several hundred dollars into the treasury. Mrs. Stranahan has ever been an active promoter of educational interests. She is a "founder" and the Brooklyn trustee of Barnard College. She is also vice-president of the alumnæ association of her alma mater. She is an ardent advocate of the higher education of women, and in that direction is always ready to respond to the call for any aid which her influence, her presence or her pen can give She has become widely known throughout the country as one of the most prominent members of the Daughters of the American Revolution Tracing her ancestry from those who fought for the liberty of the colonies, she became a member of the organization and was elected one of its vice-presidents-general, the highest tributes they have paid to her ability as a presiding officer and as a parliamentarian; but her prominence in these lines is not less pronounced than her fame in the field of literature She has written much upon many articles of interest to the public at the time when her pen gave to the press the written documents, and her opinions have carried weight and influence. These, however, having served their purpose, have passed from the public mind, yet she has a masterpiece of literature in her volume called "A History of French Painting " The fly-leaf of the work is inscribed as follows:

To
My Husband
J. S. T. STRANAHAN

This work is affectionately inscribed in recognition of the rare qualities of his service to others through his ready perception of the ties of kinship, citizenship, humanity.

The work received the highest praise in artistic and literary circles in this country and in Europe. The following extract from a review of the work by the able editor of the *Eagle,* Mr. McKelway, is here produced:

MRS STRANAHAN'S PEN.

Of the things which she might have done and still have had her book pass current as a history, Mrs Stranahan did neither. She might have contented herself with the dates and names and general allusions, or she might have made a pleasant little trip along the path of French art development, picking up a few flowers here and there, tying them into chapters and calling them a history. There are few cases in all literature in which the application of the word history is not to a great extent a sort of beneficent libel, but that of Mrs. Stranahan's production is a most notable exception. It needs the eye of no artist, either amateur or professional, to see at a glance what she had to do. There is not a page of the book that does not tell its own eloquent story of toil, which would have shaken the purposes of any but the most resolute of women The work would have been arduous enough if all the materials which she has utilized had been, by some impossible literary legerdemain, placed at her disposal with due reference to chronology and sequence. What she would still have had to do, even under those conditions, would have been exacting enough to justify the highest praise, for the manner in which she has done it.

Those who know how busy a woman she is, in other than a literary sense, are at a loss to comprehend how she found time to search out what she wanted, to wander among the shadows of the centuries that are gone, and to give them a substance as tangible as if they belonged to yesterday Tributes to her energy and determination might be made as strong as words can make them, but they are entitled to no precedence over other acknowledgments, upon which her claim is just as clear: the intuitive perceptions of a woman have been reinforced by a grasp and virility usually incident to a masculine intelligence. As a matter of fact, many have fallen into the error of supposing that the name on the title page, C. H. Stranahan, belonged to one of the sterner sex There is not the least sign of uncertainty about the touch anywhere between the covers of the book It is affirmative, vigorous and decisive, without a suggestion of dogmatism. If the material that is to be lifted into place is right, it is handled with a delicacy that is not effeminate; if it is ponderous, there is always in reserve for it a surprising degree of strength.

In her sense of relative importance of things, the author is exceedingly fortunate. Liliputians are not exaggerated into Goliaths, and giants are not dwarfed into pigmies. It is impossible not to admire the discrimination which has been shown throughout. Evidently Mrs. Stranahan's first care was to see that her own powers of assimilation were in excellent working order While it is palpable that her appetite for relevant facts was perfectly omnivorous, it is equally manifest that nothing was hastily devoured It is one thing to set a trap for the artistic honor of by-gone times in France; it is another thing to catch it Then comes the exercise of the supreme faculty of portrayal, and it is here that Mrs. Stranahan gives a momentum to her work which sends it with a sweep into the front rank. There is much in what she herself says about the true art that is suggestive of her purpose and of the manner in which she fulfills them.

She was again before the public as a member of the Woman's Board, appointed by the New York state commissioners to carry on the work of the World's Columbian Exposition, and at once was assigned an active part in organizing the Woman's Board of Managers for the Empire state, and was chosen vice-president of the board, her brilliant intellect, broad knowledge of affairs and rare executive ability well qualifying her for that exalted position She took a firm stand in opposition to the opening of the fair on Sundays, and was the only member of the board who voted in favor of closing the exposition on the Sabbath She was as resolute in her objections as she was enthusiastic and helpful in her support of many lines of work which contributed to that triumph of American art, genius and intellect Since her marriage she has given her influence in support of the the charities of the city, and for a quarter of a century was president of the Kings County Visiting Committee of the State Charities Aid Association, and for twenty-seven years was corresponding secretary of the Society for the Aid of Friendless Women and Children. The labors of Mrs. Stranahan rounded out and supplemented those of her honored husband, and no line of marked advancement in the city but felt the beneficence of their aid.

Private business investments and enterprises claimed the attention of Mr. Stranahan, and his operations along such lines were mammoth, yet he always found time and opportunity to devote to the public good. He realized as few men seem to do the great needs of humanity in the department of material, mental and moral advancement, and his labors were so far-reaching and of such varied nature that in almost every connection Brooklyn can truthfully acknowledge her debt of gratitude to him. His position in the city is indicated by the fact that through private subscriptions by his fellow citizens, a statue was erected to his honor in Prospect Park. The Rev. Richard Salter Storrs, D. D., led the movement in an address before a meeting of the Hamilton Club, called for that purpose, in which he gave a characterization remarkable in history The site was certainly appropriately chosen—in this park made possible by the effort of Mr Stranahan. This is well expressed by quoting as the inscription upon the monument, what is said of Sir Christopher Wren: "If you ask for a monument of what he has done, look around you " The idea of erecting the monument was heartily indorsed, and no one was permitted to subscribe more than a hundred dollars, but the necessary amount was soon collected, and the commission for the work given to Frederick MacMonnies, the famous Brooklyn celebrity now residing in Paris He not only had marked ability, but also the very necessary civic pride which spurred his genius to its highest effort, and has produced a statue which, when it was seen in public, was voted by critics, among them being St. Gaudens, and the press generally, to be one of the best examples of artistic sculpture in America. For many years prior to his death there was no living man in Brooklyn who had such a deep hold upon the hearts of the people, and when before was ever the statue of a private citizen erected in his home city during his own lifetime?

He passed away in Saratoga, September 3, 1898, and his funeral cortege was the first that ever took its way to the cemetery through Prospect Park. On this occasion the workmen of long-time service stood in lines of honored respect. His remains were laid to rest in Greenwood, but the very wide circle of his influence is felt and will be felt throughout all time. A contemporary biographer has said of him: "To citizens throughout Brooklyn and the state who were acquainted with his character he stood for all that is desirable in a finely developed manhood. If his word could be secured, it was as good as any bond that was ever solemnized by signature or seal; if his friendship could be won—and true worth could always win it—it was as loyal as truth is to itself, and if social order or social advancement needed a support that never bent or weakened, it could find it in him." Through all his busy career he was the soul of honor, believing honesty and integrity the best capital that a man could possess. His one particular delight was on each Sunday-school anniversary to drive up before the reviewing stand in Prospect Park and watch the inspiring spectacle of thousands of little ones, attired in bright garments, with their banners waving in air under sunny skies, marching down the long meadow which was the creation of his genius. Shakespeare's words would be a fitting epitaph for him:

"He was a man. Take him for all in all,
I shall not look upon his like again "

THEODORE LEDYARD CUYLER, D. D. LL. D.

Emerson has written:

"Knowest thou what arguments thy life
To thy neighbor's creed has lent?"

The influence of man is immeasurable by any of the known standards of the world, but its potency is no less marked, and the New England poet and philosopher, writing along the same line, has said again that every individual in greater or less degree, but always to some degree, leaves an impress upon the life of every one whom he meets. If this be true, and the great minds of all ages acknowledge that it is so, then the question propounded centuries ago, "Am I my brother's keeper?" is answered It is this everlasting truth of the brotherhood of man and the fatherhood of God that has led to the religious work of the world.

The stamp designating true nobility of character must ever find its ineffaceable tracery on the brow of one who sets himself apart from "the madding crowd's ignoble strife" and dedicates his life to the uplifting of his fellow men. A more than superficial investigation is demanded when one essays to determine the mental struggle and the spirit of unselfish devotion that must animate the man who gives all that he has and all that he hopes to be to service in the great vineyard of life, seeking reward only in that realm "where moth and rust do not corrupt and where thieves do not break through and steal." Preparations for and labors in the priesthood are perforce exacting, demanding an ever ready sympathy, a broad intellectuality and unswerving fidelity. Scoffing cynicism and careless irreverence would often be silenced if only the inner life of those who minister in holy places might be laid open for inspection. Honor is due and honor will be paid when once there comes a deeper understanding of the truth.

We are led to this train of thought through study of the life record of Dr. Cuyler, who from early manhood has devoted his labor, his thought and his energy to the uplifting of his fellow men, and whose name and work forms the most important chapter in the history of the Lafayette Avenue Presbyterian church of Brooklyn. He was born in Aurora, New York, January 10, 1822, and from Huguenots and Hollanders, who came to the shores of the new world at an early day, he traces his descent. Members of the family were particularly prominent at the bar His grandfather practiced with success in Aurora for many years, and his father, B. Ledyard Cuyler, also attained to an eminent position in the legal profession, but he died at the early age of twenty-eight years. The care of the son fell to the mother, a lady of strong Christian character, who had marked influence upon the life of her son. She always cherished the hope that he might enter the ministry, and a little pocket Bible which she gave him he learned to read when four years of age. Other relatives of the family hoped that he would become a lawyer, believing that he could attain distinction in that profession, and, while he had the mental ability to become eminent therein, he determined to enter a calling that led him into close contact with his fellow men, his services proving of the greatest good to those with whom he was associated. At the age of sixteen he became a student in Princeton College and three years later was graduated with high honors. The following year was spent in Europe, where he formed the acquaintance of Thomas Carlyle, William Wordsworth and Charles Dickens, and his visits to those celebrated English writers are among the most pleasant memories of his life. Travel broadened his knowledge, and his mind was stored with many interesting reminiscences of the sights and scenes which he viewed when abroad. Upon his return his father's family again urged him to become a member of the bar, but his mother's influence and other agencies in his life were stronger. When a young man he was asked to address a meeting in a neighboring village. Several inquirers professed belief that evening, saying that the young man made the way so plain. This brought to him a recognition of his influence and power, and he resolved to devote his activities to the cause of the Master His preparatory studies for the ministry were pursued in the Princeton Theological Seminary, where, on the completion of a three-years' course, he was graduated, in May, 1846.

His first ministerial services after being licensed to preach was as supply in the church at Kingston, Pennsylvania, where he remained for six months. Not long afterward he accepted the charge of the Presbyterian church in Burlington, New Jersey, where his labors were so successful that it was felt he should be employed in a broader field. Accordingly he left Burlington to take pastoral charge of the newly organized Third Presbyterian church in Trenton, where he remained until the summer of 1853. In May of that year he received a call from the Shawmut Congregational church, in Boston, but declined it and accepted a call from the Market Street Reformed Dutch church, in New York city, where he felt his field would be broader and more congenial by reason of the greater demands it would make upon him. His work there at once attracted public attention His earnestness, his clear reasoning, his logical arguments and his brilliant gifts of oratory attracted large audiences, and his work among young men was particularly successful For seven years he continued as pastor of that congregation, and in 1860 entered upon his important work in connection with the Lafayette Avenue Presbyterian church, of Brooklyn The exodus from New York to Brooklyn was beginning to be felt about this time, and the need for better church accommodations in the latter city had long been so pressing as to engross the attention of many earnest Christians. A conference on the subject was held May 16, 1857, by a number of gentlemen connected with Dr. Spear's "South" church, and it was decided to form a "new-school" church. Soon after its organization Professor Roswell D. Hitchcock, of the Union Theological Seminary of New York, supplied the pulpit, and during his ministry there the church society, first numbering but forty-eight souls, increased so rapidly that the little brick chapel was found inadequate to contain the audiences. It was a season of spiritual awakening all over the land,— the revival of 1858,—and Park church, for such was the name by which it was then known, shared in the general improvement and met the demand upon its accommodations by building an addition. In January of the following year, 1859, Professor Hitchcock resigned and was succeeded as pulpit supply by the Rev Lyman Whiting, of Portsmouth, New Hampshire Six months later he also resigned, and for an additional six months the congregation was without a regular minister.

About this time Dr Cuyler was offered the pastorate, but the outlook of his own church was then so promising that he declined the call Shortly afterward, however, the Dutch church began to falter in its project of planting its new edifice in the new and growing part of the city With keen foresight Dr Cuyler anticipated the rapid change that was soon to transform unpopulated districts of Brooklyn, and believed that it would prove a splendid field for Christian labor. It was then he took into consideration the offer of the pastorate of the Park church. He visited the Fort Greene section of Brooklyn, and then informed the committee which waited on him that if their congregation would purchase the plot at the corner of Lafayette avenue and Oxford street and erect thereon a plain edifice large enough to accommodate about two thousand people he would accept the call. It seemed a great undertaking for the little congregation, with its membership of only one hundred and forty people, but the committee agreed to the proposition, and within ten days the purchase of the land was effected, at a cost of twelve thousand dollars. At an additional cost of forty-two thousand dollars there was erected a splendid stone structure, modeled after Beecher's church and having also the same seating capacity Work was commenced on the new edifice in the fall of 1860, and on March 12, 1862, the completed church was dedicated. This was practically the work of Dr. Cuyler, who, in April, 1860, was formally installed as pastor.

He entered upon his work with an enthusiasm born of strong determination, firm convictions and noble purpose His brilliant oratory soon attracted the attention of Brooklyn citizens, and his forceful utterances, showing forth the divine purpose, appealed to the understanding of all thinking people The church grew with marvelous rapidity, and as rapidly as possible Dr Cuyler extended the field of his labors. In 1866 there were more than three hundred additions, and he felt that its growing strength justified the establishment of a mission. Accordingly, in Warren street, the Memorial Mission School was organized, the direct outcome of which is the Memorial Presbyterian church, now one of the strongest and most prosperous in that section of the city. The Fort Greene Presbyterian church also had its origin in one of Dr Cuyler's mission schools, which was established in 1861, with a membership of one hundred and twelve. The Classon Avenue church is also another direct branch of the Lafayette Avenue Presbyterian church—and who can measure the influence of this work? In the twenty-five years following its incorporation Dr. Cuyler's congregation contributed seventy thousand dollars to city missions, and its gifts as reported for the year 1888 exceeded fifty-three thousand dollars. The Sunday school, the Young People's Association and the various charitable and benevolent organizations became important adjuncts of the church work. The church membership in 1890 was nearly twenty-four hundred and the Sunday school numbered sixteen hundred, ranking the third largest in the general assembly.

With all these extensive and important undertakings under his supervision Dr. Cuyler also did the work of pastor as well as of teacher and leader, and perhaps no man in the Christian ministry has ever more endeared himself through the ties of friendship and love to his parishioners than he One who knew him well said of him: "He mingles freely and happily with his people. His feelings are ardent and sympathetic, his conversation is fluent and interspersed with illustration, anecdote, lively metaphor and felicitous quotations,—so that he united the gifts which elicit friendly feeling, promote freedom of social intercourse and bind a pastor to his people by the innumerable threads of friendly intercourse, rather than by one cable of profound and distant reverence Hence, he combined in an unusual degree success in pastoral labor with success in preaching He teaches his people quite as much out of the pulpit as in it. He seeks to make his church an organized band, 'who go about doing good,' in working sympathy with the poor and outcast He also diffuses a zeal, lengthening the cords and strengthening the stakes of their own influence. Dr. Cuyler is accessible both in parlor and in the pulpit One is sure of hospitality at church as well as at home."

For thirty years Dr Cuyler remained as pastor of the Lafayette Avenue Presbyterian church and then voluntarily severed his relations therewith. He addressed his people in the following words on Sunday, February 2, 1890: "Nearly thirty years have elapsed since 1 assumed the pastoral charge of the Lafayette Avenue church. In April, 1860, it was a small band of one hundred and forty members. By the continual blessing of Heaven upon us, that little flock has grown into one of the largest and most useful and powerful churches in the Presbyterian denomination; it is the third in point of numbers in the United States. This church has now two thousand three hundred and thirty members. It maintains two mission chapels, has one thousand six hundred in its Sunday school, and is paying the salaries of three ministers in this city and of two missionaries in the south For several years it has led all the churches of Brooklyn in its contributions to foreign, home and city missions, and it is surpassed by none other in wide and varied Christian work Every sitting in this spacious house has its occupant. Our morning audiences have never been larger than they have this winter. This church has always been to me like a beloved child. I have given to it thirty years of hard and happy labor, and it is my foremost desire that its harmony may remain undisturbed and its prosperity may remain unbroken. For a long time I have intended that my thirtieth anniversary should be the terminal point of my present pastorate. I shall then have served this beloved flock for an ordinary human generation, and the time has come for me to transfer this sacred trust to some one who, in God's good providence, may have thirty years of vigorous work before him and not behind him If God spares my life to the first Sabbath of April it is my purpose to surrender this pulpit back into your hands, and I shall endeavor to co-operate with you in the search and selection of the right man to stand in it I will not trust myself today to speak of the sharp pang it will cost me to sever a connection that has been to me one of unalloyed harmony and happiness. When the proper time comes we can speak of all such things, and in the meanwhile let us continue on in the blessed Master's work and leave our future entirely to His all-wise and ever loving care On the walls of this dear church the eyes of the angels have always seen it written, 'I, the Lord, do keep it, and I will keep it night and day.' It only remains for me to say that after forty-four years of uninterrupted ministerial labor it is but reasonable for me to ask for relief from a strain that may soon become too heavy for me to bear.''

A feeling of the greatest sorrow was manifest throughout the congregation. Many of the people then in the church had grown up under his active pastorate, and it was almost like a death knell to them as they heard his words. On the 16th of April, in the church parlors, a farewell reception was held, on which occasion a purse of thirty thousand dollars was presented to Dr. Cuyler—one thousand dollars for each year of his service as pastor. The gift indicated in unmistakable manner the love which his congregation bore for him. However, his friends were not limited to his own congregation, for through his writings he has become known throughout the civilized world and has many admirers among those who have been helped by his earnest and inspiring words. He has been a constant contributor to the religious journals of the country, including the Christian Intelligencer, Christian Work, The Watchman, Christian Endeavor World, Evangelist and Independent. He has prepared about four thousand articles for the press and has written seventy-five tracts, many of which have been republished in the English, German and Australian newspapers. In 1852 he published a volume entitled Stray Arrows, containing selections of his newspaper writings. He is the author of eighteen published volumes, of which Cedar Christian, Heart Life, Empty Crib,

Thought Hives, Pointed Papers for the Christian Life, God's Light on Dark Clouds and Newly Enlisted have been reprinted in England, where they have had a large sale. The Empty Crib was published after the death of a beloved boy, nearly five years of age, and the subsequent loss of a beautiful and accomplished daughter was the occasion of his writing that marvelously touching production entitled God's Light on Dark Clouds. In addition to the works mentioned he is the author of the following: How to Be a Pastor, The Young Preacher, Christianity in the Home, Stirring the Eagle's Nest and other Sermons and Beulah Land. A selection from his writings, entitled Right to the Point, has been published in Boston. Six of his books have been translated into Swedish and two into Dutch.

To a man of Dr. Cuyler's nature the needs of the world have been ever manifest and have elicited his most hearty, earnest and devoted co-operation The great benevolent movements and reform measures have received his aid, and he has labored earnestly in behalf of the Young Men's Christian Association mission schools, the Children's Aid Association, the Five Points mission and the Freedmen, while his work in the National Temperance Society has been a most potent influence in promoting temperance sentiment among those with whom he has come in contact as teacher and preacher. He has served as president of the National Temperance Society of America. In 1872 he went abroad as a delegate to the Presbyterian Assembly in Edinburg, Scotland, on which occasion he won the warm friendship of many eminent Presbyterian divines of Great Britain. His friends have been drawn from the most cultured and intelligent and have ever been an affinity between such. These include Spurgeon, Gladstone, Dean Stanley, Dickens, Carlyle, Neal Dow. Lincoln, Horace Greeley and John G. Whittier.

In 1853 Dr Cuyler was united in marriage to Miss Annie

E. Mathiot, a daughter of the Hon. Joshua Mathiot, a member of congress from Ohio. Her labors have ably supplemented and rounded out those of her husband. She has been in hearty sympathy with him in all of his church work and in his efforts for the uplifting of man and in a no less forceful, but in a more quiet way, her influence has been exerted for the benefit of God's children. Since his retirement from the ministry Dr. Cuyler has devoted his time to preaching and lecturing in colleges and to literary work. A monument to his splendid accomplishments is found in the Cuyler chapel of the Lafayette Avenue Presbyterian church, which was named in his honor by the Young People's Association of that organization in 1892. A large mission church, seating one thousand people and erected in 1900 by the Lafayette Avenue church, in Canton, China, is named the Theodore L. Cuyler church.

SILAS B. DUTCHER.

"Those who have attained the age of seventy years, as a rule, attest the fact of a sound constitution and a well spent life," said the Brooklyn Eagle editorially, July 12, 1899. "The one is a fine inheritance. The other is a fine record. Inheritance and record are both the possession of the well known Brooklynite, President Silas B. Dutcher, who was born seventy years ago today. He at once becomes a hope and a vindication. A hope he is to those who would equal his claim to respect and regard, who would match him in mentality and bodily vigor, when they reach his present years. A vindication he is to those who seek for examples to prove that three score years and ten may be really the best period of a man's life. Mr. Dutcher very likely never thought of himself either as a hope or as a vindication. He has been too busy to do so. That fact is one of the reasons why he is both. Life takes care of the fame of those who are more concerned with duty than with distinction, for distinction is a consequence best following from fidelity, energy and wisdom. It is the aroma of a career, when the career is what it ought to be."

Silas B Dutcher was born July 12, 1829, on his father's farm on the shore of Otsego lake, in the town of Springfield, Otsego county, New York. He is a descendant of an old and highly respected family His parents were Parcefor Carr and Johanna Low (Frink) Dutcher. His paternal grandparents were John and Silvey (Beardsley) Dutcher His grandmother's ancestor was William Beardsley, who was born at Stratford, England, in 1605, and came to America in 1635, settling at Stratford, Connecticut, four years later. His great-grandparents were Gabriel and Elizabeth (Knickerbocker) Dutcher. Elizabeth Knickerbocker was a granddaughter of Harman Janse Van Wye Knickerbocker, of Dutchess county, New York. His great-great-grandparents were Ruloff and Janettie (Bressie) Dutcher, who were married at Kingston, New York, in 1700 and in 1720 removed to Litchfield county, Connecticut.

Ruloff Dutcher is believed to have been a grandson of Dierck Cornelison Duyster, under commissary at Fort Orange in 1630, whose name appears in deeds of two large tracts of land to Killian Van Rensselair.

Mr. Dutcher's maternal grandparents were Stephen and Ann (Low) Frink, and maternal great-grandparents were Captain Peter and Johanna (Ten Eyck) Low, and his great-grandfather was an officer in the Continental army. Johanna Ten Eyck was a descendant of Conrad Ten Eycke, who came from Amsterdam, Holland, to New York in 1650, and owned what is now known as Coenties Slip, New York city

Mr. Dutcher attended the public schools near his father's

farm each summer and winter, from the age of four until the age of seven years. After that he had a little more schooling in the winter season and one term at Cazenovia Seminary. He began teaching school winters at the age of sixteen and taught every winter until he was twenty-two, working on his father's farm during the balance of each year. In the fall of 1851, owing to a temporary loss of his voice, which prevented him from teaching, he found employment at railroad construction, but soon became a station agent and subsequently a conductor and for more than three years was employed on the old Erie railway from Elmira to Niagara Falls, New York. He then went to New York and entered mercantile business, to which he devoted his energies through the terrible panics of 1857 and 1860 without severe misfortune. In 1868 he was appointed supervisor of internal revenue, a position which he at first declined, but was urged to accept by William Orton and other friends Against his own judgment, and, as events proved, greatly to the detriment of his financial interests, he took the office. He was unable to give attention to business, his partner was not equal to its management, and he soon discovered that all he had accumulated by twelve years of hard work was scattered and gone, and he was obliged to sell the real estate he owned to meet his liabilities.

Even as a boy he had been more or less interested in politics. His grandfather was a Democrat, and Silas was often called upon to read his Democratic newspaper to him; his father was a Whig and the result was that he had an opportunity to learn something of the claims of both parties at an early age. Before he was twenty-one he became interested in the question of freedom or the extension of slavery in the territories,—the most vital question of that day,—and while yet little more than a boy, in 1848, did some effective campaign speaking for General Taylor.

When he went to New York Mr. Dutcher resolved to have nothing to do with active politics, but the breaking up of a Republican meeting in the Bleecker building in the Ninth ward brought him out most decisively and he was quite active politically from 1856 to 1861. In 1857 he was president of the Ninth Ward Republican Association; 1858-59 he was chairman of the Young Men's Republican Committee, and in 1860 he was president of the Wide-Awakes Association. During the year last mentioned he became a member of the board of supervisors of the county of New York. His business demanded his attention and there were other reasons why, in the fall of 1861, he moved to Brooklyn in order to sever his relations with that body. William M. Tweed was a member of the board at that time and began to develop some of the schemes which eventually caused his downfall. Mr. Dutcher was not willing to vote ignorantly on any question or to act upon the representations of other members, who he believed held their personal interests above the interests of the county. As a resident of Brooklyn he again resolved to keep out of politics, but the riots of 1863 brought him in close relations with active Republicans and he found himself again in political harness. He held the office of supervisor of internal revenue from 1868 until 1872, a period of four years, at first under appointment of Hugh McCullough, the secretary of the treasury, and later under appointment of President Grant. In November, 1872, he was appointed United States pension agent, resigning that office in 1875 to accept a position in the employ of the Metropolitan Life Insurance Company, which he held until appointed United States appraiser of the port of New York, by President Grant, which latter position he held until 1880. He was superintendent of public works of the state of

New York from 1880 until 1883, appointed by Governor Cornell. At the close of his term in the last named office, President Arthur requested him to accept the office of commissioner of internal revenue, to which he replied that he had held office fourteen years and that all he had to show for that service was a few old clothes; that if he accepted the position tendered him and held it one or more years, he would retire with about the same quantity of old clothes as he had at the beginning and so much older and less available for other business, and that the remainder of his life must be devoted to making some provision for his wife and children and consequently he must decline further office-holding.

He was a member of the charter commission which framed the charter of Greater New York, appointed by Governor Morton and was appointed a manager of the Long Island State Hospital by Governor Black and re-appointed by Governor Roosevelt He was a Whig from 1850 to 1855 and became a Republican at the organization of that party. After locating in Brooklyn he was the chairman of the Kings county Republican committee for four years, a member of the Republican state committee for many years, and was the chairman of the Republican executive committee of the state in 1876. He served as a delegate to several Republican national conventions and was on the stump in every presidential campaign from 1848 to 1888.

From the time he became a resident of Brooklyn until the consolidation was consummated, Mr. Dutcher was an advocate of the consolidation of Brooklyn and New York. As a member for four years of the Brooklyn board of education, he exerted all his influence for the advancement of the public schools. As a member of the charter commission for Greater New York, he labored earnestly to secure equal taxation and home rule for the public schools, believing that the system and management were better than in Manhattan and better than any other submitted to the community. No work of his life has given him more satisfaction than the results in the charter on these two points. He has also taken an active interest in Sunday-school affairs and was superintendent for ten years of the Twelfth Street Reformed church Sunday-school, at a time when it was one of the largest schools in the state.

Mr. Dutcher resumed business to some extent in 1885, when he formed a co-partnership with W. E. Edmister in a fire and marine insurance agency, which still exists. He was one of the charter trustees of the Union Dime Savings Institution, of New York city, organized in 1859, and became president of that institution in 1885 and is now the only one of the charter trustees remaining on the board. In the spring of 1901 he was invited to and accepted the presidency of the Hamilton Trust Company. He has been for twenty years a director in the Metropolitan Life Insurance Company, is a director in the Garfield Safe Deposit Company and the Goodwin Car Company. He is a member of the Dutch Reformed church, treasurer of the Brooklyn Bible Society, one of the managers of the Society for Improving the Condition of the Poor, a member of the Brooklyn and Hamilton Clubs and of the Masonic fraternity, and he was president of the Association of the Brooklyn Masonic Veterans in 1896.

When Mr. Dutcher took up his residence in Brooklyn the population of the city was about two hundred and seventy-five thousand. What is now the Park Slope was then open fields. The small settlement known as Gowanus was all there was south of Flatbush avenue. He has seen the city grow from a little more than a quarter of a million souls to a million and a quarter He has seen the Park Slope transformed into one of the finest residential sections of the city, and he has seen the three or four churches in that part of Brooklyn increase to more than twenty. When he came the prominent Republicans of Brooklyn were Charles W. Goddard, James Humphrey, William Wall and J. S. T. Stranahan. He soon made the acquaintance of that good old Dutch mayor, Martin Kalbfleisch, whom he regarded as one of the sturdiest men he ever met. He has known every one of Brooklyn's mayors from George Hall, the first executive, down to the present incumbent of the office Mr. Dutcher has lived in Third street since 1872, and his present home is at No. 496.

His family consists of his wife and six children. He married Rebecca J. Alwaise, February 10, 1859. Mrs. Dutcher is a descendant of John Alwaise, a French Huguenot, who came to Philadelphia in 1740 Her grandmother was a descendant of John Bishop, who came from England in 1645, and settled at Woodbridge, New Jersey The children of Silas B. and Rebecca J. (Alwaise) Dutcher are DeWitt P., Edith May, Elsie Rebecca, Malcomb B., Jessie Ruth and Eva Olive. Two of Mr. Dutcher's daughters are members of the Colonial Daughters of the Seventeenth Century.

The first visit Mr. Dutcher ever made to Brooklyn was to hear Henry Ward Beecher preach in Plymouth church He has stated that he was directed, as others were, at the usual hour of church service to cross Fulton Ferry and follow the crowd. "I arrived at the church a little late," he said, "and found only standing room and but little of that. When I entered the church the congregation was singing the hymn, 'All Hail the Power of Jesus' Name,' to the good old tune of 'Coronation,' and I do not recollect of ever hearing in any other church such a volume of music. My first impression was that Henry Ward Beecher was the strongest preacher to whom I had ever listened and that first impression has never been re-

moved." Mr. Dutcher has known personally every governor
of the state of New York, from William H. Seward to Benjamin
B Odell, except Governor William C. Bouch and Governor
Silas Wright. When he went to New York, he was brought in
contact in both business and politics with men much older than
himself, among whom were Edwin D. Morgan, William M.
Evarts, William Curtis Noyes, David Dudley Field, Luther R.
Marsh, Abram Wakeman, John A. Kennedy, Washington Smith,
William Orton, George Briggs, General James Bowen and
Thomas C. Acton, very few of whom are now living. He believes
the day is not far distant when the borough of Brooklyn
will have the largest population, the greatest number of voters
and be the most important factor in Greater New York. He
predicts that the year 1910 will show Brooklyn with a larger
population than the borough of Manhattan at that date, and a
population that for intelligence, independence and a desire to
secure the best possible local government will not be surpassed
by any people in the world. Mr. Dutcher owes nothing to favor.
He "hewed his own path" and found his opportunities and improved
them; but he did not neglect the better things than success,
such as education, culture and other refining and strengthening
aids His political career has been one to note with respect.
He has never been an applicant for any office that he
has filled, and he has never become a dependent on a political
office Every public employment to which he has been called
has been a business employment, and he has fulfilled its duties
in a way to prove his fitness for private employment, and his
life exhibits a union of public and private service which is
creditable citizenship

STEPHEN V WHITE

In studying the lives and characters of prominent men we are naturally led to inquire into the secret of their success and the motives that prompted their action Success is a question of genius, as held by many, but is it not rather a matter of experience and sound judgment? For when we trace the careers of those who stand highest in public esteem we find in nearly every case that they are those who have risen gradually, fighting their way in the face of all opposition. Self-reliance, conscientiousness, energy and honesty are the traits of character that insure the highest emoluments and greatest success. To these may we attribute the success that has crowned the efforts of Mr. White.

Stephen Van Culen White was born in Pittsboro, Chatham county, North Carolina, August 1, 1831. His father, Hiram White, married Julia Brewer, and in September, 1831, the parents removed from North Carolina to Illinois, where they spent their remaining days, the father passing away in 1860 and the mother in 1868 Mr White traces his ancestry back to David White, a native of Ireland, who emigrated to what is now Wilmington, Delaware, about the year 1720 His son Charles was born about 1727, and became the father of Stephen White, whose birth occurred in 1751. The last named was the father of Hiram White, who was born August 16, 1799, and became the father of our subject He was a Baptist in his religious belief and was opposed to slavery. During the Nat Turner uprising in 1831 he defied the sentiments of the community in which he lived in North Carolina, refusing to do police duty to guard against difficulties with the slaves, and for this he was obliged to leave the state. He took his family by wagon through Tennessee and Kentucky and settled in Illinois. In the family were two sons and a daughter. One of the former, Nathaniel Brewer White, died in Florida, in the year 1888. The daughter, Jane Elizabeth Allen, is now living in St Louis

From an early age Mr White, of this review, manifested special fondness for books. He attended the Hamilton primary school of Otterville, Jersey county, Illinois, and afterward entered Knox College, being graduated in that institution on the 22d of June, 1854. Determining to make the practice of law his life work, he began reading with the firm of Brown & Kasson, of St. Louis. He worked on the *Missouri Democrat,* now the *Globe-Democrat,* and was admitted to the bar on the 4th of October, 1856. In December of that year he removed to Des Moines and opened an office for the practice of his profession. In 1861 he successfully defended the first treason case ever tried in the state. In 1864, during the illness of the United States district attorney, he took his place in the trial of several civil and criminal cases. He continued his practice in Des Moines until January, 1865, when he removed to New York city and for two years was a member of the firm of Marvin & White, Wall street brokers. During the succeeding twenty-five years he engaged in business alone, at which time he formed a partnership with Arthur B Claflin and F. W. Hopkins, under the firm name of S V. White & Company. In 1887 Arthur B Claflin withdrew from the firm, and in 1891 S. V. White & Company failed, Mr White's entire fortune having been swept away. Knowing his great ability and his incorruptible honesty, his creditors released him in full and permitted him to continue on the floor of the exchange. Eleven months after his readmission to the New York stock exchange he had paid in full, with interest, his indebtedness of nine hundred and fifty thousand dollars. For many years he was the chief operator in Delaware, Lackawanna & Western stock, which made him well known on

Wall street His business affairs have ever been conducted in the most straightforward manner and he enjoys the unqualified confidence of all with whom he has been associated

Soon after his removal to Brooklyn Mr. White became a warm personal friend of Henry Ward Beecher, and was the treasurer and president of the board of trustees of Plymouth church Though his business interests have been extensive and have made heavy demands upon his time and attention, he has ever found time to devote to the work of the church and has contributed liberally to advance its interests. He was one of the founders of the American Astronomical Society, and for twenty years owned the largest private telescope in America. It is the popular opinion that a Wall street broker has time for nothing but money making, but through a long period Mr. White has spent a considerable portion of his time in following the almost mystic courses of the stars He is a man of scholarly attainments, whose researches have been carried far and wide into the realms of scientific investigation, and at the same time he is familiar with the best works of literature, reading Latin and Greek works in the original text. He is a fluent speaker, and many beautiful and valuable prose and poetic works have come from his pen He made a translation of Dies Iræ, which has been favorably commented upon. As an indication of his ability and as a writer and orator we quote the following, for it also bears directly upon the scenes of his life work:

"Upon the occasion of the retirement of Edmund Clarence Stedman, the writer, as a member of the New York Stock Exchange. the 15th of February, 1900, his friends and fellow members of the exchange honored him by presenting to him a silver loving cup. Never before in the history of the exchange has a retiring member been thus honored. At three o'clock in the afternoon, in the board room of the exchange, about one hundred of Mr. Stedman's associates gathered around him and S V. White, a prominent Brooklyn member, presented the loving cup."

Mr White said:

"I feel it a great honor, Mr. Stedman, to have been called upon to voice the love of a thousand men who are compelled to sever their business relations with you today. I have been selected through their partiality—perchance from our long connection of thirty-one years as fellow members; perchance it is because of our abiding friendship, which has never known a break—but from whatever cause, the honor is mine

"Clarence, you and I have grown old together. I must be permitted to speak plainly for once. I must emphasize one fact, in justice to you and in justice to me. Your dual life as financier and litterateur is unique among men Your friends have met you daily for months and years You seemed ever with us— ever in this busy whirl. But at the same time you have walked and wrought in an ethereal world

"In studying your diverse walks I am reminded of a night that I spent upon Mount Washington, and in the morning, thousands of feet below us, there was a sea of clouds, absolutely impenetrable and filled with mist and fog. Above, all was clear and serene, and I saw the 'crimson streak on the ocean's cheek grow into the great sun.' All above us was brightness; all below us was mist; and so in the two departments of your life you have breathed the empyrean and you have drudged with us in the mire.

"Your literary labors have been exhausting and exhaustive. Away back in 1869 you wrote 'Pan in Wall Street' and 'Israel Freyer's Bid for Gold'; since then you have given the world 'The Victorian Poets' and 'Poets of America'; you have published 'Victorian Anthology' and 'American Anthology'; you have edited Poe in ten volumes and American Authors in eleven, and you have edited newspapers and written for the magazines in ceaseless labor. No other man has done the same. Whittier, the poet of the people, never parted from his muse, and the distant roar of the Atlantic soothed him by night and the flowers and bees and birds inspired him by day.

"The author of 'Thanatopsis' wrote that view of death while yet in college, and his later works outside of his editorial field were few and far between. Bayard Taylor gave up literature before he took up statecraft. Longfellow and Lowell are said to have lived at ease on ancestral patrimony, while Holmes wrote as a pastime to a medical practice To you it was reserved to be at once banker and poet and to achieve success in both.

"Clarence, when we roughed it together on this floor we never forgot for a moment that you lived in another realm. We had improved on the herdsmen of Admetus. When Apollo dwelt with them they did not know him as the sun god. But all through our work here we were 'on to your curves' in another sphere, and a jaunty boutonniere of laurel in memory of the lamented Daphne was tossed you in our minds day by day as you worked with us. And now I am about to do an act which brings me in touch with a great poet, whom we have mourned together.

"To be known as the friend of Whittier's friend brings an honor to one as closely as did the returning Hibernian who came from Boston to Brooklyn, after having been introduced to John L Sullivan. His companion met him with a vigorous grasp, saying, 'Put it right there, Denny; let me shake the hand that shook the hand of Sullivan.' And so it can at least be said that Whittier and I have dedicated something to a mutual friend.

"The last volume that Whittier wrote was dedicated to you in a single stanza. I dedicate to your double labors ten stanzas to make clear my admiration for your mysterious power. These are my lines:

"In the realms of high Olympus
A youthful dreamer strayed.
    Of sturdy stock
    From old Plymouth Rock,
His boyish fancy played.

"There dwelt the gods in grandeur,
And the heaven was filled with light,
    While his dauntless gaze
    Withstood its rays,
And the Immortals felt his might.

"There stood old Zeus, the father,
And there stood Ares brave;
    And the muses nine,
    With touch divine,
Their inspiration gave.

"Athene's wisdom lent its power,
Aphrodite's beauty shone,
　　And the dreamer sang,
　　In words that rang
With a sweetness all their own.

"Then up spoke sly old Hermes
(He is the banker's god)
　　And he said, 'Forsooth,
　　My earnest youth,
As a poor man do not plod

"'Below the clouds is the merchant's mart,
And commerce spreads her wings.
　　There are heaps of gold
　　And wealth untold,
And labor honor brings.'

"To earth came the poet-banker—
In Wall street's mart he stood,
　　Where they shout and yell,
　　As they buy and sell,
And he wrought there as he could.

"One day in the bright empyrean,
One day with gains bedight,
　　He bought and sold
　　And he gathered gold,
With brain and nerve aright

"With men he's the poet banker,
The banker-poet above,
　　The pride of the masses,
　　The pride of Parnassus;
With men and with muses in love.

"Oh, Clarence, our loved one! when back with the muses,
When back on Olympus once more,
　　As you look from your height
　　With eyes of delight,
You'll yearn for the 'boys on the floor.'"

In 1857 Mr. White was married to Eliza Matilda Chandler, of Staunton, Illinois, a daughter of Hiram Chandler and a granddaughter of Joseph Chandler, who was at his father's side in the battle of Bennington when the latter was killed He bore the name of Benjamin Chandler. Mrs. White is of the eighth generation of descent from Miles Standish and from John Alden and his wife Priscilla Unto Mr. and Mrs. White have been born two children: Jennie, who is the wife of Franklin W. Hopkins, a banker and broker, and they have two children, Elsie White Hopkins and Stephen V. White Hopkins; and Arthur, a stock-broker, who married Margaret Beecher, a daughter of Colonel Harry Beecher, of Brooklyn, and a granddaughter of Henry Ward Beecher. They have two children: Dorothy and Stephen Van Culen

In his political views Mr White is a stalwart Republican, recognized as one of the leading members of the party. He was a member of congress from a Brooklyn district in 1887-9, and for some years prior to that time served as a park commissioner. He takes a deep and active interest in everything pertaining to the public welfare, withholding his support from no movement or measure calculated to advance the material, social, intellectual and moral progress A member of the Plymouth church of Brooklyn, he has served as the treasurer and a trustee for over thirty years He has been a trustee of the Polytechnic Institute from 1884 until the present time, and for more than a third of a century has been a life member of the Brooklyn library. Socially he is a valued representative of the Union League, Hamilton, Lincoln and Brooklyn Clubs. He has never permitted the acquisition of wealth to affect in any way his actions toward those less successful than he, and has always a cheerful word and pleasant smile for all with whom he comes in contact.

WINCHESTER BRITTON.

Mr Britton was born in North Adams, Berkshire county, Massachusetts, April 9, 1826 His paternal and maternal grandparents were hardy, intelligent New England farmers, of pure English descent His mother's maiden name was Harrington; her grandfather was a native of Rhode Island, who very early in life removed to the town of Adams, where he became the proprietor of the land upon which more than one-half of what is now the village of North Adams is located

The paternal grandfather of Mr. Britton was a native of New Hampshire and settled in Adams when Mr Britton's father was yet a young man The marriage of his parents occurred at that place. His mother died at the early age of eighteen, when Winchester was an infant. Before her death she gave him to her father and mother, with whom he lived on their farm until he was ten years of age His father, having removed to Troy, New York, took his boy to his home in that city. One of Mr. Britton's early recollections is that of accompanying his grandfather to the tavern in the then small village of North Adams, and there reading the president's message As he read with exceeding ease and fluency, greatly to the satisfaction of his hearers, the guests and others at the hotel, it is certain that his education had not been neglected, and that he possessed much intelligence. His remarkably brilliant black eyes and his hair, which was as black as his eyes, always attracted attention, while strong and active physical powers gave abundant promise of vigorous manhood.

Not long after his removal to Troy he commenced preparing for college at the Clinton Liberal Institute, at Clinton, New York, completing his preparatory course at the Troy Conference Academy, at Poultney, Vermont. In the autumn of 1847 he entered the sophomore class (third term) at Union College. While in college he was entered as a law student in the office of John Van Buren, then attorney general of the state, where he remained about one year, during which time his collegiate studies were suspended on account of failing health. His career as a student under Mr. Van Buren was not so confining and enervating as it was in college, admitting of greater relaxation His health becoming restored, he re-entered college, where he continued until he graduated. His "chum" after returning to college and until he graduated was Chester A Arthur, then a member of the junior class, in whose easy-going habits and at that time somewhat indolent character the recognition of a future president of the United States would have seemed the wildest dream Young Britton for a considerable time was at the head of his class, but, undertaking to pursue both his legal and collegiate studies, he divided his time between the Union College and the celebrated Law School at Cherry Valley. This close application to his studies caused a second failure of his health, compelling him to abandon them. About this time the discovery of gold in California created intense excitement throughout the nation Young Britton, inspired by the hope of regaining his health by travel, determined to visit the new El Dorado Accordingly, in December, 1848, he embarked at New York on the Crescent City, bound for Chagres. The Crescent City was the first steamer that left New York for California.

He remained six weeks on the isthmus and then sailed from Panama for San Francisco in the sailing vessel Philadelphia. While on the isthmus the cholera broke out with much fatality, but, happily, young Britton, though constantly exposed to its ravages, escaped its attack

After a voyage of eighty-seven days the Philadelphia made

the port of San Francisco in safety, and the young man found himself in the land of gold, where many adventurous men soon found themselves in a short space of time transferred from poverty to wealth. Imbued with the spirit of adventure and enterprise, Britton sought the mining regions with success. After a few months he acquired interests in San Francisco, and his time was divided between that city and the mines, and he was rewarded by the acquisition of a very handsome fortune. But before he had much time to congratulate himself upon his good fortune, he learned by sad experience that riches often take wings and fly away, for in one night his fortune was all swept away by the memorable fire that nearly destroyed the city of San Francisco Yielding to an ardent desire which had possession of him, he determined to return to his home. Accordingly, in August, 1851, he sailed from San Francisco homeward. On his passage to Panama he again encountered the cholera, under many dangerous circumstances. During the seven days' voyage from Acapulco to Panama one hundred and fifty-one, or nearly one-third, of his fellow passengers died of the terrible disease; but he reached his home in safety, where he continued until the October of the following year, when he returned to San Francisco and engaged in business It was during his sojourn at home that he made the acquaintance of the estimable and accomplished young lady who subsequently, in March, 1853, became his wife She was the daughter of William W. Parker, Esq, of Albany On his return to California he took a deep interest in politics, receiving the nomination for member of the legislature of the new state, but was defeated in the canvass. He was, however, soon afterward elected a member of the common council of San Francisco, and supervisor of San Francisco county While alderman he took an active part among other things in measures for the supply of water and gas to the growing city While discharging his official duties an incident occurred deeply interesting to him and to the public, one which he will never forget

Under the peculiar customs of California at that period to be a public man, in any sense, invited personal collisions The bitter antagonism existing between John Cotter, then an alderman of San Francisco, and John Nugent, editor of the "San Francisco Herald," resulted in one of the most celebrated duels in the history of California. Mr Britton, an excellent shot, was a friend and second of Cotter. In the contest Nugent was very severely wounded and removed from the field, but Cotter was unharmed Since the duel, though as we have said Mr Britton was skilful in the use of the pistol, he has seldom, if ever, taken one in his hand

On January 1, 1853, in accordance with a promise made to his affianced, he bade a final farewell to the Pacific slope, and with a large experience, with health restored, he returned to his native land, completed his classical studies, received his college degree and returned to his legal studies.

Such was the diligence, industry and success with which he pursued them that, after the lapse of six months, he was called to the bar, and he immediately removed to the city of New York, where, without an acquaintance, he began his legal career. His married life, which, as we have seen, commenced in March, 1853, was an exceedingly happy one, but it terminated in 1854 by the death of his lovely and amiable wife, which to him was an excessively severe domestic blow. She died in Brooklyn, at the early age of nineteen, leaving an infant son, who survived her but a few months. For a time Mr Britton was heart-stricken and felt himself alone in the world. But time, which assuages sorrow, his indomitable energy and never-failing courage and professional ambition supported him, enabling him to overcome all obstacles and to attain signal success. As an illustration of the obstacles which Mr. Britton overcame in his way to success, it may be remarked that his receipts from his first year's practice in the city of New York were exactly seventy-five dollars. Not at all discouraged by this meagre return from his profession, he took an appeal to time, and with each succeeding year his income increased until it was exceeded by few in the profession.

In December, 1855, his second marriage took place; the lady of his choice was Miss Caroline A. Parker, a sister of his former wife, a lady possessing all the accomplishments and all the attributes which constitute an affectionable and agreeable wife, a tender and loving mother, capable of presiding with with graceful dignity over the home of such a man as Winchester Britton, which we may say without affectation was one of the happiest of homes Eight sons and three daughters, all of whom are living, are the fruits of this happy union.

In 1870 Mr. Britton transferred his legal business to Brooklyn, where he had resided since 1853 His professional reputation had now become so extended that he at once entered, in his new field of labor, upon an unusually large and remunerative practice, not only in the courts of the city of New York, in Brooklyn, in the surrounding counties, but also in the state courts and in the court of appeals He had been in practice in Brooklyn but one year when he was elected district attorney for the county of Kings He entered upon his official duties in January, 1872, discharging them with singular acceptability until within about eleven months before the expiration of his official term, when charges, originating in the high political excitement that prevailed, were made against him, resulting in his removal from office by Governor Dix. So little foundation was there for the charges against Mr. Britton, so devoid were they of merit, that the very next fall after his removal he was re-elected to the same office by a majority more than double that by which he was first elected.

The office of district attorney imposed great responsibility and labor upon Mr. Britton. Though criminal law practice was not exactly suited to his taste, yet after all, it had attractions for his active, energetic mind. "It gives ample room for the exercise of his well-disciplined mental energies—his power of collecting, combining and amplifying. It gives scope to his critical knowledge of statute law and the subtle rules of evidence." It was his fortune during his term of office to be called upon to conduct many exciting criminal cases, among which was the celebrated case of People versus Rubenstein, tried at Brooklyn in January and February of 1876. Rubenstein had been indicted for one of the most mysterious and atrocious murders known in legal history. The evidence against him was purely circumstantial, and many of these circumstances were remote and disconnected, and the whole crime was enshrouded in such mystery that the work of convicting the alleged perpetrator, who was defended by that powerful legal gladiator, William A. Beach, was a herculean task, but with consummate skill and great energy Mr. Britton seized upon these circumstances, blended them together, and they each tended to throw light upon and to prove the other, reaching a conclusion that overthrew the ingenious hypothesis upon which a great lawyer founded a formidable defense, resulting in the conviction of the prisoner.

No one can read the admirable and touchingly eloquent address to the jury for the defense in the case without the highest admiration None can read the closing argument of Mr Britton to the jury without equal admiration. It may be summed up in a few words: it was exhaustive, it was learned, it was eloquent, it was convincing. It left no doubt in the minds of the jury, the spectators or the bar that Rubenstein was guilty of one of the most cruel murders on record; his conviction was therefore swift and certain

Space will not permit us to give a detailed account of the many criminal trials which Mr. Britton conducted for the people, but they all tended largely to enhance his fame and to place him in the front ranks of living advocates.

Among his civil triumphs at the bar was the case of Edgerton versus Page—a leading case in the court of appeals and among the first there argued by him. This case established the doctrine of constructive eviction of a tenant by a landlord, with the qualification that no such eviction could exist unless the tenant actually left before the expiration of his term, qualifying in this respect the case of Dyett versus Pendleton. John Graham, then in the height of his fame as a lawyer, was his opponent Taking the whole history of this case, its result was a triumph for Mr Britton of which any lawyer in the nation might well be proud

Up to the time of his death, February 13, 1886, he was in the active practice of his profession, in the plenitude of professional success. There are very few, if any, important cases in Kings county in which he was not engaged

In the prolonged contest resulting in the defeat of the project known as the Bond Elevated Railroad, he was prominent, and it is not a little remarkable that the ultimate decision of the supreme court was placed upon the precise ground described in Mr Britton's brief. Among his last important arguments in the court of appeals was that made against George F. Comstock in the case of Crooke versus the County of Kings, on the part of the defendant and respondent This case was a contest on behalf of the heirs of the wife of the late General Philip S.

Crooke to establish their title to real estate of great value. Among other questions, it involved the wills of Mrs. Catlin, the mother of Mrs. Crooke, and of Mrs. Crooke, and the validity and proper execution of certain powers and trusts therein contained, and required a construction of the statute of the powers and trusts of this state which had been before the court of appeals, and necessarily became a leading case upon those subjects.

From the foregoing it will be seen that Mr. Britton was a man of untiring energy. Many of his compeers at the bar give to their profession divided allegiance; many make it second to the attractive but more ephemeral contests of the political arena, but Mr. Britton had an utter distaste for those practices and associations which are so necessary for a politician, and his abnegation of politics, except in the exercise of rational political convictions, is thorough and complete, and therefore his success as a lawyer was the reward of a constant and thorough mental elaboration and study. It was proverbial among his neighbors that none of them got home so late at night as not to see the lights burning in his well-stocked library

He was positive in his convictions, rested confidently upon them, and was not specially reserved in expressing his opinion concerning them. He was always sincere and in earnest, disliked hypocrisy, and was destitute of those platitudes which enable one to agree with everybody Therefore he was not what may be called a popular man with the masses, nor was he convivial in his tastes. With his chosen friends he was social, genial and approachable. He was especially a domestic man, and his home to him was an empire of happiness and pleasure, and he was best appreciated when seen in his family, among his children, to whom he was most tenderly attached and to whose success in life his sole ambition was directed.

On the morning of February 13, 1886, when in his library and about to leave his home for his office, he was seized with cramps in the bowels. Passing into his bed-room, he threw himself upon his bed and in less than three minutes he had breathed his last, to the indescribable shock of his wife and eldest daughter, who were with him, and to his law associate, Sumner Howe Ely, who had remained in the library waiting his return. The years of strain put upon his physical organism throughout his busy life finally caused a stoppage of the action of the heart

On the occasion of his death the courts of Kings county were adjourned as a mark of respect, and a memorial meeting was held of the Bar Association of Kings county, at which the following resolution was adopted:

"The life of Winchester Britton was at the bar, and it was as a lawyer that he was known His associates in that profession in Kings county, where he lived and largely practiced, deem it fit that they should state their appreciation of and regard for him, and their recognition of the loss which they have sustained by his death, in a public manner and permanent form. With Mr. Britton the law was not a mere trade or vocation; it was a learned and honorable profession. He considered it a duty not only to master the principles of the law, as they had been understood, but to keep his knowledge abreast of the latest application of those principles to the multiform exigencies growing out of the developing needs and business of his time. To that task he brought an acute and active intellect, an ability for work, persistent industry and a logical capacity and power of severe analysis which placed him, in the judgment of his associates, in the mind of the court and in the appreciation of the public in the very front of his profession To that equipment he added a power of advocacy and of convincing and eloquent statement that made his gifts felt in all forensic contests. He was a man of courage and determination, and to those qualities he added courtesy as a gentleman and a lawyer. He will be mourned by his associates as a lawyer and as a true and honorable friend, whose kindly manner and frank and generous courtesy had endeared him to all who had become intimate with him. The bar of Kings county tender to his afflicted family their condolence and sympathy, and they request the courts of this county to have this testimonial entered upon their minutes.''

The address of Supreme Court Justice Calvin E. Pratt was as follows:

"Mr Chairman and Brethren of the Bar: I feel I speak the sentiment of every man present on this occasion when I say we have not yet recovered from the shock caused by the announcement of the death of Brother Britton. The blow was so sudden and unexpected, the victim a man of such physical vigor, of such prominence in our profession, and so closely allied to us all by the ties of professional fraternity that the mind is dazed and language falters upon the lip. It is a duty we owe to ourselves when such a man dies to halt in our hurried march and testify to his merits as a lawyer and character as a man. What place so appropriate as this, where he made his greatest effort and where the most signal victories of his life were won, to fill the cup of honor to his memory. If I could do otherwise, which happily I cannot, the partialities of an uninterrupted friendship of twenty-seven years would only permit me to speak of the merits of our deceased brother as I observed them through that busy period Before speaking of my knowledge of him as a lawyer, I ought to allude to certain qualities which he possessed in an eminent degree, without which no man can be a great lawyer. He had a good constitution, as is popularly said, robust health, abstemious habits, a strong, vigorous body, capable of incredible labor and endurance, and the nervous energy of a trained athlete. Combined with these he had natural and acquired industry that was phenomenal, and a zeal and ambition for eminence in his profession that never abated Born and brought up in the country where men earn an honest living by labor, he early learned the lesson of self-reliance while his heart was filled with human sympathy. Added to these qualities was the effect of a thorough classical education and an extensive experience with men and affairs. Upon a mind naturally active, acute, tireless and discriminating, and, above, all, honest—such was the foundation upon which his character as a lawyer was built. As a lawyer he was profoundly learned. No man came to the trial of a cause better prepared at every point of a case, or presented his case with more zeal or learning. In equity, commercial, criminal and constitutional law he was equally skillful and successful. His points and briefs were models of terse, incisive language and clear reasoning and his oral arguments such as to challenge the attention of all in the court room, and much easier to overrule than to answer. As an advocate he had the power to grasp a case and hold it in view from the opening to the end. His power to distinguish errors and his analysis of testimony were only equaled by his power to combine all the facts of a case in a harmonious chain of logic from beginning to end His style was chaste and direct, and if true eloquence consists in the power to convince he was an orator of high degree. To sum up in a word, whatever we may say of the splendid abilities of some of our brethren in particular branches of the profession, I think it will be conceded that Winchester Britton, in the variety of the cases in which he was employed, the learning and ability he displayed at all times, and the success he achieved, he was as eminent as any man who has practiced at this bar within our recollection It is not, however, as a lawyer or advocate that his example is most to be prized, but his service in the profession to others and his qualities as a man He lived devoted to his profession and his legal brethren. While his mind and disposition were in the highest degree combative—which led him in a legal contest to neither give nor ask quarter—yet when the contest was over the hand of friendship was never refused or the animosities of conflict remembered The stores of his learning were ever open to his younger brethren and he never turned a deaf ear to one who called upon him in distress. Of him it may be truly said 'Friendship made no demands he found too exacting.' I regard it a high compliment to his character that he was not successful in politics. He was too bold, frank and outspoken to submit patiently to any defeat, but at all times, under all circumstances, maintained undaunted his own self-respect. While he was justly entitled to the highest honors of his profession and was fitted for the most responsible public station, he was better fitted to illustrate the dignity and purity of private life. His hopes, his ambition, his duty were all centered in his family. A kind and indulgent father, a loving and faithful husband, he filled the measure of his duty in every relation in life. Duty was the pole star of his existence He died as he would have wished, not from a lingering disease, but like a true knight, with his armor on and in the arena of battle, in undiminished vigor of body and without a ray of his intellect dimmed Death had no terrors for Brother Britton. He believed that the grave was but the black portal opening to a better world The career of a good citizen, an able lawyer, a wise counsellor, a steadfast friend, a kind father and a faithful husband is ended. May his surviving brethren each lead a life as pure and leave a fame as bright.''

General B F. Tracy followed with an eloquent eulogy. ''It was my good fortune,'' he said, ''to have known Mr. Britton for twenty years, and I can truthfully say that the better one knew him the better one esteemed him. He was a generous, true and faithful friend, open in speech, who never professed what he did not feel. As a keen, untiring, discriminating lawyer few surpassed him—none in this county. As a public official he was faithful and honest. I was engaged to conduct his case before Governor Dix, and now, standing here by his open grave, I declare that that prosecution was unjust and a grievous wrong— a wrong which the people afterward resented by re-electing him to his office.''

After a warm tribute to the memory of the deceased as a husband and father, General Tracy closed with the words: ''Beside his many virtues, how insignificant his faults.''

Ex-Surrogate Dailey was glad to see that nearly every county in the state was represented on that occasion The news of Mr Britton's death fell on the bar of Kings county like a pall. He remembered Mr. Britton for many years, when he was the associate of Mr. Jenks, and always to know him was to love and respect him Merit in time brought its reward, continued the speaker, talent was sure to be appreciated, our sins were sure to find us out and our virtues to become known. Mr Britton's stormy life left little but pleasant memories, and one could but admire the man who stood up against so many oppositions. He was one of the clearest thinkers of the bar, who are one by one being summoned from the great beyond ''I hope,'' said the speaker, in conclusion, ''when we are called to that higher court, we shall leave behind us that respect with which we part with our deceased brother"

Mr Freeman, a fellow collegian of Mr. Britton, who had known him nearly forty years, corroborated the previous speakers, adding that from his youth he had always found him a noble, true and generous man.

Ex-Judge Samuel D. Morris referred with pathetic regret to a difference between the deceased and himself which existed for some time, but was afterward happily adjusted. The cloud soon passed away and now the man had passed away—peace be to his ashes

Chief Judge Reynolds: "These sad occasions are occurring with alarming frequency. It seems but yesterady we were called here on a similar occasion, and then it seemed to me to be but a day removed since we were here before; and now Winchester Britton is called away without a note of warning. I see about me very few of the men who belonged to the bar twenty-five or thirty years ago "

His honor pointed out the merits and good qualities of Mr Britton as a lawyer and as a man, and was followed in this connection by Mr Shondie, ex-Corporation Counsel John A. Taylor, Robert Benedict and E. B. Barnum

Ex-Judge Gilbert was called upon and spoke briefly but feelingly of his long acquaintance with Mr. Britton and the shock the news of his death had been to him; and closed the proceedings with some references to his career and the promise there had seemed to be ahead of him.

THE TALMAGE (OR TALLMADGE) FAMILY.

This family name has been variously written in different ages Talnage, Tallmadge, Talmash, Talmaske, Tallenmache and in several other ways The family is one of the most ancient in English history and is "traditionally believed," says Burke, "to go back to Saxon times, to Salmag, a Saxon lord of the sixth century of our era." The name is found Tolmag in the Domesday Book, time of William the Conqueror, and also on the Roll of the Battle Abbey of the same century in the Norman form, Tallmache. It is found at Stoke Talmage in Oxfordshire 1135, in Norfolk 1200, at Suffolk at a very early date, and at Hampshire soon after 1300. The seat of the family in Hampshire was at Newton Stacey, an outlying manor of Barton Stacey in the city of Hampshire, in Southampton, and about ten miles northwest of Winchester, where the family had been long settled A history of this famiy is given in the Pall Mall Magazine for April, 1894, from which we extract the following:

The Tallemaches, who can trace their descent from Saxons, settled in East Anglia thirteen hundred years ago, may well claim to be the oldest family in England; and that ancient town of Ipswich, where in 1770 the corpse of one of their ancestors— an Earl of Dysart—lay in state on its way to Hilmingham, is appropriately the starting point where an excursion may be made to inspect the grand old noted hall which lies in stately solitude some miles to the north.

To inherit the traditions of a long line of noble ancestors whose integrity has never been questioned, is something to boast of, even in these leveling-up days, and with justifiable pride might the present head of the family replace the old distich taken long ago from the manor house:

Where William the Conqueror reigned with great fame,
Bentley was my seat and Tallemach was my name.

The connection between the American and English branches has been fully established.

Thomas Liehford, an English lawyer, who came to Boston

in 1638 and returned to England in 1641, kept a note-book of legal memoranda recently printed, in which occurs the following entry, page 294:

"William Talmage, of Boston, in New England, Thomas Talmage, Robert Talmage and Richard Walker, husband of Jane Talmage, deceased, sons and daughter of Thomas Talmage, brother of John Talmage, of Newton Stacey, in the county of Southampton, deceased, make letter of attorney to Richard Conving and William Dowlying, overseer of the will of the said John, deceased, to receive of the executor and administrator of the last will and testament of Symon Talmage, our brother, and of John Talmage, aforesaid, the sums of money due unto us by the will of the said John Talmage, and a certificate under the probate seal (L. S)" On page 311 is "A Letter of Attorney to William Talmage, Thomas Talmage and Robert Talmage aforesaid, and Richard Walker, to Mr Ralph King, to receive the money of said overseer, dated 3rd September, 1640."

James M B Dwight, of New Haven, who has collected considerable data of the Talmage family, says, "these memoranda show conclusively that there were three brothers Talmage who came to America: William, Thomas and Robert, and a sister Jane, who married Richard Walker, of Lynn These came from England to New England in 1630, and no others are known to have come to America in the Colonial period The record also establishes the fact that they were children of Thomas Talmage, of Newton Stacey, in the county of Southampton, or Hampshire, England. It also proves that they had an uncle, John Talmage, who left each of them legacies in his will; and also a brother, Symon Talmage, who also mentioned them in his will, and referred to these legacies These three brothers and sister's husband gave a power of attorney to Ralph King to receive the money. Still more recent advices carry the trace backward nearly to 1300, where the head of the line stands Sir William Talmach." (See Collins' "Peerage.")

The family heraldry is arms, Argent, a fret sable; crest, a horse's head erased, or, with wings expanded pelletee.

The elder of the brothers Talmage, who came to America, William, settled in Boston, and died leaving only one daughter. Thomas Talmage, the second of the three, settled in Lynn, Massachusetts, was admitted freeman in Boston in 1634, and was allotted there two hundred acres of land, showing that he was a man of considerable means and that he was one of the largest landholders in the town. He removed to Southampton, Long Island, in 1642, and joined the colony from Lynn which settled there. (This town was named from Southampton, England, the birthplace of Talmage) He removed, in 1649, to East Hampton with his son, Thomas Talmage, Jr., who became the first recorder or town clerk of the town. The Long Island and New Jersey branches of the family are descended from Thomas Talmage, Sr., and Thomas, Jr., the recorder, also known as Captain Thomas Talmage.

Captain Thomas Talmage, Jr , was a man of education with a scholarly and elegant handwriting, which resembles that still taught at the famous school at Manchester, so near his English birth-place. He was appointed lieutenant in 1665, and afterward captain. He died in 1690, and had as issue: Thomas, Nathaniel, John and Enos.

Enos Talmage, a son of Captain Thomas, was born at East Hampton in 1693, died at Elizabethtown, New Jersey, in 1725 He was the progenitor of the New Jersey branch of the family. His children were Daniel and Thomas.

Thomas Talmage (1st), the second son of Daniel Talmage, was born at Elizabeth, New Jersey, March 1, 1722; died there February 7, 1790. He married Hannah Norris, and had as issue Daniel, John and Enos. He married, secondly, Elizabeth Week and had a son named Thomas

Major Thomas Talmage (2), a son of Thomas and Elizabeth (Weeks) Talmage, was born at Basking Ridge, New Jersey, October 24, 1755, died at Somerville, New Jersey, October 2, 1834, at his estate known as Mount Verd He was a member of Captain Ten Eyck's company in the war of the Revolution and participated in all the principal battles which took place in New Jersey. He married Mary, a daughter of Captain Goyn McCoy, supposed to be a representative of the McCoy family of Pennsylvania. Their children were: David, born at Somerville, New Jersey, April 21, 1783; Thomas, born about 1799; Samuel Kennedy Talmage, born at Somerville, New Jersey, in 1798, who went to Georgia and became president of Oglethorpe University and was chaplain of the Confederate congress; and Goyn Talmage, born also at Somerville, in 1778.

David Talmage, the eldest child of Major Thomas (2d) and Mary (McCoy) Talmage, was born at Somerville, April 24, 1783, was a man of considerable prominence and held several public positions. He served three successive terms as a member of the New Jersey legislature, was sheriff of Somerset county, a position of great honor and importance in those days He married Catherine Van Nest, a descendant of Lieutenant John Brokaw, of the First Battalion, Somerset county, New Jersey, who was killed at the battle of Germantown, October 4, 1777. She was a niece of Abraham Van Nest, of Westchester, New York, philanthropist and donor of Van Nest Chapel at Westchester. The children by this marriage were: Phebe, Rev. Richard, Sarah, Peter Van Ness, Daniel, the Rev. John Van Ness, the Rev. Goyn, Catharine, David, Mary and the Rev. Thomas DeWitt.

Colonel Daniel Talmage, fifth child of David and Catharine (Van Ness) Talmage, was born in Somerville, February 10, 1816, and died in Brooklyn, New York, March 15, 1869.

The New York *Sun* in an article on the Talmage family says: "The best known one among the Talmage boys, except the Tabernacle preacher, was Colonel Daniel Talmage, the founder of the great rice house in New York, now styled Dan Talmage's Sons, and possessing branches in Savannah, Charleston and New Orleans. Dan Talmage was a famous politician in central New Jersey and an ardent Democrat, who worked for his party as if it was his bread and butter, and yet who would never accept an office of any sort until he was pressed by a governor he had done more than anyone else to elect, when he became a colonel on the executive staff, bought fine uniforms and spent hundreds of dollars in entertaining his friends. He was warmly liked by those who knew him and they mourned his loss. He gave a great deal in a quiet way for charity, and it is said that this son, the present head of the firm, inherited this trait and gave one-tenth of his income to the needy.

Colonel Talmage was one of the leading merchants of his day and the founder of the great rice house of Daniel Talmage's Sons. He was the first merchant in this country to establish the sale of rice as a regular article of merchandise. Previous to this the southern planters had been in the habit of shipping rice to their northern agents on commission and receiving in exchange such articles of domestic and household goods as they required for personal use. The business proved a great success from the start, and this firm is known far and near as the pioneers in this business. The old sign of Daniel Talmage still remains over the door just above the sign of the present firm. Colonel Talmage married, in December, 1839, Hannah Aymar Fowler, a daughter of Pexcil Aymar Fowler and Hannah Kip, of New York city, a descendant of the French families of Le Brum and Quereaux.

The issue of this marriage was John Fowler Talmage, who

was born in Brooklyn July 27, 1842, and married, April 26, 1865, Isabella Van Syckel, ninth in descent from Major William Phillips, commander of the Yorkshire forces in 1665, and seventh in descent from Thomas Carhart, secretary to Governor Dongan.

Major Thomas Talmage (3d), the second child of Major Thomas (2d) and Mary (McCoy) Talmage, was born at Somerville, New Jersey, about 1799. He was an enterprising, sagacious and practical farmer. During his life he filled many important positions of trust in church and state with honor and credit to himself and benefit to the community He married Sophia Van Vichten, a daughter of Michael Van Vichten, son of Dirck, son of Hon Michael Dirckse Van Vichten, son of Dirck Teunise, son of Teunise Dirckse.

Teunise Dirckse Van Vichten came to New Amsterdam in the ship "Arms of Norway" in 1638 with his wife, child and two servants, by way of Rotterdam, probably from Veghten on the Veghten river near Utrecht He settled at Greenbush, opposite Albany, where he had a farm as early as 1648. He had a son named Dirck Teunise, who was born at Veghten, Holland He married Janetza Michaelja Viulandt He removed to the Catskill before 1681, and resided where the old Van Vechten house now stands, which is the third built on the same site It was built in 1750. They had twelve children, of whom Michael Dirckse was the third. The latter was born November 28, 1663, married first Marthja Perker, and secondly Janitja Damon, and removed to New Jersey with his brother Abraham before 1699, and he had a child named Dirck, born September 16, 1699, on the Raritans. His family bible is at the Bible House in New York city. His will was dated the 17th of April, 1777, and probated the 4th of February, 1872. He was one of a company of eight who bought, May 3, 1712, the Royce plantation of fourteen hundred and seventy acres. He was one of the assistant judges of Somerset county in February, 1711 He gave the land upon which the first Dutch church of Raritan was originally built in 1721. The church was destroyed in the time of the Revolution, and the next building was erected near the town of Somerville. He had seven children, of whom Dirck was the fifth.

The last mentioned was born September 16, 1699, and died November 29, 1781. He married first Judith Brockholst, and secondly Deborah Antonides, and thirdly, in 1759, Sarah Middah. His farm was the camping ground of the Revolutionary armies, and his house that of a bounteous hospitality to officers and men. General Greene left a handsome mahogany table there as a token of appreciation of kindness received in this hospitable mansion. This table is now a treasured heirloom in the family. He had five children, of whom Michael was the fourth. The latter was born November 13, 1764, as shown on the tombstone, but the Dutch bible says November 16, 1776 He died December 29, 1831. He married, April 10, 1787, Elizabeth La Grange, a daughter of John La Grange, and had eight children, of whom Sophia was the sixth. Sophia was born July 11, 1801, and married Thomas Talmage Thomas Talmage, by his wife, Sophia (Van Vechten) Talmage, had as issue Samuel and John Frelinghuysen.

Dr. Samuel Talmage, just mentioned, was born at Somerville, New Jersey, February 20, 1831, studied medicine with his father-in-law, Dr. Ephraim Clark, of Staten Island, and entered the medical department of the University of the City of New York, and was graduated in 1870 He subsequently removed to Brooklyn and became associated with his brother John F , who had already acquired a large practice He adopted the new system of homeopathy and continued with his brother until the latter's death, and is still (1901) engaged in practice in Brooklyn. At the breaking out of the Civil war he was commissioned by the governor of New Jersey captain of a cavalry company. In early life he contributed occasionally to the weekly periodicals, but his time has since been wholly absorbed in his profession He married, in 1863, Arabella M. Clark, a daughter of Dr. Ephraim Clark, of Staten Island.

John Frelinghuysen Talmage, A. M., M. D., second child of Major Thomas (3d) and Sophia (Van Vechten) Talmage, was born at Somerville, New Jersey, March 11, 1833, and was named after his mother's brother-in-law He was brought up on his father's farm and received his early education at the village academy under the personal tuition of his father's pastor, the Rev. T W. Chambers, D. D., of New York, who at that time was settled in Somerville. Young Talmage entered Rutgers College, New Brunswick, and took his place in the second term of the sophomore class. He was graduated in 1852, his diploma bearing the signature of Theodore Frelinghuysen, president

After his graduation he traveled extensively in the southern states and for a time filled the professorship of ancient languages in an Alabama college, now extinct. At Huntsville, that state, he made the acquaintance of Drs. Burrill and Gillson, physicians of the homeopathic school of medicine, and became interested in their methods, witnessing some remarkable cures effected by them. He was thus led by his own observation to abandon the convictions of earlier years and adhere to the school of Hahnemann. For six months he pursued his medical studies with his friends in Huntsville, and on his return north attended a course of lectures in the medical department of the University of the City of New York The following summer he entered the office of Dr. A. Cooke Hall, of Brooklyn, one of the most distinguished physicians of the new school of scientific medicine of that period. In 1859 he received his graduating diploma from the University Medical College, in which at that time the eminent Dr Valentine Mott was emeritus professor of surgery.

Soon after this Dr. Talmage became associated with his preceptor, Dr. Hall, as partner, and continued these relations for twelve years. For one year he acted as physician of the Brooklyn Orphan Asylum, and during that time met with uniform success in the treatment of epidemic and other diseases of a difficult nature. He was afterward appointed to the department of diseases of women in the Brooklyn Homeopathic Dispensary, but was compelled to resign after one year's experience, owing to the large increase in his private practice. At the time of the last visitation of the Asiatic cholera in the city in 1866, he issued a private circular containing hints and suggestions for his patients. Though intended only as a private circular, it soon came to the knowledge of others, and so admirably did it meet a great pressing emergency that various public journals, such as the "Eagle" and "Union" of Brooklyn, the "New York Tribune," the "Springfield (Massachusetts) Republican" and others reproduced it at length with emphatic commendations of its form and matter It has since become a standard medicine for that epidemic, and thousands of sufferers have been benefited by it.

After the death of Dr. Hall, Dr. Talmage naturally succeeded to a large portion of his practice, which, added to his own, occupied every moment of his time, and in 1870 he associated with him his brother Samuel, who had taken up the study of medicine at a later period than his younger brother. The former continued in active practice until his death, June 30, 1897, and was at that time one of the leading practitioners of the new school of medicine in this part of the country

He was for many years identified with the Church of the Pilgrims Under General Meserole he served as surgeon of the Eleventh Brigade, N. G. S. N. Y. He was one of the charter members of the Brooklyn Club, which relation he resigned, and at the time of his death he was a member of the Hamilton Club. His father, Thomas Talmage, was an uncle of Rev. T De Witt Talmage, another cousin of Hon. Thomas Talmage, a former mayor of Brooklyn.

Dr. Talmage married, in 1863, Miss Maggie A. Hunt, a lady of great personal attractions, the youngest daughter of Thomas Hunt, Esq., widely known as one of the merchant princes of New York.

The issue of this marriage were Thomas Hunt (deceased), Lilian, who married John Murray Mitchell, Edward Taylor Hunt and John Frelinghuysen.

Goyn Talmage, the fourth son of Major Thomas and Mary (McCoy) Talmage, was born at Somerville, New Jersey, in 1778. He married Magdalene Terhune, a descendant of an old Long Island family Their children were Thomas Goyn, Catharine, Maria and Mertine The last mentioned married Edward Patterson, of Philadelphia, who was the father of Hon Edward Patterson, judge of the supreme court of New York city.

Hon. Thomas Goyn Talmage, son of Goyn and Magdalene (Terhune) Talmage, was born at Somerville, New Jersey, in October, 1801, spent his early life on his father's farm and came to New York city at the age of eighteen, entering the employ of Abraham Van Ness, then engaged in the saddlery-hardware business on Hanover Square. He resided for some time on Stone street, near Broad, where two of his children were born. He began his public career as early as 1827, when he was elected alderman of the first ward on the Democratic ticket, and from that time until his death was almost constantly in public office, but always for public good and not for self-aggrandizement, as his record abundantly proves He moved to Greenwich village in the ninth ward about 1832, residing on Hammond street, now Eleventh street. He was elected alderman from this ward about 1836, and became president of the common council He was elected to the state legislature in 1833, during the administration of Governor Silas Wright, with whom he enjoyed intimate relations. He was largely instrumental in the passage of the Union Ferry bill, which was of great commercial importance to the city of Brooklyn. He moved to Brooklyn in 1840 and from that time until his death was identified with its interests, and favored every movement tending to its growth and prosperity He settled on the property of his second wife, Sarah J. Van Brunt, which consisted of a farm of thirty-four acres lying between Smith and Eighth streets and extending from Gowanus creek to the Flatbush line It was on a portion of this farm that the gallant Marylanders who fell at the battle of Long Island were buried Mr. Talmage was elected alderman of the eighth ward of Brooklyn after a residence there of three years and was elected mayor of the city in 1845. A foundation for a city hall was undertaken during the administration of his predecessor, but for lack of funds only one story of the building was completed, and the debris removed, and plans for the present city hall were made and adopted and the present building was constructed under his administration Largely through the efforts of Mr. Talmage the debt was liquidated, and not long after the building completed.

The most important work of his life, however, was in connection with Prospect Park, Brooklyn, of which he was the originator and chief promotor He introduced and carried through the state legislature the bills of 1858-'59 and '60 for the creation of the park, and was untiring in his efforts until the work was fairly under way The three first commissioners appointed by the legislature were Thomas G. Talmage, E. C. Litchfield and Charles Stanton. When they found they were likely to meet with opposition from the Republican side of the house, Mr. Stranahan, a Republican, was added to the commission. The conception of the enterprise was due to Mr. Talmage, and this he prosecuted with unabated vigor and energy up to the day of his death, which was caused from a cold contracted while advocating the measure at Albany Without detracting from the honors awarded to another, they should be equally shared by him who fell at his post of duty a martyr to the cause to which he had devoted the best years of his life. It is noteworthy also that the man who conceived this enterprise was a descendant of one of the oldest families on Long Island, among whose descendants are found some of the brightest and most distinguished statesmen, patriots, orators and learned divines of the country

Mr Talmage was three times married. His first wife was Dorothy Miller, daughter of Colonel David Miller, of Morris county, New Jersey. One of her brothers, Hon. Jacob Miller, was a United States senator from New Jersey for about sixteen years, and was the contemporary of Clay, Webster and other distinguished statesmen of that period. Another brother was William Miller, United States minister to France There were four children by this marriage: David M , Mary Louise, William Henry and Tunis Van Pelt. Mr. Talmage married secondly Sarah J. Van Brunt, a daughter of John Van Brunt, and two children were the issue of this marriage: Jane Elizabeth, who married Rev Henry Vonbac, and Adrian The third wife of Mr. Talmage was Harriet Joraleman, a daughter of Judge Tennis Joraleman, from whom a principal street in Brooklyn derives its name By this marriage there was one child, Frederick T

Tunis Van Pelt Talmage, fourth child of Hon. Thomas Goyn Talmage, was born in Clinton, New Jersey, in July, 1832, during the temporary sojourn of his parents at that place Until he was eight years of age his childhood was spent in New York city Since 1840 he has resided in Brooklyn, and was educated at the public schools of the two cities. At the age of seventeen he went to California as one of the "Forty-niners," returning in 1852, richer only in experience. He began business in Brooklyn that year as a street contractor. He graded Sixth, Seventh, Eighth, Ninth and Tenth avenues and all the streets between First and Ninth streets. In 1857 he started in the retail coal business, and since 1882 has been engaged in the wholesale coal trade.

He was engaged actively in local politics for many years. His first public office was that of supervisor, to which office he was elected from the eighth ward in 1860 for a two-years term, and in 1862 was elected alderman of the same ward, the second year of his term serving as president of the board. He represented the fourth district in the state legislature in 1874-5, introducing and carrying through one of the most important measures ever enacted for the people of Brooklyn, but more especially for his own constituents. This was the readjustment of Prospect Park taxes, which, instead of requiring the few property holders whose property was contiguous to the park to bear the entire burden of taxation, was distributed throughout the entire city. He claimed that as the whole city was benefited equally by the park, other property holders should share equally the burden of taxation By his strenuous efforts to overcome the strong opposition to the measure he made many friends in both parties

In 1865 Mr. Talmage came within one vote of receiving the nomination for mayor, his opponent being Mayor Kalbfleisch. He ran on the independent Democratic ticket in 1867, but was defeated. From the first day he entered public life he has been actively connected with the Twenty-second Ward Improvement Association.

During the Civil war, as one of the supervisors he served on the relief committee which gave genuine assistance to the widows whose husbands were killed on the battle-field He assisted in raising the Fifty-sixth Regiment (of which his brother was major), and was commissioned captain by Governor Morgan. He went with his regiment to the front in 1863 during the invasion of Pennsylvania by Lee's army, and remained in active service until all danger was passed, after which he resigned his position.

Until within the past few years he has been actively identified with the Reformed church. Since 1898 he has been connected with the Park Congregational church, of which he is a trustee

He married, in 1853, Magdalene Van Nest de Forest, daughter of John I de Forest, of New York Their children are: Magdalene, who married Francis E. Dodge, and has children named Frank, Linden and Helen; William De Forrest, unmarried; Katherine A., who married William H Force and has two children,—Katharine and Magdalene

THE RAPELYE AND ALLIED FAMILIES.

DESCENDANTS OF JORIS RAPALIE, OF LONG ISLAND.

According to recent discoveries, Gaspard Colet de Rapella (of Rapella), the founder of the Rapalye family of America, belonged to the celebrated Coligny family of France, and was a nephew of Admiral Coligny, who suffered martyrdom for his religious belief at the instigation of Queen Catharine, of Navarre, being one of the victims of the massacre of St. Bartholomew. The titles which he bore were Gaspard de Coligny, Marquis de Chatillon, Admiral of France, Colonel of French Infantry, Governor of Picardy, Isle de France, Paris and Havre

"The house of Coligny was," says a well known authority on French heraldry, "next to those of Montmorency, Rohan, Leval and a few others, and, always excepting the semi-royal house of Lorraine, one of the first in France The ancestry of the family was traced back to the first Duke of Burgundy. In the sixteenth century they had been a great house for four hundred years and more. They founded the Abbey of Le Mirerir in 1121; those of Montmerle and Crillon in 1202. Humbert de Coligny is said to have followed Conrad III in the second Crusade, but his name does not occur in the Cartulary of Jerusalem or in the lists of Families d'Outre Mer. * * * The place from which they took their name is a small town or village in the department of Ain on the line from Lyons to Strasburg, some forty miles west of Geneva and twenty-five miles north of Main. About one hundred years before the birth of Admiral Coligny the family removed from Coligny to Chatillon-sur-Loing, from which place they took their title The Admiral's father, high in favor with Francis the First, was marshal of France, governor of Picardy, lieutenant of the principality of Orange and the county of Guienne."

Of Admiral Coligny it is said:

"He received in 1577 the Collar of the Order and the command of the French Infantry He acted against the English at Boulogne and negotiated the treaty which restored the place to the French in 1550. In 1557 he commanded the infantry in the campaign of Lorraine and was engaged in the taking of Metz, Soul and Verdun, and in the sieges of Rodermark, Damvilliers, Ivry and Montmedy Fighting under the Duke of Vendome in Picardy, he carried by assault Hesden and Seronanne.

"Espousing the cause of the Protestants, he incurred the animosity of Queen Catharine of Navarre, and was assassinated August 24, 1572. The monument erected to his memory recites briefly his virtues, his achievements and the honors he had won

The armorial bearings of this noble family are described as: Coligny-Chatillon: de gueules a l'aigle d'argent becquee membree et couronnee d'azur ongles d'or couronnee, de due centier; une demi-aigle poses de profil, couronnee de becquee d'azur. Supports: deux limions, d'argent affrontes assis et accoles de gueules. Devise (motto), Je les prouve tous. Issue, au dixieme siecle des comtes souverains de Bourgogne, cette maison illustre a pour chef de nom et d'armes le marquis de Coligny-Chatillon au chateau de Choye, Haute-Saone."

"The origin of the Rapelye family," says a recent writer in the Brooklyn *Eagle*, "has often been erroneously stated as being of French or Dutch extraction; but the true origin of the family is Italian, they having come from Rapelia, a town in Italy, from which place they emigrated to France in the fifteenth century The first mention of the family of which we have any detailed account is Gaspard Colet de Rapella, who was a nephew of the celebrated Admiral Coligny Gaspard Colet was born in Chatillon-sur-Loing, a town in France, in 1505. He was an officer in the French army, and a staunch Protestant, and during the religious persecutions in that country he was compelled to flee to that haven of refuge, Holland, in 1548. There he settled and married the daughter of Victor Antoine Jansen, or in plain English, Johnson, of Antwerp, and had three children The first he named after his uncle and himself, namely, Gaspard Coligny; the second preserved the family name, Abraham Colet; the third was a daughter, Briekje, and she married her cousin, Victor Honorius Jansen, and had one son, named Abraham, who became an historical painter He married the daughter of Hans Loedwick, of Amsterdam, and had three sons, William, Joris and Antoine

"The two eldest determined to leave Holland and emigrate to America. They sailed from Rochelle, in France, in 1623, and settled at Fort Orange, now Albany William died unmarried, but his brother, whose full name was Joris Jansen de Rapalie, married Catalyntie Trico, of Paris, France, and, dropping the name of Jansen, assumed that of Rapalie, and became the founder of the entire Rapelye family of this country. The younger brother, Antoine, who also emigrated to this country, in 1631, preserved the true family name of Janssen, and was the founder of one branch of the family in this country."

Joris Rapelie removed from Fort Orange to New Amsterdam in 1626, and resided there till after the birth of his youngest child. On June 16, 1637, he bought from the Indians 235 acres of land, called Runnegaconck, now embraced within the city of Brooklyn. He became the first settler on Long Island, and his eldest child, Sara, who was born on June 9, 1625, was the first white child born on the island She married Hans Bergen, and they in turn became the founders of the Bergen family of Brooklyn. Joris was the leading man and took a prominent part in the public affairs of the colony. He died soon after the close of the Dutch administration, his widow surviving him many years. Their children were:

I Sara, born June 9, 1625, married first Hans Bergen, and secondly Teunis Gysbert Bogert

II Marritie, born March 11, 1627, married Michael Van De Voert.

III Jannetie, born August 16, 1629, married Rem Remsen de Breck.

IV. Judith, born July 5, 1635, married Peter Van Nist

V. Jan, born August 28, 1637, married Marya Maer, and had no issue.

VI. Jacob, born May 28, 1639, was killed by the Indians.

VII. Catalyntie, born March 28, 1641, married Joremus Westenhout.

VIII Jeronemus, born June 17, 1643, married Annetie, daughter of Van Teunis Dennis

IX. Annetie, born February 6, 1646, married first Martin Ryerse, and secondly Joost Fransz.

X. Elizabeth, born March 28, 1648, married Cornelius Derrick Hogeland.

XI. DANIEL, born December 29, 1650, married Sara, daughter of Abraham Clock

Daniel Rapalie, youngest child of Joris Rapelie, was born on Manhattan Island December 29, 1650, later removed to Brooklyn, and died there December 26, 1725. He was a man of high standing and respectability, and was an elder in the Brooklyn Reformed Dutch church. He married, May 27, 1674, Sarah, daughter of Abraham Martensen Clock. The latter was one of the early proprietors of New Amsterdam. His name appears on an old map of New Amsterdam, the location being Hanover Square, and the tradition being that this name was given to it by the family of Daniel Rapelie, by his wife. Sara (Clock) Rapelie had issue: Joris, born March 4, 1675; Daniel; Catharine, who married Joseph Van Clief; Annetie; Mary, who married Elbert Hegeman; Sarah, who married Peter Luyster; and Daniel, born March 5, 1691, who married, October 17, 1711, Aeltie, a daughter of Johannes Cornell. He removed to Newtown and bought the farm on Flushing Bay.

Lieutenant Joris Rapelie, eldest son of Daniel and Sara (Clock) Rapelie, was born in Brooklyn March 4, 1675 He was the chief brewer of the town, held the position of lieutenant in his Majesty's forces, and resided in Newtown. In the building of the edifice of the Reformed Low Dutch church congregation of Newtown, December 2, 1731, it is said that "encouraging advance having been made in obtaining subscriptions (amounting to £277 12s.), the congregation, on May 27, 1732, appointed their brethren and faithful friends, Abraham Remsen, Isaac Brogaw, Joris Rapelie, Abraham Lent, Nicholas Berrien and Abraham Brinkerhoff, a committee to superintend the building of the church, who forthwith entered upon arrangements for the work "

Lieutenant Joris Rapelie married Agnes, daughter of Cornelius Berrien. He was a man of education and prominence. In 1669 he settled in Flatbush, and in 1685 removed to Newtown, where during the previous year he and his brother-in-law, Abraham Brinkerhoff, bought over four hundred acres of land at the head of Flushing Bay His wife was Jannetje, daughter of Jan Stryker. Lieutenant Joris Rapelie, by his wife Agnes (Berrien) Rapelie, had issue, Daniel, Cornelius, Abraham, Jane, John, Jacob and Jeromus.

DESCENDANTS OF JOHN RAPELYE, FIFTH CHILD OF JORIS

John Rapelye, fifth child of Lieutenant Joris and Agnes (Berrien) Rapelye, was born June 11, 1711, in the house which his father, Joris, built. This is still standing and in good preservation, being the property of the Elliott family, of Corona. In 1743 John and his brother Jeromus bought the paternal estate, which they divided, John retaining the farm more recently occupied by Robert Willett. He died of consumption February 11, 1756. He married, January 12, 1733, Maria, daughter of Abraham Lent, son of Ryck, eldest son of Abraham Rycken, who assumed the name of Lent. Their children were: George, born October 22, 1733; Anna Catrina, born August 10, 1736, who married Jacobus Riker; Abraham, born November 21, 1739; and Daniel, born August 15, 1745, who married Ellen, daughter of William Livisay.

George Rapelye, eldest son of John and Maria (Lent) Rapelye, was born October 27, 1733 After the Revolution he settled at Communipaw, New Jersey, and on March 22, 1791, was accidentally drowned in coming to New York. His remains were recovered and buried at Communipaw He married Mary, daughter of Colonel Bernard Bloom, of Newtown His widow died June 4, 1819, aged eighty-six, and was interred at Newtown Their children were: John, born February 7, 1757; Bernard, born August 27, 1759; and George, born March 14, 1763. The latter married Anna, daughter of Paul Vandervoort, and being knocked overboard by the boom of a vessel, was drowned in the East river May 28, 1789, leaving issue two sons, George and Paul, the first of whom was also drowned at New York several years after Thus by a singular fatality a father, son and grandson, each bearing the same name, met a watery grave. Paul occupied the farm upon Newtown creek formerly owned by Thomas Alsop

John Rapelye, eldest child of George and Mary (Bloom) Rapelye, was born February 7, 1757. He purchased a farm in Newtown from Captain William Weyman, and resided in the old farm house, which is still standing, being occupied by the son and daughters of his son-in-law, Benjamin Moore He married Lemma Boice, of New Jersey, and died April 5, 1829. She died September 15, 1832 They had issue George I., Jacob, Jane, who married Benjamin Moore, and Mary. The eldest son, George I, was born in Nova Scotia, his parents and grandparents having gone there with many other loyalists at the close of the Revolution Both their sons became two of the most prominent members of the Rapelye family. George I., the eldest son, was born February 7, 1787, and came with his parents to Newtown, first locating for a few years at Bowery Bay, and afterward purchased Captain William Weyman's farm He lived there for the rest of his life—a period of almost ninety years, dying on April 23, 1883, at the ripe old age of ninety-six years and two months. He was familiarly known as "Uncle George," and for the latter part of his life was the oldest inhabitant of the town. He was a vestryman of St. James' Protestant Episcopal church of Newtown village, and held that and the office of warden for a period of sixty years He held several town offices, notably that of commissioner of highways, and also inspector of turnpikes. He was the last of his generation.

Jacob Rapelye, the second child of John and Lemma (Boice) Rapelye, was born in Newtown September 8, 1788. When he was twenty-one years of age he became a clerk in the

United States Bank in New York city, but on the breaking out of the war of 1812 he obtained a commission as first lieutenant of artillery, and was very active in the defense of New York city. He was afterward appointed adjutant to General Izard and did active duty throughout the war, and at its close he removed to Charleston, South Carolina, and engaged in the drygoods business In 1816 he received the appointment of deputy secretary of state of South Carolina. During the insurrection of the negroes in that state Mr. Rapelye was placed by the governor on a committee of investigation, and he did much in restoring public safety

In 1828 Mr. Rapelye settled in Brooklyn and made his home at the corner of Atlantic avenue and Clinton street, where the South Brooklyn Savings Bank now stands After living there for many years he removed to 145 Columbia Heights When he came to Brooklyn he entered into the real estate business, with Mr Charles Hoyt as his partner, and he was largely instrumental in the widening and improvement of Atlantic avenue and in the opening of Clinton and Court streets He was also interested in the establishing of South Ferry and did much to further the work In 1837 he invented a machine to clean the streets, the brooms of which were on long arms which revolved like a windmill; but on its first trial it was destroyed by an angry mob who thought that its use would throw them out of employment!

Mr Rapelye, in connection with Cornelius J. Bergen and Alexander Bergen, took a very active part in the opening of that part of South Brooklyn that is near Carroll Park In 1853 he bought one hundred acres of land at Newtown and named the tract Laurel Hill. There Mr. Rapelye built himself a fine mansion and made it his home up to the time of his death, August 21, 1867 Always of a kindly and charitable disposition, he possessed many friends He was identified with the Protestant Episcopal church, and rendered material aid toward the building of St Luke's, the first St. John's and Emanuel churches of Brooklyn. He married, September 9, 1818, Elizabeth Van Mater, and had issue: Margaret, born December 11, 1819; Lemma Ann, born at Laurel Hill September 17, 1821, and died January 31, 1824; Catharine, born at Charleston, South Carolina, December 26, 1822, and died at Newtown December 18, 1895; John, born in Newtown December 30, 1824, died December 10, 1825; Gilbert Van Mater, born at Newtown August 18, 1826, and resides at Rhinebeck, New York; John, born August 4, 1828, and died August 10, 1844; Augustus, born March 29, 1830, and died February 7, 1900; Lemma Ann, born September 11, 1831, and died November 26, 1874; Mary Elizabeth, born June 11, 1833, died May 29, 1866; and Jane Moore, born September 28, 1839, and died September 17, 1883.

Augustus Rapelye, seventh child of Jacob and Elizabeth (Van Mater) Rapelye, was born in Brooklyn March 29, 1830, and died February 7, 1900 After his father's death he resided for some years at Laurel Hill, where his father had previously settled In June, 1885, he married Miss Helen Schroeder, of Woodside, a daughter of Herman Schroeder, of an old and highly honored family of German descent. Mr. Rapelye in 1890 removed to Newtown village and purchased the Sackett-Moore place, where he resided until his death For many years he conducted a real-estate business in New York, but about 1890 he retired from active business life and occupied his time with his many home pursuits. He was a public-spirited man and took an active interest in town and church affairs For a number of years he was a member of the board of education for district No 1 of the old town of Newtown, and on the retirement of Judge Garretson from the presidency of the board he was elected to that position, continuing until the consolidation of the town with Greater New York He took a great interest in the school and was a most active and useful member of the board. In church affairs he was one of the most distinguished laymen in the Protestant Episcopal diocese of Long Island. For some years he was warden and treasurer of St. James' church, of Elmhurst, of which he had been a faithful member for many years, and was the chairman of all the important committees of the vestry of that church. He was a member and secretary of the standing committee of the diocese of Long Island, and was one of its trustees as well as a member of the missionary committee. He was a lay delegate from St. James church to the arch-deaconry of Queens and Nassau in 1898, and was a delegate to the general convention of the Protestant Episcopal church in America, held in Washington, D C He was treasurer of the jubilee fund of thirty thousand dollars, which was added to the Episcopal fund of the diocese to celebrate the twenty-fifth anniversary of Bishop Littlejohn's episcopate Mr. Rapelye was an intimate and confidential friend of the bishop, and was greatly respected and esteemed by all the clergy throughout the diocese.

At the time of Mr Rapelye's death the standing committee of the diocese of Long Island paid a graceful tribute to his memory by a series of resolutions, beautifully engrossed, which were presented to his widow The following, from these, show the estimate in which he was held by his associates in the diocese: "A layman of such exalted personal worth; so useful to the community, so devout and helpful as a son of the church; so ambitious for the extension of the heavenly kingdom—was truly an important factor in any diocesan life; was an enthusiastic friend and supporter of all measures and agencies which he believed would promote the interests of the Redeemer's cause within these borders "

Mr. Rapelye was also connected with St. Paul's church in Woodside, in which he was an active and prominent worker He was also in charge of a mission Sunday-school at Laurel Hill, where he did much good work. He was a member of the Long Island Historical Society, and was prominently connected with the Holland Society of New York, of which he had been a member ever since its organization He was likewise one of the organizers and a member of the board of directors and secretary of the Citizens' Water Supply Company of Newtown.

As a public-spirited citizen and a noble-hearted Christian, Mr. Rapelye held a prominent place in the community. He was a fit representative of a family that helped to plant the standard of Christianity on Long Island, and his name will ever be kept in remembrance by those with whom he was so long associated.

LINE OF CAPTAIN JEROMUS RAPELIE, YOUNGEST CHILD OF LIEUTENANT JORIS AND AGNES (BERRIEN) RAPELIE (JORIS, DANIEL, JORIS).

Captain Jeromus Rapelie, youngest child of Lieutenant Joris and Agnes (Berrien) Rapelie, was born September 14, 1717. He bought the homestead half of the paternal farm on Flushing bay, and succeeded his father in business He held a commission as captain of militia, was a man of great resolution and energy, and is said to have been a man of large and heavy frame, while his wife was remarkable for her diminutiveness. He married Wyntie, a daughter of Abraham Lent, a son of Ryck, eldest son of Abraham Rycken, who assumed the name of Lent.

An interesting incident is related of Wyntie Rapelie, showing the strong political differences that divided neighbors and friends at the beginning of the Revolution Mrs Maria Rapalie, mother of George Rapalie and grandmother of the last Cornelius, was spending a social afternoon with her neighbor, the wife of Captain Jeromus Rapelie. At the tea table the good hostess had prepared to serve up her choicest tea, not recognizing the right of congress to deprive her of her favorite beverage. But her guest, who entertained opposite views, declined to partake, and upon being pressed for her reason, replied: "Cousin Wyntie, I cannot do it; it's against my principles " Overcome by a sense of their unhappy position, both fell to weeping. Mrs Rapelie adhered to her purpose, though the two friends lived to drink tea together in more auspicious times.

Captain Jeromus Rapelie, by his wife Wyntie (Lent) Rapelie, had issue: George, born December 12, 1739; Abraham, born December 10, 1741; Daniel, born November 27, 1743, died September 9, 1762; Jacobus, born February 15, 1746; Cornelius, born August 10, 1748; Jeromus, born August 23, 1751; and John, born March 9, 1755, and died September 9, 1776.

Cornelius Rapelie, fifth child of Captain Jeromus and Wyntie (Lent) Rapelie, was born at Newtown August 10, 1748, resided in Newtown until the close of the war, and then went to Nova Scotia and remained some years. On his return he took charge of the tavern (now the Rapelye House), which he carried on until his death. He married, November 17, 1780, Maria, daughter of his cousin, Jacobus Riker.

Jacobus Riker was born in 1736 and named after his uncle, Jacob Van Alst. He remained on the paternal farm at Newtown He married, February 20, 1761, Anna Catrina, daughter of John Rapelye, and May 1, 1770, after his father's death, bought the homestead. In the Revolution he desired to take no part, and only by cirumstances and influences peculiarly adverse was he found, like many others, to yield an apparent compliance with loyalist measures. But his observation and own bitter experience during that reign of terror had the effect of attaching him firmly to the Republican party, with which from the peace of 1783 he uniformly acted in exercising the right of suffrage. He was a man of considerable ingenuity, and thoroughly Dutch in language and habits Faithful in the practice of useful industry, prudence and strict integrity, he enjoyed the respect and confidence of his fellow townsmen He served as an elder in the Dutch church at Newtown. Maria, his eldest child, born March 27, 1762, was married to Cornelius Rapelye. Jacob Riker was the son of Abraham (3rd), son of Abraham (2d), son of Abraham Riker, the ancestor.

Cornelius Rapelye, by his wife Maria (Riker) Rapelye, had issue: Grace, born August 20, 1782; Jeromus, born May 27, 1784, at Newtown; Jeromus, born at Shelburn, Nova Scotia, May 27, 1788; James Riker, born in Nova Scotia, January 3, 1790; and George, born in Newtown February 15, 1793.

George Rapelye, the last mentioned, was born in Newtown, February 15, 1793, and became a prominent New York merchant and carried on the wholesale grocery business on Catharine street for many years, where he accumulated a fortune. He owned a fine residence on Madison street, which was then a fashionable part of the city, making his summer residence at the present Rapelye homestead in Astoria. He married Jane Maria, daughter of James and Adrianne Suydam, son of Captain Lambert, son of Hendrick (2d), son of Hendrick Rycken

Hendrick Rycken, a member of the Riker family, came from Suydam, Holland, in 1665, and settled in New Amsterdam, at what was called Smith's Fly, where he purchased a house and land in 1678. He removed to Flatbush with his wife, Ida Jacobs, and acquired a large estate His children took the name of Suydam.

Hendrick Suydam, son of Hendrick Rycken, became a farmer at Bedford (a part of Brooklyn), where he bought a farm of his father in 1698   He died subsequent to 1743. By his wife Bennetie he had Lambert Hendrick (3rd) and Elsie.

Captain Lambert Suydam, eldest child of Hendrick (2d) and Bennetie his wife, resided at Bedford. In 1749 he was commissioned captain of the Kings county troop of horse. He died in 1767. He married Abigail Lefferts and had Hendrick, Bennetie, Jane, Ida and Jacobus.

Jacobus Suydam was born at Bedford, December 4, 1758, became a New York merchant and resided at Bedford In 1794 he bought the estate of William Lawrence, in Newtown, and lived there until his death, June 11, 1825. He married Adriana, daughter of Captain Cornelius Rapelye, and had issue: Lambert, Cornelius Rapelye, Abigail, Adriana, James, Jane Maria and Henry

Jane Maria married George Rapelye, and had a son named Cornelius.

Cornelius Rapelye, only child of George and Jane Maria (Suydam) Rapelye, was born in New York November 16, 1833. His mother died during his early childhood, and he was raised by his aunt, Grace Rapelye Trafford, who did her best to supply the place of a mother. She was the widow of John Trafford, and her son became prominent in the public affairs of Astoria and did much for its growth and development. He purchased a set of chimes for the Church of the Redeemer, with the request that his remains should be buried in the churchyard and that these chimes should be rung on each recurring anniversary of his birthday. This request has been strictly observed, and the set of bells are known as the "Trafford chimes." Cornelius Rapelye, under the careful training of his aunt, grew up an exemplary youth. A certificate of his scholarship has been preserved, which shows his good standing at school. It reads: "Monthly Certificate of Approbation of the Male High School,

78 Crosby Street. Awarded to Cornelius Rapelye of the Fifth Class for his Industry, Punctuality and Good Deportment during the past four weeks. [Isaac F Bragg, Principal.]" It is an old proverb, "Show me the boy and I'll show you the man," and it proved true in his case. He was not obliged to labor for a living, having inherited an ample fortune; but he was never idle and his time was profitably employed. He was punctual in all his engagements, and his good deportment was shown in his daily walk and conversation, which was that of a true gentleman,—courteous, kind, considerate and obliging It might be truly said of him,

"His life was gentle; and the elements
So mixed in him that Nature might stand up
And say to all the world, This was a man."

He was quiet and reserved and of an even temperament. He won the confidence of his fellow men without an effort. His words had no uncertain sound or double meaning.

Astoria, the home of his childhood and manhood, owes much to him as a public-spirited citizen. He not only encouraged but was an active promoter of all public improvements, and had great confidence in the future of his native town. Of a modest and retiring disposition, he could not be induced to accept public honors, but was generous in his support of friends who did accept them. In his works of benevolence and charity he followed the injunction, "Let not thy right hand know what thy left hand doeth." He accepted offices of trust and responsibility in his business connections where he felt that he could be useful. He was president of the Astoria Ferry Company for many years and a director in other corporations.

He was long an elder in the Astoria Reformed Dutch church, to which he was at all times a liberal contributor, and when the church edifice was destroyed by fire he was foremost in the work of erecting the new church edifice, being a member of the building committee At the time of his death, November 20, 1890, the consistory of the church adopted the following resolutions:

Whereas, Almighty God, our heavenly Father, by His messenger Death has, in His inscrutable providence, removed from the midst of us our brother, Elder Cornelius Rapelye,

Resolved, That while we know and are sure that "He doeth all things well," and "will have compassion according to the multitude of his mercies," yet we cannot refrain from giving some expression to our sense of the great loss sustained by his family and friends, the Church and this church in particular. An earnest, upright man, a true and affectionate husband, a consistent and devoted elder, a firm and faithful friend has obeyed the call of the Master, "Come up higher."

Resolved, That in the consistent walk and conversation of Elder Rapelye, and in his unostentatious devotion to the spiritual and temporal welfare of the church, he has shown an example worthy of being followed by those with whom he had been intimately and harmoniously associated for so many years

Resolved, That Consistory extend to his family its sincere sympathy, with earnest prayers that the Saviour will sustain them in their affliction. And, rejoicing in the knowledge that they "sorrow not even as others which have no hope," and in the firm belief that we shall one day meet again with all the loved ones gone before, we say to our brother, "Only 'Good night,' beloved, not 'Farewell!'"

Resolved, That this action be recorded in the minutes of Consistory, and in the minutes of the Eldership, and that a copy thereof be sent to his family, and published in the Christian Intelligencer By order of Consistory

JOHN J HALSEY, Clerk.

Astoria, Nov 21, 1890.

Referring to the above resolutions, his pastor, for whom he entertained the warmest friendship, said:

"In the set of resolutions framed by consistory, the word 'unostentatious' occurs. It is a word peculiarly expressive of our brother's character. For nearly two years, though his pastor and intimate friend, I did not discover anything unusual in the quiet and simple life he led. Then slowly it began to dawn upon me that here was one of the most widely misunderstood of men. One by one, ten by ten, I began to stumble over the recipients of his bounty. Men whom he had made, I found, and many of them too. He would not speak about it; he would almost resent the intrusion of a word concerning his benefactions; but, that he was no unimportant factor in the helping and healing agencies of the world, and that he conscientiously distributed far more upon others than he cared to use upon himself, let the hungry whom he has fed, the homeless whom he has sheltered, the unfortunate whom he has rescued, this day testify.

"In little matters he was particular, precise, a man of methodical habit and conservative taste. When he bought, he bought his money's worth, and could not endure to be cheated. But in matters of moment and largest concern, easy, generous, untroubled over loss, and (what to my mind is evidence of lofty character) never dictatory where he had given largely and had every right to dictate.

"Witness his connection with this church. Nineteen years ago he made a confession of his faith, and became a member of this family. Five years later he was elected deacon, and five years subsequent to that he was ordained elder. In the letter of acceptance which he wrote on the occasion of his election to the deaconate this significant sentence occurred: 'The Master's cause will be strengthened, and *our church* prospered, if anything I can do or say will help. The underscoring ('*our church*') is his own, and indicates how complete even then was his identification with the work of Christ as carried forward by this church. How he loved its services! How he cherished its fellowship!—so faithful he was to its every meeting, so fond of its music, so quietly appreciative of all things good that came from the pulpit or the pew! More enthusiastic than was his nature he appeared, on the occasion of his return to us this fall 'So good to be home again,' he said; 'so blessed to sit in the dear church again, and join in the worship of God!' Perhaps he may have had some premonition of trouble; perhaps he began to look upon this church as, in some sense, the monument which he had builded. It would have been a work impossible without his aid; it would even now be groaning under the burden of debt, had he not quietly and all unsolicited interposed with the guaranty of a sum exceeding his first munificent subscription."

Referring to his public efforts and personal relations, his pastor said:

"While never actively engaged in business life, he still found abundant occupation in the management of the estates to which he had fallen heir. Nor was there wanting an interest in matters of public benefactions, and in those affairs which naturally concern the citizen. It is perhaps forgotten by this time that he was largely, if not chiefly, instrumental toward the completion of those enterprises which had been originated and promoted by his cousin, the late Cornelius Rapelye Trafford (with whom was associated the late Stephen A. Halsey and others), such as the laying of sidewalks, the setting of lamps and the general improvement of the village before it became a part of the Long Island City. He was also one of the incorporators of the Hunters Point and Steinway Horse Car line, as also one of the first to respond in almost every matter of public concern The Astoria ferry owes its present development and prosperous condition largely to the courage with which he undertook its resuscitation at a time when it affairs were critical. He had faith enough to cling to it, and foresight to know that ultimately it would prosper At the time of his death he was president of the company, an honored member of the Citizens' Committee, as also of the Law and Order Society, out of which the citizens' committee grew; he was ever ready to aid in its work, with advice where advice was needed, with money where money would help In politics a Democrat, and loyal to his party, he could nevertheless be independent of party lines, a warm advocate of law and order, a citizen zealous for the public weal.

"Concerning his character and private life I feel 1 can speak, if not with authority, at any rate with appreciation For nearly six years past, an intimate acquaintance in the home, in the church, and in the official board of the church, has given me excellent opportunity for knowing him and abundant reasons for loving him From the day when first I came to Astoria—when his kindly word decided my acceptance of your call to this pastorate—up to the day of death, I have received from him uniform courtesy; gentlemanly consideration always, and, when I have needed it for personal or parish work, the most substantial encouragement, the most gratifying friendship. His was no gushing manner which gave promise of what he could not perform, but the plain, unpretentious bearing that begets no enthusiasm perhaps, but what is far better, a confident assurance that he will do what he has agreed to do—that he *can* do very much more Had he been smitten with a love for vulgar conspicuousness, what great display he might easily have made—what abundant opportunity to make what the world calls a 'figure' in life! But who that knew him ever found hint of boastfulness or swagger? Who ever found him offensively assertive? As natural for him to be unassuming and modest as to be steady, honest and gentle.''

Mr. Rapelye loved the old home of his ancestors at Astoria, but he purchased a beautiful summer residence at Kidder's on Cayuga Lake, where he spent many happy days with her who had been his life-long partner and helpmeet. Before her marriage she was Miss Lydia L Hyatt, daughter of John B. Hyatt, of Newtown, and Ann Burroughs, daughter of Thomas and Sarah Burroughs. The Burroughs family have filled an important place in the history of the world. Among the first of the name mentioned is that of Captain Stephen Burroughs, an English navigator, who accompanied Chancellor as second in command in his voyage to discover a northeast passage around the eastern continent in 1553. Three years later he had chief command of another expedition equipped with the same object He doubled Cape North, touched at Nova Zembla, discovered the island Wygaltz and reached north latitude seventy degrees three minutes—a higher point than had been reached by any previous navigator. He published in England an account of his observations. He was the first who observed the declination of the magnetic needle.

The following armorial bearings were granted June 27, 1586, in the reign of Queen Elizabeth, to William Burroughs, Esq : "Clerk and comptroller of the Queen's Navy, son of Walter Burroughs, at Northam, near Barnstable in the county of Devon.'' Arms—Azure; a bend wavy; argent, between two fleurs de lis, ermine The family of Burroughs have been highly honored by their sovereigns at different periods, and always distinguished for their loyalty and great learning.

John Burroughs, the progenitor of the American family of this name, was born in Dorsetshire, England, in 1617, and is found at Salem in the Massachusetts Bay Colony in 1642. He was a member of the long parliament that assembled November 3, 1640, which was dissolved by Cromwell, and with many others fled from England to escape religious persecution He removed from Salem, Massachusetts, to Newtown, Long Island, of which he was one of the patentees in 1666. He was a fine penman, and filled the office of town clerk for eleven years. He was a man of resolute character and a warm advocate of popular rights. He died in August, 1678 His will is on record in the surrogate's office in New York city. He left issue Jeremiah, Joseph, John, Joanna and Mary.

Joseph Burroughs, son of John (1st), was a worthy citizen and a liberal supporter of the Presbyterian church. He died February 16, 1738. His son, John Burroughs, married Margaret, daughter of James Renne. He served the next year as constable of the town, and was subsequently justice of the peace. He owned land at Trenton, New Jersey, and was also interested in the New Cornwall mines. He died in Newtown July 7, 1750, and his widow died July 11, 1767. Their children were John, Samuel and Joanna.

John Burroughs (2d), son of John (1st), married, April 26, 1747, Sarah Hunt, then the widow Smith. He inherited the paternal farm, and died February 18, 1755, leaving an only child, Joseph. The latter occupied the paternal estate, was a leading man in the Episcopal church, and died December 24, 1820, in his seventy-third year. He was twice married—first to Lydia, a daughter of Thomas Hallitt, by whom he had issue John, Thomas, Joseph, Hallitt, Anna and Benjamin.

Thomas Burroughs, son of Joseph, succeeded to the paternal farm, and married Sarah, daughter of George Wyckoff, of Flatlands He died September 20, 1835, leaving issue: Lydia, who married George Rapelye; Sarah, who married Charles H. Roach; Joseph; and Ann, who married John B. Hyatt; and George Wyckoff Burroughs Ann became the mother of Lydia Hyatt, who became the wife of Cornelius Rapelye, and still resides at the old homestead in Astoria.

ROBERT HENRY GOLDER, M. D

Robert Henry Golder, M D, a prominent physician of Staten Island, residing in Rossville, borough of Richmond, is a representative of an old and honored family. His grandfather, Archibald Golder, was a native of Maryland, where the family resided for many years, having its seat at Annapolis He served during the Revolutionary war with the rank of captain He died presumably at Annapolis or Baltimore. He married Matilda Johnson, a member of one of the oldest and most famous Maryland families Her father, Reverdy Johnson, was one of the leading lawyers and statesmen of his day, and served as chancellor of the state of Maryland Reverdy Johnson, son of said Reverdy Johnson, was even more famous than was his sire He also was a distinguished lawyer, and served as attorney-general in the cabinet of President Zachary Taylor. He had previously served as United States Senator, elected in 1845, and in 1863 was again elected to that body. In 1868 he went to England as Minister Plenipotentiary, and negotiated the famous Johnson-Clarendon Treaty, which was rejected by the senate. It is a noteworthy fact that the question under discussion (that of the "Alabama Claims")

was eventually settled under another administration on substantially the same principles which he laid down. Returning to the United States in 1869 he resumed the practice of his profession, continuing until shortly before his death, which occurred in Annapolis, February 10, 1876

Archibald Golder had children: 1. Archibald, married and resided in Baltimore, had a son George, who was a physician. 2. George, served in the war of 1812, and was wounded in action; married and resided in Baltimore 3. Robert, died a bachelor. 4. Henrietta, unmarried. 5. John, see forward.

John Golder, born in Annapolis, Maryland, May 23, 1783. He was an accomplished lawyer, practicing in Philadelphia, to which city he removed in 1818, and thence to New York city. He was a prominent Free Mason. He was also the author of a number of literary works, among which were the lives of Chief Justice W. Tilghman, of the Supreme Court of Pennsylvania, Patrick Henry, and a book on "Deliberate, Forensic and Pulpit Eloquence." In 1812 he married Margaret McMaken, of Philadelphia, who was of Scotch-Irish descent. Her mother's family—the Scotts, who were nearly allied to the family of Sir Walter Scott—came to this country about the middle of the eighteenth century, and settled mostly in Bucks county, Pennsylvania. He died in Morrisania, New York, March 21, 1864

Dr. Robert Henry Golder, son of John Golder, was born in Philadelphia, Pennsylvania, September 23, 1820 He graduated from the medical department of the University of the City of New York in 1851, and established himself in the village of Rossville, Staten Island, where he has conducted a successful and remunerative practice to the present time. He is deeply devoted to the interests of the community, and has ever taken an active part in the promotion of every worthy movement and object. He is a communicant of St Luke's Protestant Episcopal Church, and the oldest living member. He is a member of Richmond Borough Medical Society, to which he was elected president for several successive terms. He was the only living physician of Staten Island who knew Dr. S. R. Smith, the founder of the Smith Infirmary at Castleton, and is at present the only surviving physician in Richmond county, and also the only survivor who was present at the laying of the corner stone of the hospital building.

Dr. Golder married Catherine V. Dunham, born in New Brunswick, New Jersey, November 18, 1824, daughter of Ephraim and Elizabeth (Vaughan) Dunham. Of this marriage have been born a son, Valentine Mott, born September 17, 1848, died December 29, 1878, and a daughter, Margaret Dunham, who survives.

ROBERT L COOPER, M. D.

Robert L Cooper, M. D., an able and experienced physician and surgeon of New York city, with offices located at No. 321 West Fifty-ninth street, was born in Richmond, Virginia, January 6, 1876. He is a son of Frederick T. and Edmonia (Davenport) Cooper, the former dying in New York, September, 1904, the latter residing in New York city.

Dr. Cooper's early education was obtained in the public and high schools of his native city, from both of which he was graduated with honors. He came to New York in 1895, attended the Dwight Scientific School, from which he was graduated the following year, and then began the practical study of medicine in the Long Island Hospital College, being graduated from that institution in 1899. He began the practice of his profession almost immediately after graduation and this was marked with success from the beginning. He rapidly won the confidence and esteem of his fellow practitioners as well as of his patients, and for many years has held an assured and enviable position in the profession. He is a man of enterprise and progress, and in spite of the manifold demands made upon his time by the necessities of his calling, devotes a considerable portion of his time to the perusal of medical literature, thus keeping well advised of all innovations and discoveries in that line. He is a member of the County Medical Society, National Association of Physicians and Surgeons, Medical Chirurgical Society, Medical Pharmaceutical Society and Alumni of Long Island Hospital College His fraternal affiliations are with Plymouth Rock Lodge, Knights of Pythias, and the A. T. Stewart Association He is a member of the Bethel Methodist Episcopal Church, while his wife is a member of St Philip's Protestant Episcopal Church.

He married, April 10, 1901, in New York city, Lottie Frances Meredith, born in Chicago, Illinois, daughter of Frank and Laura Meredith.

ROBERT CORNELIUS FRASER, M. D.

Robert Cornelius Fraser, M. D., an experienced and successful physician and surgeon of the city of New York, who makes a specialty of electrical treatment, has his offices located at No 329 West Thirty-fifth street.

Francis Cornelius Fraser, father of Robert Cornelius Fraser, M. D., is a native of British Guiana, South America, where he is professor of languages in Bishop's College, in Demerara He married Princess Charlotte Bacon, born in British Guiana, died in 1881, and their children are: 1. Litchfield B., a mechanical engineer, at present in charge of the British Guiana Gold Mines Company. 2. William R., a mechanical engineer. 3. Susan Christina, married ——— Grant, a pharmacist of Demerara. 4. Robert Cornelius, see forward. 5. Ada Zerolina, married.

Robert Cornelius Fraser, M. D., son of Francis Cornelius and Princess Charlotte (Bacon) Fraser, was born in Georgetown, Demerara, British Guiana, South America, April 15, 1871. His early education was acquired under the able tuition of his father in Bishop's College, and he also studied languages under the preceptorship of the following eminent men: Professor Clarke, of Barbadoes, British West Indies; Professor Daniels, who was connected with the Lady Mico Institute of Antigua, British West Indies; and Rev. H. M. Joseph, now a professor in the high school in Washington, District of Columbia. During his tuition under the first two instructors he learned the art of printing in the office of a newspaper called *The Argosy*, in Georgetown, British Guiana. While serving his apprenticeship to the printing trade, he also studied stenography without the aid of a personal teacher, and at the end of his five years apprenticeship was offered and accepted the position of reporter on a paper entitled *British Guiana Gazette* He filled this position very acceptably for fifteen months and then took up the study of nursing and the art of compounding medicines in an estate hospital under the tuition of a Mr. Abel. He passed a very creditable preliminary examination in 1888 and entered the Colonial Hospital of British Guiana to perfect himself in these studies. A few months later he was graduated from that institution, receiving a diploma as competent head nurse and pharmacist. During the following two years he was manager of the Tuschen de Vrienden Plantation Hospital, filling the position to the great satisfaction of all concerned. He came to the United States in August, 1892, and in the fall of that year matriculated at the Leonard Medical College of Shaw University, Raleigh, North Carolina, where he gave his entire attention to the study of medicine for the next three years. He came to New York in 1895, and continued his medical studies at the Eclectic Medical College for one year, being graduated from that institution with honor May 6, 1896. In July of the same year he passed with credit and honor an examination by the New York State Medical Board, and immediately commenced the practice of his profession in the city of New York, where he has attained a high reputation as a physician and surgeon. He compounds most of his prescriptions, and is a strong advocate of electrotherapeutics. His offices are fitted up with an X-ray apparatus, and the most modern and scientific electrical appliances are at hand. With these he has been uniformly successful in treating many serious cases He is progressive in his methods, but does not believe in discarding old and tried methods before the newer ones have been proven superior. He is associated with the following organizations: County Medical Society; Mount Olive Lodge, No 2, Free and Accepted Masons of New York, Royal Arch Masons; Mount Calvary Commandery, No. 1, Knights Templar; Philomathean Lodge, No 646, Grand United Order of Odd Fellows; Lincoln Fountain Lodge, No. 3, True Reformers; Guild of St. Cyprian, of which he is medical examiner; Mount Horeb Tabernacle, Sons and Daughters, Brothers and Sisters of Moses; West Indian Benevolent Society of New York, of which he is the medical examiner; Emanuel Lodge, Knights of Pythias, grand member and grand medical register of same for New York district; Lily of the Valley Lodge, Household of Ruth.

He married, December 29, 1901, Lillian P. Taylor, of Richmond, Virginia, and they have one child, Lillian Cornelia, born December 28, 1902. Both he and his wife are consistent members of St James Presbyterian Church.

RICHARD A. TAYLOR, M. D.

Richard A. Taylor, M. D., whose offices are located at No. 267 West Fortieth street, has attained more than an ordinary share of success as a physician and surgeon. He was born on the island of St Kitts, British West Indies, September 17, 1869.

His early education was acquired in the public schools and by means of private instructors in his native town, and upon coming to New York, in 1889, he continued his studies under private tuition in the city of New York. Later he took up the study of medicine, entering Leonard Medical College, Raleigh, North Carolina, from which he was graduated in the class of 1901. He continued his medical studies in the Long Island Hospital College, being graduated with honors from that institution in 1903. While a student at the Leonard Medical College he carried off the prizes for Chemistry, Physiology and Obstetrics. He has been a liberal contributor to newspapers and magazines, and was at one time associate editor of the *"New York Pilot,"* a newspaper. He is a member of the County Medical Society, St. John's Lodge, No. 29, F and A. M., Manhattan Lodge, and True Reformers, being medical examiner for the two last mentioned He is one of the rising physicians and surgeons of the city, possesses the confidence and respect of his patients, and his fellow practitioners predict a bright future for him.

YORK RUSSELL, M D

York Russell, M. D., an efficient and successful medical practitioner of the city of New York, with offices at No. 317 West Thirty-sixth street, has acquired an enviable reputation for his zeal and earnestness and his careful observance of the laws, written and understood, of his profession. He was born in Barbadoes, British West Indies, May 29, 1867, son of York and Maria (Stewart) Russell, both deceased.

He enjoyed the advantages of an excellent literary education in the public and grammar schools of his native town, and this was supplemented by a course in St. Joseph's College, from all of which institutions he was graduated with honor. Upon the completion of his college course he was appointed principal of a school, and conscientiously performed the duties connected with this position for a period of fifteen years. He then decided to take up the study of medicine, resigned his position as principal in 1894 and came to the United States. He matriculated at the Howard University, Washington, District of Columbia, from which he was graduated in 1898, after which he came to New York and was licensed to practice medicine and surgery by the board of regents, December 12, 1899. He established himself in his profession immediately and has been in continuous practice since that time, having a lucrative and constantly increasing practice. He is a man endowed with more than an ordinary share of brain power, and is possessed of a forceful, determined character. His classical education is far beyond the average, and he devotes as much time as he can spare from his professional pursuits to reading. He is associated with the following organizations: Member of the County Medical Society; member and medical examiner of the Marine Benevolent Society, and many fraternal orders.

He married, May 31, 1888, Lillian E. Harris, also a native of Barbadoes, and they have children: Claudine, born April 11, 1889; Chester De Witt, born May 11, 1890. Both he and his wife are consistent members of the St. Philip's Protestant Episcopal Church.

JOHN MILTON WILLIAMS, M. D.

John Milton Williams, M. D., a well known physician and surgeon of New York city, with offices located at No. 265 West

Thirtieth street, has a large and constantly increasing practice. He was born in the city of New York, February 24, 1860, son of John and Elizabeth (Jones) Williams, both deceased. His preliminary education was acquired in the public schools of the city and he then became a student of College of the City of New York. His medical studies were pursued in the Long Island College Hospital, from which he was graduated in the class of 1883. From that time until 1885 he was engaged in the practical pursuit of his profession, with a large amount of success. For some years thereafter his time was spent in extensive traveling, throughout the United States, Canada, Europe and Central America. Upon his return, in 1889, he again took up the practice of his profession, in which he has been continuously engaged since that time. He has the confidence and esteem of his patients and fellow practitioners, and his practice is a lucrative one. He is associated with the following organizations: Medico-Chirurgical Society of Greater New York; Adelphic Union Lodge, No. 14, Free and Accepted Masons; Lone Star Chapter, No. 2, Royal Arch Masons; Northwest Commandery; King David Consistory, No. 3, New York city. He is a member of the Protestant Episcopal church of the Messiah. He has held the office of medical sanitary inspector of the city of New York. He married, August, 1896, in New York, Albertina M. Connover, who died December, 1900.

PETER AUGUSTUS JOHNSON, M. D.

The life and success of Dr. Peter A. Johnson is an illustration of what a man can accomplish under very discouraging circumstances, if actuated by energy and perseverance.

Dr. Johnson was born at Eatontown, New Jersey. In his early youth he was brought up in the family of Frederick W. Stevens, of New York, a gentleman of wealth, and, what is far more important, possessed of a philanthropic spirit Seeing promise of superiority in the young colored boy in his employ, he sent him to school, and afforded him many advantages in the hours not devoted to the duties of his daily labors. These advantages the boy appreciated, and his energies were soon found to be in a congenial field Mr Stevens possessed a country seat at Newport, Rhode Island, and the boy went to Rogers high school, in that city Some years previously he made the acquaintance of Rev. Alexander Cromwell, D. D , a colored minister, who had come from England and who was an excellent Latin and Greek scholar, and from him he received both sympathy and assistance One day he saw in a newspaper a notice that there would be a night class of the high school under the tuition of Professor Tilton, who had been master of Philips Academy in Andover, Massachusetts He joined that class with one other colored boy, but the latter soon dropped out. Professor Tilton inquired his history, and found him possessed of a superior mind, and well deserving of assistance In this class he remained till the senior year. He then returned to New York and became acquainted with Professor Clark, who was the principal of the Collegiate Institute, at the corner of Fourth and Macdougal streets Notwithstand ing the prejudice which might be expected to be shown to the young colored student, the professor told him he should be admitted to any class for which he could pass the proper examination. The result was that he was promptly admitted to the senior class The other students, who at first manifested some displeasure, soon discovered that it would require all their labor and ability to keep pace with the new student, and they soon became his warmest friends, and his scholarship was recognized as superior He afterwards went through the Long Island Medical College, and studied under Dr Edward J. Messner, who was to him like a father and gave him all the assistance in his power. He graduated from Long Island College Hospital in 1882, and has ever since been in active and successful practice in New York Dr. Johnson was chief of staff of Macdougal Memorial Hospital, and is at present the president of the Medical Chirurgical Society (a colored institution), also state vice-president of the National Medical Association and chairman of executive committee of that society He is a member of the County Medical Society Among the medical fraternity Dr Johnson is recognized as a practitioner of skill and ability, and enjoys the respect and friendship of some of the most celebrated physicians of New York

JOSEPH FRANK THORPE, M. D.

Joseph Frank Thorpe, M. D , a general practitioner of surgery and medicine, with offices at No 58 West Ninety-ninth street, New York city, was born in Barbadoes, British West Indies, November 23, 1861. He is a son of Francis W. and Mary (Duchess) Thorpe, both deceased

He acquired his early education in the public schools, notably S David's high school, under the instruction of a tutor who was a graduate of the University of London, England Upon the completion of his classical studies he became the principal of Vaux Hall and S. David's public schools, positions which he filled with credit and honor to himself and satisfaction to all concerned for a period of fifteen years. Having decided to take up the study of medicine he resigned his principalship and came to the United States He matriculated at the Howard University of Washington, District of Columbia, and was graduated from that institution of learning in the class of 1903 He began the practice of his profession in New York city in November of the following year, and has met with a marked degree of success His earnest devotion to his profession has won the confidence of his patients and his practice is a rapidly growing one He is connected with the following organizations: County Medical Society of Greater New York; Medico-Chirurgical Society of Greater New York; Livesey Comet Lodge, No. 3312, Grand United Order of Odd Fellows; Majestic Lodge, No 7, Knights of Pythias; Court Calanthe Lodge, No 336, Knights of Pythias, of which he is the medical examiner. He married, in Barbadoes, Clarissa Smith, principal of a girls' school in Barbadoes, British West Indies, and their children are: Stanley H., Winifred E , and Enid F He and his family attend the Protestant Episcopal church.

THOMAS S. P. MILLER, M D.

Thomas S P. Miller, M. D , a general practitioner of medicine and surgery in the city of New York, with offices at No. 250 West One Hundred and Twenty-fourth street, is one of those energetic characters who seem to find time to accomplish their own duties well and bear a goodly share of those of their neighbors. He is not alone an able, experienced physician, but he has taken an active part in the political interests of his country, and bore a gallant part in the late Civil war. He was born in Charleston, South Carolina, July 10, 1846, son of the late Gabriel and Nancy (Pierson) Miller.

In early life Thomas S. P. Miller removed to Portland, Maine, where he acquired a good public school education and took a course in the business college of Bryant & Stratton. His classical education was acquired under the able tuition of Rev. Dr O T Tuckerman He read medicine in the office and under the preceptorship of Dr. Samuel H Tewksbury and also attended a course of lectures at the Portland School for Medical Instruction, supplementing this with a varied course of studies in Bowdoin College, Brunswick, Maine. He then entered the medical department of the Howard University at Washington, District of Columbia, in 1871, and was graduated with honor three years later in the class of 1874 After this he attended a short course of lectures in the Long Island Hospital College, and June 12, 1874, feeling himself well equipped for his life work, he commenced the practice of his chosen profession in the city of New York His efforts were crowned with success from the very beginning, and his practice is a large and lucrative one. Although there are many demands made upon his time by his numerous patients, he makes the best possible use of the odd moments and is continually adding to his store of knowledge. He makes personal investigation as far as his time will permit of all the discoveries and innovations which have been made in the science of medicine during the past years, and if found practical and available they are adopted by him. During 1873 and a part of 1874 he was professionally connected with the Freedmen's Hospital, in Washington, District of Columbia. During the troublous times of the Civil war he was with Captain N E. Elfwing, of the Forty-eighth Regiment, New York Volunteers, at the siege of Fort Pulaski, Savannah river, near Daufiskie Island, South Carolina, the storming of Fort Wagner, and other important conflicts of the war. He has been actively interested in political affairs, and in 1883 was an Independent Republican candidate for assembly, and was a regular candidate for alderman for the United Labor party of eleventh assembly district. He has served as a member of the board of trustees of the Metropolitan Art Association He is connected with the following organizations: Member of the New York County Medical Society for twenty-five years; charter member of the MacDonough Memorial Hospital and Dispensary of New York; past master of Hiram Lodge,

No. 4, Free and Accepted Masons; Widow's Son Chapter, No. 5, Royal Arch Masons; commander in chief of Lucidius Consistory, Ancient Arabic Scottish Rite Masons; member of Alucias Temple, Knights of the Mystic Shrine; P. N. H.; Hamilton Lodge, No. 710, Grand United Order of Odd Fellows; past vice-supreme chancellor and supreme medical director of the Knights of Pythias.

He married, October 31, 1879, in New York, Amanda Cooper, of Augusta, Georgia. He and his wife attend services at St. Philip's Protestant Episcopal church.

ALBERT S. REED, M. D.

Albert S. Reed, M D., a highly valued general practitioner of medicine and surgery for the past ten years in the city of New York, with offices now located at No. 314 West Fifty-second street, owes his marked success to his indefatigable zeal and diligence. He was born in Beaufort, South Carolina, August 11, 1869, son of Harry G. and Mollie (Gardner) Reed, the former deceased, the latter still living in South Carolina.

Dr Reed received his early education in the public schools of Beaufort, South Carolina, then matriculated at Lincoln University, Pennsylvania, from which he was graduated in 1891. He returned to his native city, was appointed clerk in the office of the sheriff, his brother being sheriff of Beaufort at that time, and also served in the capacity of deputy sheriff for some time He performed the duties of these offices very efficiently for about one year. He then came to New York city, entered the New York Homeopathic Medical College and Flower Hospital, and was graduated from these institutions in 1895. He engaged in the practice of his profession one year later, May, 1896. He takes his profession very seriously, and his intelligence, earnestness and sympathy have endeared him to a large circle of patients. He is a member of the Medico-Chirurgical Society, president of the Southern Beneficial League, and examining physician of Howard Union Lodge. Both he and his wife are active members of the Baptist Temple, and he is a member of the board of trustees. He married, January 25, 1905, Daisy P. Cargile, a graduate of Louisville high school and of New York Business School.

HON. THERON R. STRONG.

Hon. Theron R. Strong, deceased, was a son of Judge Martin Strong, of Litchfield, Connecticut, and his wife, Sally Harrison Strong, and was born at Litchfield, Connecticut, November 7, 1802. He received a thorough training in his profession in the office of his father, and in 1826 commenced practice at Palmyra, Wayne county, New York. He resided there for a period of twenty-seven years, during which time many honors were conferred upon him.

For five years he was district attorney of Wayne county, and was a master and examiner in chancery for a long time. He was elected to Congress in 1839 and served his district for two years in that office. In 1842 he was a member of the legislature of New York. In 1851 he was elected a judge of the Supreme court and filled that honorable position creditably for eight years During one of these years he was a member of the Court of Appeals and his numerous decisions, then rendered, are often quoted with approbation for the force and cogency that characterized them. The celebrated Cancemi case was twice before the highest tribunal of the state while he was a member of it, and on both occasions he delivered the opinion of the court. More opinions emanated from him while a member of this court than from any other judge, except Judge Denie. After retiring from the bench, Judge Strong resumed the practice of his profession at Rochester, New York, in which city he resided from 1853 to 1867. During that period his business was very extensive, and he was on one side or the other in almost every important case arising in the Seventh Judicial district. He removed to New York city in 1867, and was at the time of his death the senior member of the firm of Strong & Shepard, and engaged up to that time in active practice in the United States and state courts. Judge Strong had the reputation of possessing a mind eminently candid and judicial, of considering all questions submitted to him with care and circumspection and wisely deciding upon all the facts. He died at his residence, No. 61 West Forty-sixth street, May 14, 1873.

GOLDSBROW BANYAR.

For more than half a century one of the most conspicuous characters in the life of New York city, and ranked among its most prominent citizens, was Goldsbrow Banyar, Esq. He was born in London, 1725, and came to America at the early age of fourteen. He had scarcely arrived at manhood before he began a long career of official life, and he lived long after the Revolution.

In 1746 he was appointed Deputy Secretary of the Colony of New York, and in that capacity had full charge of the recording of wills, and volume after volume are certified by the elegant signature of Goldsbrow Banyar. He was also Deputy Clerk of the Council, and of the Supreme Court In 1752 he was made Register of the Court of Chancery, and in 1753 was Judge of Probate. He remained in office till the beginning of the Revolution, when all his public engagements ceased with the termination of the Royal government. When the Whigs assumed the direction of affairs he retired to Rhinebeck, where he lived a quiet life, undisturbed by the war that shook the country. The fact that he had held office under the Royal government caused him to be ranked among the Loyalists, but no overt act in hostility to the American cause was ever urged against him. When peace returned he removed to Albany, where he was for many years a very prominent citizen, taking a great interest in the internal improvements of the state and contributing to all a liberal support. In the latter part of his life he was afflicted with blindness, and was led about the streets by a colored servant. He died in Albany in 1815, at the advanced age of ninety-one, and left to his descendants a large fortune and a more enduring inheritance in the recollection of his many virtues and the example of a life devoted to duty.

Among other property Goldsbrow Banyar was the owner of various very extensive tracts of land in Schoharie and adjoining counties. Of his descendants we will add an extended account Goldsbrow Banyar married, in 1769, the widow of John Appy, who was the Judge Advocate of the Royal forces in America. Their children were a son, Goldsbrow Banyar, and a daughter, Martha. The former married Maria Jay, daughter of Peter Jay, a member of a very illustrious family. He died in 1826 without issue. Martha Banyar married Jacob Le Roy, who had a son, Goldsbrow Banyar Le Roy, and a daughter, Harriet, who married Campbell P. White.

In a petition presented to the legislature by Goldsbrow Banyar Le Roy it is stated that his grandfather, Goldsbrow Banyar, Esq., late of Albany, had in his will left him a large part of his estate as residuary legatee, on the condition that he took the name of Goldsbrow Le Roy Banyar His name was accordingly changed by a special act of legislature passed March 1, 1816.

Goldsbrow Le Roy Banyar was a prominent and useful citizen, possessed of a large estate, born March 9, 1802, died in 1866, leaving a large amount of property to his nephew, John

GENEALOGICAL AND FAMILY HISTORY 169

Campbell White, born in New York city, March 17, 1817, son of Campbell P. and Harriet Banyar (Le Roy) White, on condition that he assume the name of Goldsbrow Banyar, and that was accordingly done He also left liberal legacies to his nieces, Catharine E Stewart, Ann White, Mary Martha White and Cornelia Le Roy White.

TOWNSEND—VAN RENSSELAER FAMILIES

Among the earliest settlers on Long Island were three brothers, John, Henry and Richard Townsend, whose descendants are numerous and their record honorable. These brothers were natives of Norwich, England, and came to this country in 1645, or, as another account states, in 1638. They were members of the Society of Friends, "called by the world's People in scorn, Quakers," as one of their number expresses it, and it is a singular fact in the history of religious sects that the society who came preaching and practicing peace toward all mankind, found not peace but a sword. They settled in Flushing and were soon in trouble with Governor Stuyvesant, whose persecutions of the Quakers is the only serious fault that can be laid to the charge of the famous personage known in the pages of the veracious Diedrich Knickerbocker, as "Peter the Headstrong." It is to the everlasting credit of his wife, Judith Bayard, that it was through her influence that the persecution was greatly lessened A complaint against John Townsend was that "he was among the principal persons in Flushing who resisted the Dutch mode of choosing Sheriffs, protesting against the adopted course in the Fatherland, and who refused to contribute their share to the maintenance of Christian, pious, reformed ministers." He with several others was summoned before the Director General and Council, January 23, 1648. In consequence of this persecution they left Flushing and went to

Warwick, Rhode Island, where all three of the brothers are said to have been members of the Provincial Assembly, besides holding other offices. In 1656 they returned to Long Island, and with others obtained a patent for Rusdorp (now Jamaica). Here they were still beset by their former religious difficulties Henry was particularly obnoxious, and John "neither concealed nor compromised his opinions " In 1657 Henry was sentenced to pay "Eight Pounds, Flanders," or leave the province within six weeks, his crime being "having called together Conventicles." The people held a meeting and remonstrated As a result "the Town Clerk, the magistrates and John Townsend were arrested and held in bail of Twelve Pounds." They were condemned

to pay one hundred pounds, Flanders, and remain arrested until paid. The matter seems to have been settled in some way, for they still remained. Henry and John Townsend with others were accused of "entertaining the Quakers," and Henry was again imprisoned. It is stated that before 1676 John Townsend had occupied "8 acres of land at the Fresh Water, in New York," "and made large improvements, and enjoyed the same divers years," but was obliged to leave the same "through the Indians and other difficulties." This tract was probably in the vicinity of James street and the Bowery. John Townsend died in 1668, was buried on his own land on Long Island, and was probably the first person buried in the graveyard at Fort Hill. He left a wife, Elizabeth, and children: James; Elizabeth, wife of Gideon Wright; Rose, Ann, Sarah, George and Daniel. His widow died about 1671

The history of Oyster Bay begins with the purchase made from the Indians in 1653, by which Assiapuns, alias Mohanes, an Indian Sachem, sold to Peter Wright, Samuel Mayo and William Leverich, all the land situated upon Oyster Bay, bounded east by Oyster river, and west by Papaquatunk river, with all the islands "excepting one island commonly called Hog Island " The consideration was "6 Indian coats, 6 kettles, 6 fathoms of wampum, .6 hoes, 5 hatchets, 3 pairs of stockings, 30 all blades or muxes, 20 knives, 3 shirts, and as much Peegue as will amount to 4 Pounds Sterling." What this last article was we leave to others to decide. The original purchasers accepted as partners Thomas Armitage, Anthony Wright and John Washburne, and then began the building of the town To these were added Daniel Whitehead, Robert Williams and Richard Holbrook. Then came William Smith "and old John Titus." They laid out twenty lots "beginning at mill river, and so east to the Barbor side " The purchase money not being paid, "the Indians began to be very unruly and disturbed," and the amount was raised by the help of Mr. Briant, of Milford. Richard Holbrook was "the first man as a purchaser that got up his house at Oyster Bay " Such was the testimony of Nicholas Simkins, December 20, 1683, he being then "aged 53 and an inhabitant of Mosketo Cove."

To this place came the Townsends. John Townsend was a magistrate in 1684 Henry Townsend was here before September 16, 1661, when he had a grant of a mill stream. On the third day of seventh month, 1667, he wrote a letter to the inhabitants of Huntington, protesting against their trespassing, and the three brothers were present at Town meetings. In 1669 they had orchards in bearing, and shortly after Thomas Townsend purchased Fort Neck, a tract estimated as four miles square. The grant of the hill stream to Henry Townsend was upon the condition that he "build a mill such as at Norwalk, on the main, or an English mill" They were careful to provide that if the mill should cease for half a year, it should revert to the town He was to have one-tenth for toll, but if the amount increased "so the miller be not discouraged," he was to have less. His "toll dish was to be true, and to be struck when taking the toll." In 1673 he built a saw mill. The house built by Henry Townsend in 1683 was standing for many years. The homestead of John Townsend was owned in recent years by Rev. Aaron Johnson. Mark Meggs came from Southampton, and was an early resident A meeting house was built, but disappeared before 1709 Such was Oyster Bay when Henry Townsend was a resident He was Town Clerk and surveyor His dwelling house was on the main street "the next house but one to Quogue Lane" In 1683 he built a new house "on the Hill," giving the old house to his son Henry Notwithstanding his unpleasant experience in Rusdorp (Jamaica), he seems to have had an affection for the place By the will of Richard Grassmore he had "housing and lands" there, and gave them to the poor of the place and also £176 in money. His whole life was one of active usefulness even in old age. He died probably in March, 1695, at an advanced age. After the custom of the Friends, his grave is marked only by a rough stone bearing the initials H T Henry Townsend married Anne, daughter of Robert Coles. His children were: Henry; Rose, wife of Joseph Dickinson; Susannah, wife of Aaron Furman, Jr.; Mary, wife of John Wright; and Elizabeth, who died unmarried, September 13, 1680

Henry Townsend, the eldest son, married Deborah, daughter of Captain John Underhill famous in Long Island history. He left children: Henry; Robert; and a daughter, who married ———— Ludlam

Henry Townsend, the third of the name, married Eliphal, daughter of John Wright and Mary Townsend, his cousin. After the death of his uncle, known as "Mill John," he was appointed surveyor. He had a reputation for prudence and thoughtful care He died a young man in 1709, leaving three sons: Isaac, Henry and Absalom

Henry Townsend, the fourth of the name, married Elizabeth Titus and moved to Orange county, New York Their children were: Henry, born 1725; Nicholas; Peter; Phebe; Elizabeth; Martha, and Absalom.

Henry Townsend, the fifth married Anne Wright, who died September 17, 1825, at the age of ninety Her husband died March 28, 1803 Their children were: Betsey, who married Lewis Carpenter; Henry; Zebulon; Noah; Phebe, who married ———— Wright: and Charles, who died unmarried in 1799.

Henry Townsend, the sixth, married Mary Bennet Their children were Isaiah, John, Mary A., Samuel, William, Peter A, Hannah, Charles, and Noah The last three sons died unmarried.

Among the descendants of John Townsend was Samuel Townsend, who was the father of Solomon Townsend, born in 1746. In his twentieth year his father placed him in command of a brig. At the beginning of the Revolution he was captain of the ship "Glasgow " He went to Paris and obtained from Franklin a certificate of American citizenship. He returned to this country, went to Chester, Orange county, where he married Anne, daughter of Peter Townsend Here he purchased property adjoining that of his father-in-law, and established extensive iron works. It was at these works that the great iron chain was made which was stretched across the river at West

Point. At a later date he removed to New York and carried on an extensive business in iron. He established a manufactory of bar iron on the Peconic river on Long Island. He was also prominent in politics, and was a member of the Legislature at the time of his death, March 27, 1811.

Isaiah Townsend, born 1777, died 1837, married Hannah, daughter of the above mentioned Solomon Townsend. Both he and his brother John moved to Albany in 1799 and established an iron furnace. They were prominent merchants. Isaiah's children were: Isaiah, Jr ; Anna, wife of Henry H Martin; Robert; Franklin; Howard; Frederick; and Mary, wife of General William H. Walker. Of these sons, Robert married Harriet Monroe At the beginning of the Civil war he entered the navy, and served on the blockading squadron off Charleston, and on the Mississippi under Commodore Porter. He was commander of the gunboat "Essex," and died on the China Station in 1866, while in command of the United States Steamer "Massachusetts."

Franklin Townsend married Anna, daughter of Rufus King, of Albany. He was twice adjutant-general of the state, and was mayor of the city of Albany.

Frederick Townsend married Sarah, daughter of Joel Rathbone, of Albany In April, 1861, he went to the front as commander of the Third Regiment, New York Volunteers. He served through the war and was made brevet-brigadier-general in 1865.

Isaiah Townsend married Harriet, daughter of his uncle, Samuel Townsend, of Orange county.

Dr. Howard Townsend, the fifth child of the family was born November 18, 1823, and died January 16, 1867. He was graduated from Union College in the class of 1844 His professional education was obtained in Philadelphia, and he spent a year and a half in perfecting his medical knowledge in Paris. Upon his return he was made a professor of materia medica in the Medical College in Albany. Dr. Townsend married Justine Van Rensselaer, fourth daughter of Stephen Van Rensselaer, the son of the late Patron of the Great Manor of Rensselaerwick, who married Harriet Elizabeth Bayard, daughter of William Bayard of New York.

Their children were: 1. Stephen Van Rensselaer Townsend, born in Albany, October 20, 1860, died at Hempstead, Long Island, January 15, 1901. He married Janet Eckford King, daughter of Cornelius Low and Janet (De Kay) King, and left three daughters: Janet King, Margaret Schuyler and Justine Van Rensselaer Townsend. One son, Stephen Van R. Townsend, died before him.

2. Justine Van Rensselaer Townsend was born in Albany, December 5, 1862, and died in Paris, March, 1881. She married, February, 1877, Thomas H. Barber, an officer of an artillery regiment, United States Army. She left no children.

3. Harriet Bayard Townsend, born March 23, 1864, married, April, 1886, Thomas H. Barber They have two children: Thomas H , born January, 1889, and Justine Van Rensselaer, born March 31, 1901.

The Townsends of Albany held a high position, not only due to their ancestral descent, but to their own intrinsic ability and excellence. They were men of the highest sense of honor and exerted a wide and beneficial influence, and were not only honored but beloved.

Howard Townsend was born in Albany, New York, in 1858, and received his early education at the Albany Academy. He entered Harvard University in 1876 and was graduated in the class of 1880; he studied for one year at the Harvard Law School and for two years in the office of Jenkins & Cooper, attorneys of Albany, New York He was admitted to the bar in 1883 and moved to New York, where he entered the law office of Julien T. Davies, whose partner he subsequently became, the firm name being Davies, Short & Townsend Mr. Townsend withdrew from the firm in 1893. He was for many years interested in the creation of the State Hospital for the Treatment of Incipient Consumptive Patients, and when the Legislature created this institution Mr Townsend was appointed by the governor one of its trustees and was its first president

He is a governor of the New York Hospital, a trustee of Roosevelt Hospital, vice-president of the New York Association for Improving the Condition of the Poor, and manager and secretary of the House of Rest for Consumptives. He is a member and governor of the Union Club, and a member of the Century, University and other clubs. Mr Townsend has his summer home at Southampton, Long Island He married (first) Sophie Witherspoon, daughter of the late Charles D. Dickey She died in January, 1892. He married (second), October, 1894, Anne Langdon, daughter of the late Eugene Langdon. Mr. Townsend's children are as follows: By his first marriage: Sophie Witherspoon Townsend, born February, 1889; Howard Townsend, born in 1890, died in 1891. By his second marriage: Anne Langdon Townsend, born 1898; Howard Van Rensselaer Townsend, born 1900; Eugene Langdon Townsend, born 1902; and Philip Schuyler Townsend, born 1906.

It remains to show the lines of descent of this branch of the Townsends from various ancient families of the state

VAN RENSSELAER LINE

Killiaen Van Rensselaer, the first patroon, was born at Niewerkerk, Guilderland, Holland, and settled in Amsterdam, where he was a merchant in precious stones and pearls. He was a director of the Dutch West India Company. In 1635 he received from the Director General a grant of the immense tract of land called the Manor of Rensselaerwyck This manor was twenty miles in width on each side of the Hudson, and twelve miles north and south from Beeren, Island of Cohoes. Over this tract he held full power as a feudal lord. He married (first) Killegonda Van Bylant; (second) Anna Van Weely. By the first marriage he had a son, Johanes, and by the second, three children: Jeremias, Nicholas and Richard. Johanes, the eldest son, had a son Johanes, who married Elizabeth Van Tweller, and had a son, Killaen, who married Anna Van Rensselaer, and died without issue His widow married William Nicoll, the Patentee of Islip. The line of descent is as follows:

1. Kilian Van Rensselaer, died 1647. 2 Jeremias, who married Maria Van Cortlandt. 3 Kilian, who married Maria Van Cortlandt. 4. Stephen, born 1707, died 1747. He married Elizabeth Grosbeck, who died 1729. 5. Stephen, born 1742, died 1769 He married, in 1764, Catherine, daughter of Philip Livingston, signer of the Declaration of Independence. 6. Major General Stephen Van Rensselaer, born in New York, 1764; died January 26, 1839, married (first) Margaret, daughter of General Philip Schuyler (her sister Elizabeth married Alexander Hamilton); (second) Cornelia Paterson, daughter of Governor William Patterson, of New Jersey. 7. Stephen Van Rensselaer, who married Harriet Elizabeth Bayard, daughter of William Bayard. Their children were: Margaret S., wife of De Peyster Douw; Wilmot Johnson; Cornelia P., wife of Nathaniel Thayer, of Boston; Stephen; Catherine, wife of Nathaniel Berry; Justine, wife of Dr. Howard Townsend; Bayard; Harriet, wife of T. Schuyler Crosby; Eugene, now living at Berkeley Springs, West Virginia.

THE SCHUYLER LINE.

1. Philip Pieterse Schuyler, the ancestor, was a magistrate in Albany, where he died March 9, 1684. An emblazoned window was placed by him in the first church in 1656. He married Marguarita Van Schlectenhorst, December 12, 1650. 2 His son Johanes was born in 1668, died July 25, 1747 He was mayor of Albany 1703-6 He married Elizabeth Staats. 3. Their son, Colonel Johanes Schuyler, born 1697, died 1747, married Cornelia Van Cortlandt, October 18, 1723. He was mayor 1741-2. 4. Major-General Philip Schuyler, born November 11, 1733, died November 18, 1804. 5 His daughter Margarita, married General Stephen Van Rensselaer. 6. His son, Stephen Van Rensselaer, married Harriet Elizabeth Bayard. 7. Their daughter, Justine Van Rensselaer, married Dr. Howard Townsend.

VAN CORTLANDT LINE.

Oloff Stevense Van Cortlandt, a soldier in the employ of the Dutch West India Company, came in the ship "Haring" with Governor William Kieft in 1638. He soon attained prominence. Was Schepen in 1654; Commissioner to treat with Connecticut, 1663; Member of Council under Governor Andross. His descendants are found in almost all of the noted families of the state. He married Anatje Lockermans, sister of Gouvert Lockermans, whose daughter Elsie was the wife of the famous, but ill-fated, Jacob Leisler. Stephen Van Cortlandt, son of Oloff Stevense, was the proprietor of Van Cortlandt Manor in Westchester county. He married Gertrude Schuyler. Their daughter Cornelia married Colonel Johanes Schuyler, who was the father of General Philip Schuyler, whose daughter Margarita married General Stephen Van Rensselaer, from whom the line has been traced.

Another line of descent from Oloff Stevense Van Cortlandt is from his son Stephen Van Cortlandt, whose daughter Margaret married Samuel Bayard, whose line is here traced.

THE LIVINGSTON LINE.

Robert Livingston, of Ancram, the First Lord of the Manor of Livingston, born 1654, died 1728. His son, Philip Livingston, the second Lord of the Manor, born 1686, died 1749. His son, Philip Livingston, born 1716, died 1778. He was member of Assembly 1759-1769. In 1768 he was Speaker. As member of the Provincial Congress he signed the Declaration of Independence. His daughter Catharine married Stephen Van Rensselaer, who was the father of Major-General Stephen Van Rensselaer, from whom the line has been given.

The Townsends are also descended from the Livingstons, in another line. Robert Livingston, the first Lord of the Manor, had a daughter, Margaret, who married Colonel Samuel Vetch, whose daughter Alida married Stephen Bayard, from whom they are descended, as seen by the Bayard line.

THE BAYARD LINE.

This family is said to be descended from an uncle of the Chevalier, *"sans peur et sans reproche"*

Rev. Lazare Bayard married, 1601, Judith De Vos, and had children: Judith, wife of Governor Peter Stuyvesant, and Samuel, born 1609. The latter married Anna, sister of Peter Stuyvesant, and his children: Balthazar, Petrus and Nicholas.

Nicholas Bayard was the father of Samuel Bayard, who married Margaret, daughter of Stephen Van Cortlandt. They had among other children, a son, Stephen Bayard, born 1700, died 1757. He married Alida Vetch, daughter of Colonel Samuel Vetch and Margaret Livingston

Their third child, William Bayard, born June 1, 1729, died in Southampton, England, 1804. He married Catherine McEvers Their son, William Bayard, Jr., died 1826. He married in 1783 Elizabeth Cornell, daughter of Samuel Cornell, Esq , of Newbern, North Carolina. Her sister Hannah married Herman Le Roy, October 19, 1786.

Their daughter, Harriet Elizabeth Bayard, married Stephen Van Rensselaer, whose daughter Justine married Dr. Howard Townsend.

CLINTON—JONES FAMILIES.

The Clintons, who were for more than fifty years the ruling power of the state and have left an imperishable record in the history of our country, were descended from William Clinton, a grandson of Henry, second Earl of Lincoln, who was an officer in the army of Charles the First. After the downfall of that monarch he fled to the continent and afterwards went to Scotland and married a lady of the family of Kennedy, the heads of which were Earls of Cassilis. He then went to Ireland, where he died, leaving a daughter Margaret, and a son James, then two years old.

James became an officer in the army of Queen Anne, and married Elizabeth Smith, a daughter of one of Cromwell's officers. They had three children: Mary, Christian and Charles, who, after the death of their parents, came to America and settled at Little Britain, in Ulster county, New York.

Charles Clinton was judge of Orange county. He was lieutenant-colonel of De Lancey's Regiment in the expedition against Fort Frontenac, in which two of his sons, James and George, were also officers. He died in 1778. He married, in Ireland, Elizabeth Denniston They were the parents of seven children, three born in Ireland, and four in America Of the former, two died young; the other, Catherine, married Colonel James McLaughry, of the Revolutionary army The four children born in America were: 1. Alexander, a physician, who married Maria Kane He left no issue 2. Charles, also a physician, who died unmarried. 3. James Clinton, brigadier-general in the Revolution, was born at Little Britain, August 9, 1736, and died there,

December 22, 1812. He was promoted major-general at the close of the war

The fourth son was George Clinton, famous in the annals of our state. He was born at Little Britain, July 26, 1739, and died in Washington while in office of vice-president, April 20, 1812, in his seventy-third year. He married Cornelia Tappan, and had five daughters and one son, George Washington Clinton, who married Anna, daughter of General William Floyd, signer of the Declaration of Independence. They had one son, George W. Clinton, who left no issue, and the name of this branch of the family became extinct.

One of the daughters died in her thirteenth year. Another daughter, Cornelia, married "Citizen" Genet, minister of the French Republic to the United States. The others married into the Van Cortlandt and Talmadge families, and had many descendants.

General James Clinton married (first) Mary De Witt; (second) Mrs. Mary Gray, a widow. By the first marriage there were seven children:

1. Alexander, who, when scarcely more than a lad, was lieutenant in Colonel Lamb's Regiment of Artillery in the Revolution, and served till its close He was drowned in the Hudson river in his twenty-second year.

2. Charles, who married Elizabeth Mulliner, and had three children: Mary De Witt, wife of Captain Robert Gourley; Alexander, who married Adeline A. Hamilton; and Ann Eliza, who married James Foster, Jr.

3 De Witt Clinton, Mayor of New York, and Governor of the state. He married (first) Maria, daughter of Walter Franklin; (second) Catherine, daughter of Dr Thomas Jones.

4 George Clinton, who married Hannah, daughter of Walter Franklin, and sister of Maria, who married his brother, De Witt Clinton.

5 Mary, who married (first) Robert B. Norton; (second) Judge Ambrose Spencer. By the first marriage there were two children: Clinton Norton, who married Sally Pearsall; and Mary, wife of Alexander C. Spencer.

6. Elizabeth, who married Lieutenant William Stewart, of the Revolutionary army.

7. Katharine, who married (first) Samuel L. Norton, brother of her sister Mary's husband; (second) Judge Ambrose Spencer, her sister's widower.

By his second marriage General James Clinton had six children: James, who died young; Caroline, wife of Judge Charles A. Dewey; Emma L., who died unmarried; James Graham, who married Margaret Conger, and had one son: De Witt; Letitia, wife of Dr. Francis Bolton, had two sons: Thomas, and James Clinton Bolton, who married Laura Tallmadge; and Anna, wife of Lieutenant Edward Ross, U. S. A.

De Witt Clinton, governor of the state, had by his first marriage ten children, four of whom died young. The others were: Charles Alexander, who married Catharine Howe; James Henry, who died at sea; George William, who married Laura C. Spencer; Mary, wife of David S. Jones; Franklin, who died unmarried; and Julia, who died unmarried

George Clinton, the younger brother of De Witt, married Hannah Franklin and had three children: Mary Caroline, who married Henry Overing; Franklin, who died young; and Julia Matilda, who married (first) George C Tallmadge, (second) James Foster, Jr

George Clinton, whose life and labors are so large a part of the state and nation, passed his early life at Little Britain. He was for many years surrogate of Ulster county. The beginning of the Revolution found him ready for the struggle and foremost among the defenders of the rights of his country. He was commissioned as brigadier-general, and was dangerously wounded when the British took Fort Montgomery, in the Highlands He was a member of the Convention at Philadelphia which adopted the Declaration of Independence, for which he voted, but before it was engrossed and ready for signature, at the request of Washington, he hastened to New York to defend the passes of the Highlands His day of glory was when he, as governor of the state, rode at the side of Washington when they entered New York City after the evacuation. For twenty-one years he held the office of governor, was twice vice-president of the United States, and died in office, honored and respected, in 1812. The name and reputation of De Witt Clinton are too well known to require extended mention here. To the end of his life he was connected with almost every office in the power of the

Gov George Clinton

people to bestow. While United States senator he resigned that high position to become mayor of New York, which office he held 1803-1807, 1808-1810, 1811-1815. His career as governor of the state for nine years, and his long struggle for the Erie canal, which was crowned with success when the Great Lakes were united with the sea, are too well known to be repeated here In the midst of his usefulness, the "Great Governor" died suddenly at his residence in Albany, in 1828. Leaving none of the name who could fill his place in the world, he might be said to be the last of the Clintons. A magnificent monument to his memory was prepared at the instance of his countless friends. This was exhibited for a while in the City Hall Park, in New York, and now stands over his honored grave in Greenwood cemetery.

The country residence of De Witt Clinton was at Maspeth,

Country Seat of Gov. De Witt Clinton, Maspeth, L.I.

Long Island. The house was built many years before the Revolution by Judge Joseph Sackett. He died about 1756, and his son, William Sackett, sold it to Walter Franklin, February 28, 1776 Upon his death in 1780, it was left to his daughter Maria, who married De Witt Clinton, and they occupied it as a country seat during the remainder of his life. After his death in 1832 it was sold under a partition suit, and in 1842 it was purchased by Hon. David S. Jones, who took the deed in the name of his wife, Mary Clinton Jones, who was one of the children of Governor Clinton. They occupied it until the death of Judge Jones, May 10, 1848, and it was sold by his widow the following year. The view here given was made when it was in its original form and beauty. Since then it has passed through many hands, and

Walter Franklin's House.

now presents all the aspects of decay, and in a few years it will be swept away by the "march of improvement." Mrs. Mary Clinton Jones died in Portland, Oregon, August 10, 1872, aged sixty-five.

Walter Franklin was a merchant of great ability and extensive means In 1762 he purchased from the heirs of Robert Benson a large lot at the junction of Queen (now Pearl) and Cherry streets. Upon this he erected one of the most beautiful houses in the city, and afterward noted as the residence of President George Washington Walter Franklin left it to his daughter Hannah, who married George Clinton, a younger son of De Witt Clinton, who made it his temporary residence in 1816. After the death of Hannah Clinton it remained unchanged until 1856, when the heirs destroyed the building and erected stores in its room. The enterprise was not successful, and the stores being mortgaged were sold to Robert R. Morris. When the Brooklyn bridge was built the upper stories of the stores were removed. The mansion, when Washington occupied it, was No. 3 Cherry street. About 1826 the numbers were changed, the even numbers being placed on the north side of the street.

THE JONES FAMILY.

The ancestor of this family, one branch of which is so closely allied with the Clintons, was Major Thomas Jones, who was born 1665 at Strabane, County Tyrone, in the Province of Ulster, Ireland. His parents came from England, but the family is originally from Northern Wales. He was an officer of James the Second, and was engaged in the battle of the Boyne 1690, and Aughrim 1691. After the defeat he fled to France and then embarked for the West Indies and was on the Island of Jamaica when Port Royal was destroyed by the great earthquake July 7, 1692; he then came to Rhode Island and finally made his permanent residence at Fort Neck, in Queens county, Long Island. He married Freelove, daughter of Thomas Townsend, who died in July, 1726, from whom he obtained the grant of a very large tract of land at Fort Neck He built there, about 1696, the first brick house on Long Island, which stood until about 1833 when it was removed by his great-grandson, David S. Jones, who erected near the same site a mansion to which he gave the Indian name of Massapequa.

Major Thomas Jones was a man of wealth and influence He was commissioned by Lord Cornbury, sheriff of Queens county in 1709, and in 1710 was appointed ranger-general of the Island of Nassau or Long Island. He died at his residence in 1713. His eldest son, David Jones, who was born September, 1699, inherited most of the paternal estate. He was a lawyer

JONES
Coat of Arms

and a man of great attainments. From 1737 to 1738 he was a member of the Provincial Assembly, and for thirteen years was speaker. In 1758 he was appointed judge of the Supreme Court and held the office until 1773 He died October, 1775, and few men shared more largely in public confidence and respect.

His eldest son, Judge Thomas Jones, was admitted to the bar in 1775, and was clerk of Queens county from 1757 to 1775 He married Anne, daughter of Chief Justice De Lancey. In

1769 he was made recorder of New York City and retained the office for several years He was appointed judge of the Supreme Court in 1774 and held the office during the Revolution. Being an intense Loyalist his property was confiscated and he went to England, where he died many years later. His journal, which is a complete Tory history of the Revolution, was published a few years since by the New York Historical Society, and edited by his descendant, Edward Floyd De Lancey.

David Jones was the ancestor of the branch known as the Floyd Jones family. The stately mansion built by Judge Jones before the Revolution is now owned by that family.

William Jones, the third son of Major Thomas Jones, was the father of Samuel Jones, who was born July 26, 1734. He was admitted to the bar in 1760, and by his application and talents soon became distinguished for his legal acquirements and took a high stand among his contemporaries. He was a member of the convention held to consider the propriety of adopting the Constitution of the United States and gave his vote for its adoption. About this time he was chosen, with Colonel Richard Varick, to revise the laws of the state, a task which was performed to general satisfaction. For many years he represented the southern district in the state senate and to him we owe the preservation of many of our most venerable institutions, which the rude hand of innovation was ready to hew down. He was appointed recorder of the city of New York in 1789. He was also a member of common council, and a judge of mayor's court. He was made comptroller of the state in 1797, and held this office till his retirement from public life. In the spring of 1800 he retired from business and professional pursuits and purchased from one of his brothers the place where he was born, residing there until his death, and enjoying all the pleasures of country life. His long and useful career was terminated by his death, November 25, 1819, having reached his eighty-sixth year, and the highest honors were paid to his memory.

Judge Samuel Jones married Cornelia, daughter of Elbert Haring, July 17, 1768 Her father was the owner of the famous Haring (or, as it is more commonly called the Herring farm) which, on the west side of Broadway, extended from Waverly Place nearly to Bleecker street, and included a large part of

Washington Square and a larger tract at the north part of Bleecker street. Upon her part of the farm Cornelia street was laid out and perpetuates her memory, and Great Jones street was named in honor of her husband The children of Samuel Jones and his wife Cornelia were: Samuel, Thomas, William, Elbert and David S. Jones.

Samuel Jones, the eldest son, was also a noted lawyer, and held among other important positions that of chancellor of the state, judge of the Court of Appeals and presiding justice of the Superior Court of the city of New York. He died in 1853.

He left a son, Samuel Jones, who was also a noted lawyer and was justice of the Superior Court and clerk of Court of Common Pleas. He died in 1892.

David S. Jones, the youngest son, was born November 3, 1777. He was also a lawyer of the highest professional and social standing He held few public offices, but in 1812-1813 was corporation counsel of New York, and in 1836-1837 was judge of Queens county. He was closely related by blood or marriage to all the old and leading families of New York, and was the intimate friend of Irving, Cooper and, in a word, of all the prominent men of his day He was to the time of his death a trustee of Columbia College, of the New York Society Library and General Theological Seminary. He was also a director of the Bank of the Manhattan Company, and one of the founders and a director of the Phoenix Bank, and trustee and guardian of large estates He died May 10, 1848.

Mr. Jones married (first) Margaret, daughter of Dr. Thomas Jones, of an entirely different family. She was a granddaughter of Philip Livingston, one of the signers of the Declaration of Independence. Her sister, Catherine, was the second wife of De Witt Clinton. He married (second) Susan Le Roy, daughter of Herman Le Roy. Her younger sister was the second wife of Daniel Webster (Third) Mary Clinton, eldest daughter of Governor De Witt Clinton. The children of David S Jones by his first wife were: Henry, Philip L., and William Alfred, all of whom died without issue By his second marriage to Susan Le Roy, who died May 26, 1832, he had two children: Herman Le Roy, who married Augusta L., daughter of Mayor Ambrose Kingsland, and has children: Herman Le Roy, Kingsland and Mary; 2. Mary, who died unmarried. By his third marriage, to Mary Clinton, June 11, 1833, he had four children: De Witt Clinton, Walter Franklin, Julia C. and Florence C.

In this sketch only a few names comparatively have been given, but the various branches have furnished a lieutenant-governor, as well as judges, senators, members of assembly to the state for generations. In short, the Jones family has furnished legislators and jurists to the colony and state for more than a century.

De Witt Clinton Jones, son of Hon. David S. Jones, was born June 30, 1834, at the residence of his father, No. 2 Bond street, then one of the most fashionable quarters of New York. He was educated at the school of Rev. Dr. Mühlenberg at College Point, Long Island, and at Mr. Marlborough Churchill's Military Academy, at Sing Sing, New York, and graduated from Trinity College, Hartford, in 1854. He then attended a two years' course at the Rensselaer Polytechnic Institute at Troy and left in 1857, the year before graduating, to accept a position on the Chicago, St. Paul & Fond du Lac railroad. Here he was actively engaged as a civil engineer when the financial difficulties of 1857 caused a suspension of railroad enterprise. He returned to Poughkeepsie where his mother had a country seat, commenced the study of law and was admitted to the bar in 1859. He entered the office of Mr. John T. Crosby whose niece he afterwards married. He, with Mr. P. W. Ostrander, formed a partnership with Mr. John P. Crosby in 1867, under the firm name of Crosby, Ostrander & Jones. During the continuance of this partnership Mr. Jones was interested in many important law suits, and conducted the large real estate business of the firm. He was one of the original incorporators of the elevated railroad on Greenwich street, patented by Mr. Charles T. Harvey, which was the forerunner of the elevated railway system. Mr. Jones went with his family to Portland, Oregon, in 1871, and there practiced his profession. The following year he obtained an appointment on the United States Coast Survey under his

DeWitt Clinton Jones

friend General Michler, and was engaged in the survey of the San Juan archipelago and the channel of the Columbia river, at Astoria. In the fall of 1873 he went to San Francisco and formed a business relation with Hon. Delos Lake, a leading lawyer, which continued several years. He then entered into partnership with Hon. Nathaniel Bennett, formerly one of the judges of the Supreme court, and was for a time attorney for the Pacific Mail Steamship Company, and in many important cases gained a well merited reputation as an able lawyer. He returned to New York in 1882 and entered the office of Coudert Brothers, where he remained two years and then recommenced practice by himself, principally confined to real estate and counsel business and to corporation matters.

Mr. Jones married, December 18, 1860, Josepha, second daughter of the late William Henry Crosby and Josepha Neilson, his wife, who was a daughter of Dr John Neilson, son of Col. James Neilson, of New Brunswick, New Jersey, distinguished officer in the Revolution. William H. Crosby was formerly a professor in Rutgers College, and brother of Rev. Dr Howard Crosby, who was a son of Dr. Ebenezer Crosby, surgeon on Washington's staff, Professor in Columbia College and member of the Cincinnati. William H Crosby was a nephew of Col. Henry Rutgers, and inherited a large part of the Rutgers farm. Mrs Jones was also a lineal descendant of Gen. William Floyd, and of Johanes DePeyster, anciently Mayor of New York.

The children of Mr. DeWitt Clinton Jones are: 1. De Witt Clinton, Jr., born December 28, 1862. He married Bessie Duncan Cannon, daughter of Henry Rutgers Cannon and Mary Brinkerhoff. They have two children, DeWitt Clinton Jones, third, and Rutgers Brevoort. 2. Mary Franklin. 3. Henry Crosby. 4. Ellen Roosevelt, wife of Frederick Glover Pyne.

They have three children, Frederick Cruger, Schuyler Neilson and Charles Crosby.

The residence of William B. Crosby, of which a view is given, was built about 1740 by Henry Rutgers. It stood on the block bounded by Cherry, Monroe, Clinton and Jefferson streets, and was one of the finest residences in the city. It remained an interesting relic of the past until 1868.

Residence of Wm. B. Crosby, Esq.

L'HOMMEDIEU FAMILY.

The ancestor of this family was Pierre L'Hommedieu, of La Rochelle, France. He married Martha Peron, and their son, Benjamin L'Hommedieu, was born in 1656 and came to America about 1686. He married Patience, daughter of Nathaniel Sylvester, the owner of Shelter Island. The ancient family Bible of Benjamin L'Hommedieu is now in possession of his descendant, Sylvester Youngs L'Hommedieu, of East Orange, New Jersey, and from it the following record is copied *verbatim*:

"The first *temps* that I com to this country I lande at Rod Island the first, 168. ."

GENEALOGICAL AND FAMILY HISTORY 195

Benjamin L'Hommedieu, son of Benjamin and Patience L'Hommedieu, was born on Monday, the 3rd of December, 1694. Hosea L'Hommedieu, son of Benjamin and Patience L'Hommedieu, was born on Sunday in April, 1697. Peter L'Hommedieu was born on the Sabbath day, 19th of August, 1699. Grizzel L'Hommedieu was born 20th of April, 1701. Sylvester L'Hommedieu was born January 7, 1703. Susanne L'Hommedieu was born Thursday, December 14, 1704. John L'Hommedieu was born Saturday, January 11, 1707. Patience L'Hommedieu died 1719, the 2nd of November, at 10 o'clock in the night, and was 55 years of age, born in the year 1664, first of November. "The Lord received her soul." Next to this is the following, almost illegible: "My father Nathaniel Sylvester dyed June 13, 1688 My mother, Grizzle Sylvester dyed June 13, 1687 (?)" Benjamin L'Hommedieu died January 4, 1749, aged ninety-six His daughter Grizzel married Samuel Hudson. Susanne married Jonathan Tuthill.

Benjamin L'Hommedieu, son of Benjamin (1), married (first) Mary Conklin, who died June 19, 1730. He married (second) Martha Bourne. The children by the first marriage were: Benjamin, born November 21, 1717, "Thursday morning at 2 o'clock;" died in 1718. Sarah and Elizabeth. The only child by the second marriage was Ezra L'Hommedieu, of whom a more extended notice will be given. He was born August 30, 1734.

Hosea L'Hommedieu, son of Benjamin (1), married Freelove Howell. Their children were: Constant, born November 22, 1720, died March 29, 1725. Patience, born December 13, 1721. Joseph, born May 20, 1723. Hosea, born May 31, 1726. Nathaniel, born May 3, "on Friday about 11 o'clock in the morning, 1728 " And Timothy, born October 23, 1729

Peter L'Hommedieu, son of Benjamin (1), married Sarah

Corwin. They had one son, Constant L'Hommedieu, born February 5, 1730. He married Deborah, daughter of John and Dorcas Young. She was born March 23, 1732. They had children: Nathaniel, born August 19, 1762, died July 19, 1832. William, born June 10, 1759. Deborah, born June 24, 1764. Sarah, born August 1, 1767. Hannah, born at Southold, September 21, 1769, died at Red Mills, New Jersey, April 17, 1854. John, born January 31, 1772. Betsey, born October 23, 1774.

John L'Hommedieu, son of Benjamin (1), married Mary Hudson, and had children: John, Benjamin, Henry, born 1741, and Mary

Sylvester L'Hommedieu, son of Benjamin (1), died March 9, 1783, and is buried in the churchyard at Southold. He married Elizabeth Booth in 1737. Their children were: Elizabeth, who died September 6, 1754. Grover, born August 3, 1741; and Samuel, born February 20, 1744.

Of this family, Samuel L'Hommedieu married Sarah, daughter of Ebenezer White, of the Southampton family, November 26, 1776. Their children were: Sylvester; Ezra; Phebe, who married ———— Fosdick; Charity; Elizabeth; Mary; Charles and Samuel, born June 25, 1785. Samuel L'Hommedieu, the father of this family, died March 17, 1834, aged ninety. His wife died November 18, 1822, and both rest in Oakland Cemetery, Sag Harbor, Long Island.

Grover L'Hommedieu, brother of Samuel, married (first) Esther Vail, December 27, 1763. Their children were: Elizabeth; Giles, born April 28, 1766, married Abigail Reynolds, of Norwich, Connecticut, no children; Mary; Susanne, born March 13, 1770, married James Gordon, December 5, 1816; Ezra, born March 12, 1772; Sarah; Esther; Joseph; Lucretia; William, born November 17, 1783, died young; Abbey, who married Gurdon Smith; and Joshua, who died unmarried. Grover L'Hommedieu married (second) Elizabeth Tracy. Their children were: William, born October 6, 1793; Stephen, born March 16, 1796, married Mary Clark, August 24, 1835; Benjamin, born March 6, 1798; Maria, Fanny and Nancy. Of this family, Ezra L'Hommedieu left children: John, Grover, William, Joshua, Samuel, Harriet and Laura.

Nathaniel L'Hommedieu, son of Constant, son of Peter, son of Benjamin (1), married Ann Burcham, April 8, 1806 Their children were: William A, born July 24, 1807, died in New Orleans, May 31, 1841; Nathaniel C., born March 4, 1810; Elizabeth, wife of ——————. Suydam; Ann Amelia, born August 7, 1813, died November 23, 1835; Sylvester Youngs, born October 16, 1816, died August 20, 1840. Of this family, Nathaniel C. L'Hommedieu married Jane M. Hepburn, August 29, 1838. She died August 19, 1866 Their children were: Ward B., born August 5, 1839, died at Hong Kong, China, May 28, 1862; and Sylvester Youngs, born March 24, 1842. Nathaniel C. L'Hommedieu, the father, died April 30, 1901.

Sylvester Youngs L'Hommedieu married Abby Caroline Baldwin, September 15, 1875. Their children are: Frank Arnold, born June 23, 1876; Sylvester Y., born November 15, 1878; Nathaniel Constant, born August 28, 1882; Augusta Dean, born June 27, 1889; and Nathalie Constant. Frank Arnold L'Hommedieu married Noella Virginia Colquitt, October 14, 1905.

Sylvester Youngs L'Hommedieu, a prominent citizen of Orange, New Jersey with extensive business interests in New York, is the possessor of the ancient family Bible of his honored ancestor, Benjamin L'Hommedieu, which is treasured with care as a precious heirloom of the past.

Nathaniel L'Hommedieu, son of Hosea, son of Benjamin (1), married ————— Mulford, of Southampton, Long Island. His eldest son was Henry Mulford L'Hommedieu, commonly known as Mulford L'Hommedieu, who had a son, Henry L'Hommedieu, whose son, Wallace L'Hommedieu, was the father of Hon. Irving L'Hommedieu, of Medina, New York, late State Senator.

Ezra L'Hommedieu, son of Benjamin, son of Benjamin (1), was one of the most distinguished men of Suffolk county. He was born August 30, 1734, and died September 28, 1811. He was graduated from Yale College in 1754, and was a delegate to the Continental Congress from 1777 to 1783; also in 1787-8. He was a member of the New York Legislature from 1777 to 1809, except in 1793. Helped form the first State Constitution and was a member of the Council of Appointment. For twenty-six years he was clerk of Suffolk county. His first wife was Charity Floyd, sister of General William Floyd, "The Signer." She died in 1785, and he then married Mary Catharine Havens, June 15, 1803. She died February 4, 1837, aged thirty-one, and left three daughters. The present representatives of this illustrious man are the daughters of Professor Eben Horsford, who has an estate on Shelter Island.

Samuel L'Hommedieu, son of Sylvester, son of Benjamin (1), was one of the most prominent citizens of Sag Harbor, Long Island. He was Lieutenant of Militia, and his commission from Governor Tryon is in the Long Island Historical Society. With other prominent Whigs he fled to Connecticut and settled in New London After the war he returned to Sag Harbor and carried on the manufacture of ropes and cordage, which was continued by his son Samuel. He was Justice of the Peace, and for long years was known as "Old 'Squire L'Hommedieu," and was also a member of Assembly, and in both positions he was held in high honor. One of his daughters, Mary, married Rev. J. L. Gardiner, father of late Samuel L. Gardiner, a noted lawyer of Sag Harbor.

Previous to 1774 a Joseph L'Hommedieu, whose life we do

not know, married a daughter of Ephraim Hildreth, of Southampton, Long Island

Henry L'Hommedieu, born 1741, son of John, son of Benjamin (1), was the great-grandfather of Hon. Frederick L'Hommedieu of Deep River, Connecticut, to whom the writer is under great obligations for information granted

SAMUEL L'HOMMEDIEU.

Benjamin L'Hommedieu, the ancestor of the family, of whom a more extended notice has been given, had among other children a son John, born Saturday, January 11, 1707. He married, February 25, 1727, Mary Hudson and had children: John; Henry, born 1741; Benjamin and Mary. In his will he mentions Benjamin as being his second son.

Benjamin L'Hommedieu married Jemima Thompson, born 1735, died 1807, and in his will mentions his sons Samuel, Joseph and Daniel, and his granddaughter, Jemima, daughter of his son Samuel.

Samuel L'Hommedieu was born January 15, 1763, died March 21, 1845. He married Esther Downs, born 1735, died September 4, 1842. He was born and lived at Upper Aquebogue, in the present town of Riverhead, Long Island When a young man Samuel L'Hommedieu paid his attentions to Esther Downs, born 1735, died September 4, 1842, who declined his offer of marriage and married Ezekiel Petty. Some years afterward, when she was a widow, Mr. L'Hommedieu renewed his suit with better success They were the parents of children: Joseph; Daniel; Jemima; and Samuel, who died at the age of twenty-one.

Joseph L'Hommedieu was born at Upper Aquebogue, 1806, and died July, 1877. He married (first) Deborah Benjamin, and had children: 1. Daniel Benjamin, married Chilla Raynor and had children: George, Edward and two daughters. Daniel B., died February 22, 1905, aged seventy-five years. 2. Samuel, died young 3. Jane, married George Barber and had children: Deborah, Henry, Charles, William G., Frank, Joseph and George. He married (second) Susan Higbie and had children: John W., married (first) Marian Towns, (second) Ellen Gilbert, (third) Annie Reeves. He died 1901, leaving children: Nellie, Susan and Roswell. 2. Marietta, married David Andrew Havens and had children: Elizabeth, wife of Captain Charles A. Day, and Grace, wife of William E. Newton. 3 Huldah. 4. Samuel, see forward. 5. Joseph, married Eliza Estelle Benjamin and had children: Harrison, Nathan Benjamin, Carl, Percy and Lulu. 6. David Benjamin. 7. Esther, married David Leedham and had children: Caius and Esther.

Samuel L'Hommedieu, well known in the marine mercantile business of New York, was born at Baiting Hollow, in the town of Riverhead, February 11, 1843. When he was eleven years of age he went to live with Captain Harry Gardiner, of Quogue, and remained there five years, attending the public schools. At the beginning of the Civil war he "went on the water" as a steward on the sloop "Diligent," Captain John Brown, and afterward on the schooner "Selah B. Strong," and various other vessels After that he became connected with the towing business, and by his diligent labor and intelligence rose to be the general manager of the "White Star Towing Line," consisting of a fleet of thirteen tugs and employing one hundred men. There are also a number of vessels, schooners and barques sailing to southern ports. From his long and extensive experience Mr. L'Hommedieu holds a high position among seafaring men and very few men are better acquainted with marine interests. Mr. L'Hommedieu is the owner of the old homestead at Baiting Hollow. He and his sister, Mrs. Jane Barber, are the last survivors of his father's family. Mr. L'Hommedieu

Clement C Moore

married Cornelia, daughter of George Wells. She died, leaving one daughter, Florence Cornelia, who was killed by falling from a bicycle at the age of eleven years.

Harrison L'Hommedieu, now living at Babylon, Long Island, has children: Arthur, Samuel and Edith.

Daniel L'Hommedieu has children: Harry, Edna, Florence and Joseph, all residing in Babylon.

CLEMENT C. MOORE AND HIS HOME.

The American ancestor of the Moore family was Rev John Moore, who was born in England about 1620. He came to America and was living in Lynn, Massachusetts, in 1641 From there he moved to Southampton, Long Island He had a "planting lot" laid out for him in that place, April 6, 1641, and May 30, 1644, he was one of the delegates to Hartford. He was one of the "freemen" in 1649 About 1651 he left Southampton, and on September 25 of that year we find him as minister at Hempstead. Mr. Moore died at Newtown, September 17, 1657. Rev. John Moore married Margaret, daughter of Edward Howell, the founder of Southampton His widow married Francis Doughty, son of Rev. Francis Doughty His children were: John, who moved to New Jersey; Captain Gersham; Captain Samuel; Joseph, who moved to Southampton, Long Island; and Elizabeth, wife of Content Titus.

Captain Samuel Moore married Mary, daughter of Thomas Reed He died suddenly, September 19, 1717, leaving children: Captain Samuel; Benjamin; Joseph; Nathaniel; Mary, wife of Nathaniel Woodward; Elizabeth, wife of Isaac Hicks; Sarah, wife of Daniel Coe; and Margaret, wife of John Protten, Jr.

Benjamin Moore, the second son, married, December 17, 1710, Anna Sackett. Their children were Lieutenant Samuel, born December 5, 1711; Mary, who married James Renne; Anna, wife of Thomas Hallett; Sarah, wife of Samuel Moore; Dr. Benjamin; Elizabeth, wife of William Hazzard; Patience, wife of Joseph Lawrence; and John, who died in 1827 at the age of ninety-eight.

Lieutenant Samuel Moore died April 7, 1788. He married Sarah, daughter of John Fish, of an honored family. Their children were: Sarah, wife of Thomas Barrow; Patience, wife of Daniel Titus; Jacob; Benjamin; William; and Judith, who married Rev. Thomas Lambert Moore

Benjamin Moore, afterward the honored bishop of New York, was born October 16, 1748. In his early years he was sent to a school in New Haven Some years later he entered Kings College, New York, and was graduated in 1768. He then studied theology under Rev. Dr. Samuel Auchmuty, rector of Trinity church For several years he taught Latin and Greek in New York and in May, 1774, went to England, and on June 24 was ordained deacon by the bishop of London, and was ordained priest June 29. Upon his return to New York he was made an assistant minister of Trinity church. He was chosen rector of the church in 1800, and on September 5, 1801, he was unanimously called to the high office of bishop, and was consecrated on September 11 of the same year His diocese embraced a very large extent of country. He was constantly visiting his many churches, and new ones were built and dedicated In addition to this he held many high positions and was president of Kings College from 1801 to 1812.

Among the many episodes of his eventful life may be mentioned the fact that he was present at the death of Alexander Hamilton, and administered the sacrament to him in his last moments He was also one of the assistants at the inauguration of President Washington. After a most useful and honored life Bishop Moore died February 27, 1816, in his sixty-sixth year.

His remains were placed in the vault of Grove Bend, at the Rector street side of Trinity churchyard Bishop Moore married Charity, daughter of Major Thomas Clarke, of whom a more extended notice is here given Their only child, Clement Clarke Moore, was born July 15, 1770.

House of Clement C. Moore.
("There "Night Before Christmas" was written).

Of Clement C Moore it may be said that he was born and lived surrounded by all the advantages that could make life pleasant and render it useful. Receiving his preliminary education under the care of his honored father, he entered Kings College, being graduated in 1798, and receiving in later years the degrees of A. M and LL D. He was one of the trustees of the college from 1821 to 1857, and clerk of the board for many years. From 1821 to 1850 he was professor of Greek and Oriental languages in the General Theological Seminary in New York, and for the last three years of his life was professor Emeritus Among other acquirements he was an excellent musician, and was voluntary organist in St. Peter's church, on Twentieth street, where a mural tablet is erected to his memory. He died in Newport, Rhode Island, July 10, 1863.

Clement C. Moore married Catharine Elizabeth Taylor,

> 'Twas the night before Christmas, when all through the house
> Not a creature was stirring, not even a mouse;
> The stockings were hung by the chimney with care,
> In hopes that St. Nicholas soon would be there;
> The children were nestled all snug in their beds,
> While visions of sugar-plums danced in their heads;

November 20, 1813. She died April 4, 1830. Their children were: 1. Margaret Elliott, born June 6, 1815, married, October 1, 1835, Dr. John Doughty Ogden, and died April 13, 1845 2. Charity Elizabeth, born September 14, 1816, died December 14, 1830. 3. Benjamin, born August 24, 1818, married Mary Elizabeth Sing, died September 6, 1886. His widow died February 24, 1895. 4 Mary Clarke, born September 2, 1819. She became the second wife of Dr. John Doughty Ogden, February 3, 1848, and died April 11, 1893. 5. Clement, born January 3, 1821, died unmarried May 13, 1889. 6. William Taylor, born October 8, 1823, married (first) Lucretia Post; (second) Katharine E. Robinson. He was killed by a carriage accident in the Champs Elysees, Paris, May 19, 1897, and left no children. 7. Katharine Van Cortlandt, born May 1, 1826, died unmarried July 29, 1890. 8. Marie Theresa, born December 15, 1826.

Benjamin Moore the eldest son, left children: Clement C., born September 19, 1843; Casimer De Rham, born June 28, 1851; Elizabeth; and Katharine Theresa. All now living in New York.

Capt Thomas Clarke

Dr John D Ogden left a large family, who are also the descendants of Clement C. Moore

Captain Thomas Clarke was born in England in 1692, and when he came to America was a retired officer of the British army. In 1745 he married Mary, daughter of Richard Stilwell. Upon being rallied for marrying a young wife in his old age, he replied that the Clarkes were not in their prime until after sixty. That he was in his prime is evidenced by his being the father of a family, who were: Mary, who married Richard Vassal; Charity, who married Rev. Benjamin Moore; and Maria Theresa, who married Viscount Barrington, a cousin of Theodosia Bartow, wife of Aaron Burr. On August 16, 1750, Captain Clarke purchased from the heirs of Jacob Somerindyck a large farm on the west side of the city, bounded south by the land of Sir Peter Warren and Yellis Mandeville, west by the Hudson river, north by Brant Schuyler and land of Widow Cowenhoven, and east by land of John Horne. It contained over ninety-four acres and the price was one thousand and fifty-nine pounds, or two thousand six hundred and forty-seven dollars. This tract extended from Nineteenth to Twenty-seventh street and east to near Eighth avenue. Here he erected a magnificent mansion and called it "Chelsea," a name which the neighborhood still retains. When Lord Howe sailed up the river on July 12, 1776, several shots were fired at Captain Clarke's mansion, which presented a very conspicuous prospect. Shortly afterward the house was burned and the owner, who was very sick, was with difficulty rescued from the flames. It was rebuilt by his widow with greater grandeur. In this mansion Clement C. Moore was born, the larger part of the farm having been left to Rev. Benjamin Moore and his wife. It remained as the elegant home of an honored family until the advance of the great city rendered it unfitted for a country residence. It stood on the top of a high hill which overlooked the river. It was destroyed in 1850, and the hill, leveled to its base, went to fill up water lots in Tenth avenue. The exact location of this interesting mansion was on the south side of Twenty-third street about two hundred feet west of Ninth avenue. The poem of the "Visit of St. Nicholas," far better known as "The Night Before Christmas," which has made the name of the author famous forever, was written by him in 1822 as a Christmas gift for his children. A copy was made by a young lady who was visiting the family, who, upon her return to her home in the city of Troy, sent it to an editor, and it was first printed in the Troy *Sentinel*, December 23, 1823. A little picture was attached showing St. Nicholas and his sled and "tiny red deer," a spectacle ever dear to the minds of children. It attracted immediate attention and has been printed in more forms and in greater numbers than any poem ever written by an American.

The Hebrew Lexicon which he prepared, and which was the first printed in this country, and other works upon which he bestowed so much time and labor, have been superseded by works of far deeper research, but the man is yet to be born who can write anything to supersede the little poem which has made Santa Claus and his tiny red deer living realities to thousands of children throughout our broad land.

THE BROWER FAMILY.

Among the earliest settlers in New Amsterdam was Adam Brower, whose descendants still remain after more than two and a half centuries. In 1647 he is mentioned as "at present residing on Long Island." In that year he sold to Dirck Van Schelhuyne "a house and lot north of the begun graft, between the lot of Jan the Cooper on the west, and Egbert Woutersen on the east." This was on the north side of Beaver street, east of Broadway. The line of descent is as follows:

Adam Brower married Magdalena Verdon, March 10, 1645. Their son Jacob married Anetje, daughter of William Bogardus and Wyntie Sybrants, January 7, 1682 Their son Jacob married Pieternella, daughter of Jan De La Montagne and Anetje Josephs Waldron, October 28, 1709. Their son Johannes married Susanna Deroilhet, October 9, 1734. They were the parents of Johannes Brower, who was baptized in 1747, and died April 13, 1823. He married Catharine Duryee, March 22, 1769. Their son John was born September 6, 1774, and died November 1, 1804 He married Magdalen Duryee, December 15, 1796 They were the parents of John J. Brower, who was born January 7, 1804, and died October 8, 1878. He married Sophia Wyckoff Olcott, May 20, 1835. Their children are: Cornelia L., wife of Rev. Charles H McCreery; John, who married Sarah L. Beckley; Catharine H , wife of W. Wheeler Smith; Henry Wyckoff, who married Diana Horton; and William Leverich.

William L. Brower is a devoted member of the Collegiate Reformed Dutch church of New York and an elder, worshipping at the Middle Collegiate church, Second avenue and Seventh street, and as a member of the consistory of the Collegiate church he serves upon many of its most important committees, including the finance committee and board of church masters. He has been superintendent of the Middle Church Sunday school since 1887.

Mr. Brower was received into the full communion of the Collegiate church on February 2, 1870, on confession of faith, was installed as a deacon in 1873, and continued to serve as such until 1897, when he became an elder He is very familiar with the usages of the Reformed Dutch church and with the history of the Collegiate church, both his paternal and maternal ancestors for many generations having been connected with the former, his paternal ancestors having been identified with the Collegiate church throughout its existence. His father, Mr John I. Brower, was in its communion for many years and also a member of its consistory.

While Mr. Brower is deeply interested in all that concerns and contributes to the general welfare of the Collegiate church in all of its congregations and their various channels of helpful influence, his time and energies being generously given in the discharge of his duties as a member of the consistory, it is to the work of the Middle church that his affections and untiring service are especially devoted.

When the church at Lafayette place and Fourth street was taken down, Mr. Brower was one of those who were firm in the belief that the Collegiate church should continue to maintain a

Wm L Brower

church and place of worship in that section of the city and minister to the spiritual welfare of all who could there be reached, and in the new Middle church at Second avenue and Seventh street he has earnestly applied himself to the work there conducted. In this church no pew rentals are charged, the seats being free to all, and the edifice is kept open daily "so as to afford any persons who might be religiously and devoutly disposed opportunity for rest, meditation and prayer."

Mr. Brower has made the following gifts to the Collegiate church:

A communion service for the sick. (See Year Book of 1894, page 136)

Mural tablets in the Middle church in memory of—
  I. Peter Minuit.
  II. The Krankenbezoekers,
      Sebastian Jansen Krol and Jan Huyck.
  III. The Rev. Jonas Michaëlius
      (See Year Book of 1901, page 330.)

Tablets erected in the Middle church, memorials to those who perished in the "General Slocum" disaster.

HEWLETT FAMILY.

The family of which George W. Hewlett, produce dealer, whose place of business is located at No. 180 South street, New York, one of the worthy, respected business men of the city, is a member, was founded by George Hewlett, who married, 1680, Mary Baylis, died 1722

Daniel Hewlett, son of George and Mary (Baylis) Hewlett, died 1757-58. He was united in marriage with Sarah Jackson. Daniel was the first of the family to settle in Merrick, Queens county, Long Island.

George Hewlett, son of Daniel and Sarah (Jackson) Hewlett, born 1725, died 1787. He married, 1754, Elizabeth Williams, who bore him the following children: Ann, 1755, died 1824; married 1774, Hewlett Townsend. Mary, born 1757, married, 1781, Richard Townsend. George, born 1763, died 1847; married Jane Williams.

George Hewlett, only son of George and Elizabeth (Williams) Hewlett, born 1763, died 1847. He married Jane Williams, who bore him one child, Israel Horsefield.

GENEALOGICAL AND FAMILY HISTORY 213

Israel Horsefield Hewlett, only child of George and Jane (Williams) Hewlett, was born in Merrick, Long Island, 1814, died 1889. He was a farmer by occupation, and spent his entire life in Merrick. He was an active politician in the ranks of the Republican party, but was never in any sense of the word an office seeker. He served in the capacity of assessor. He was a member of Morton Lodge, Free and Accepted Masons, Hempstead, and a member of the Society of Friends. He married, 1832, Eliza A. Hewlett, daughter of Charles and Sarah Ann (Platt) Hewlett, and died September 20, 1859. Their children were: 1 Henry P , born 1832, died 1890; married, 1856, Charity Jarvis Mott, two children: Jesse M., born 1858, married, 1882, Margaret Mott, residing at Freeport, Long Island; and Henry P., born 1867, died 1872. 2. Fannie N., born 1835, died 1890; married, 1855, William S Willetts, of Jericho, and their children are: Elizabeth R , born 1857; Frederick, 1858; Ann Eliza, Mary W., Allen O , James, Martha J. 3. Charles, born 1836, married, 1863, Mary L. Edwards, and resides at Little Neck, Long Island; one child, Frederick E , married, 1895, Cornelia Van Nostrand. 4. George W., born September 28, 1838, mentioned hereafter. 5. Sarah Elizabeth, born 1840, died 1885; married 1865, Coles C. Hegerman 6. Rev. John C., born 1842, a minister in the Protestant Episcopal church, now stationed at Boston, Massachusetts. 7. Mary W., born 1844, married Benjamin Wooley, no issue 8. William W , born 1847, a physician, practicing his profession at Babylon, Long Island; married, 1872, Ella Pittman, has two sons: Harold, born 1873, married, 1898, Winifred Roberts, and Percy, born 1875; also two children who died in childhood. 9. Benjamin P., born 1847, twin to William W., died in infancy. Israel H. Hewlett married (second), 1863, Margaret Dorland, and their children were: Jane W., Eliza, Nellie, Sarah, married ——— Ackerley

George W. Hewlett, third son of Israel H. and Eliza A. (Hewlett) Hewlett, was born at Merrick, Long Island, September 28, 1839. He acquired his education in the district schools of Merrick, and his boyhood days were spent upon the homestead farm. He enlisted in Company H, One Hundred and Nineteenth New York Regiment, August 19, 1862, and served three years in the Civil war. In 1864 he was transferred to the Veteran Reserved Corps, where he held the rank of sergeant. He was honorably discharged at Washington, D. C., June 30, 1865. After remaining in Washington one month, he returned to the east and accepted a position in a clothing store in Brooklyn, New York. He subsequently became bookkeeper in a wholesale house in New York and remained in this employ for fourteen years, and in 1880 engaged in his present business, dealer in produce, wherein he has gained a reputation for integrity and uprightness. He is a member of Altair Lodge, No. 601, Free and Accepted Masons, and Constellation Chapter, No. 134, Royal Arch Masons, Brooklyn.

Mr. Hewlett married, in Brooklyn, New York, June 14, 1872, Susan O. Mott, born in Brooklyn, New York, daughter of Jesse and Experience Mott. Their children are: Ella E., born February 14, 1874; Eliza Ann, born November, 1875, married, 1900, Edwin L. Hitch, residing in Brooklyn, New York; Harry P., born October 1, 1877

ALBERT G. RICHTER

Albert G Richter, owner and operator of the Centennial Iron Works, located at No 190 Elm street, New York, is a native of New York city, born April 2, 1868.

His father, Herman Richter, the founder of the business above mentioned, was born in Zwicken, kingdom of Saxony,

Germany, November 5, 1837. His boyhood days were spent in his native land and he was there educated and learned the trade of machinist. He came to America, hoping that by so doing he would improve his financial affairs, and for many years was employed in Roach's shipyard, Mr Roach being one of the largest shipbuilders in this country. In 1867 Mr Richter engaged in business on his own account at No. 409 Broome street, in the manufacture of all kinds of iron work for buildings, and conducted business there until 1875, a period of eight years. In 1876 he removed his business to the present site, No. 190 Elm street, and there continued until his death, in August, 1902. He enlisted in Company B, First United States Artillery, was wounded at the battle of Williamsburg, Virginia, March 4, 1862, and was discharged on account of disability He was a member of Koltes Post, No. 32, Grand Army of the Republic He was married to Theresa Koch, a native of Saxony, daughter of George and Herminie Koch, and their children were: Ludwig, born August 15, 1864, in New York, married Matilda Ludiman, has two living children: Stephen and Eleanor. Ernest, died in childhood. Albert G., whose name heads this sketch. Ernest, died in childhood. Herman. Theresa, wife of August Bohl, two children: William and Herman. Frederick W.

Albert G. Richter was educated in the public schools, and St Matthew's Lutheran Church school. After completing his studies he learned the machinist's trade with his father, subsequently becoming a partner in the business, and after the death of his father purchased his interest in the estate and is now sole owner. In addition to the manufacture of all kinds of iron work for buildings, special attention is given to alterations and repairs, and in all the transactions conducted since the establishment of the business the utmost integrity has been observed

Mr. Richter is a member of Eichen-Kranz Singing Society, Pioneer Lodge, No. 20, Free and Accepted Masons, Old Hoboken Turtle Club (which is over one hundred years old), and the Employers' Association of Architectural Iron Workers.

Mr. Richter was married in New York, November 25, 1900, to Katherine Frederica, daughter of William and Amelia Frederica. They have no living children.

ADOLPH LOWENBEIN.

Adolph Lowenbein, deceased, during a long and active career known as a man of much business ability and enterprise and sterling character, was a native of Bavaria, born in the village of Brux, April 27, 1828, a son of Nathan Lowenbein, born in 1792.

Mr. Lowenbein received a limited education in his native land, and was trained to the trade of upholstering, of which he was master at a youthful age. When only thirteen years old he came to the United States, and at once obtained employment at his trade. In 1846, when only eighteen, he engaged in business for himself, in Christopher street He developed this to larger proportions, and further enlargements necessitated various removals—to Broome street, and later to the corner of Hudson and Broome streets. At a later day he purchased a piece of property comprising three buildings at the corner of Hudson and Dominic streets These he demolished, erecting in their stead a mammoth edifice, where he carried on an extensive furniture and upholstering business, numbering among his patrons very many of the best hotels, business houses and private citizens of the city. He also extended his activities to the lumber business, importing and exporting, and had the distinction of being the first to introduce American walnut to European markets, and to bring into this country French veneering from

France. He was also actively interested in various other business enterprises, industrial and financial. His death occurred July 20, 1878, aged a little more than fifty years.

Mr. Lowenbein married, in New York city, Miss Hannah Engle. Of this marriage were born children named as follows: 1. Sarah, who became the wife of D. S. Hess, of New York city. 2. David. 3. Morris. 4. Ernest. 5. Henry. Two of the sons, to be further referred to, are associated in business under the firm name of A. Lowenbein's Sons.

David Lowenbein was born in New York city, August 2, 1854. He received his preliminary education in the city schools, and pursued a collegiate course in European institutions of learning. After completing his education he returned home and entered his father's establishment. On the death of the parent, David Lowenbein, with his brother Morris, organized the firm of A. Lowenbein's Sons, furniture dealers and decorators, and removed to Fourteenth street, where they remained until 1888, subsequently to Twenty-third street, and in 1901 to 383 Fifth avenue, its present location. The house is known as one of the leaders of its class, and enjoys a large patronage of the wealthiest classes. Mr. Lowenbein is prominent in military circles; is captain of Company F, Twenty-second Regiment, New York National Guard; saw service in the Spanish-American war, and is a member of the military order of Veterans of the Spanish war. He is a Republican in his political affiliations. He married, in New York city, Miss Harriet Martens.

Morris Lowenbein, junior member of the firm of A. Lowenbein's Sons, was born in New York city, October 6, 1856. He began his education in the city schools and took collegiate training in Germany. Returning to the United States he joined his brother David in the business which now engages their attention. He is a member of the Freundschaft Club of New York city. He married, April 6, 1880, Miss Helen Axmacher, and they have one living child, Edna.

Ernest Lowenbein was born in New York city, October 23, 1858. He was educated in the New York city public schools, private schools in Germany and Cornell University, graduating from the last named institution in 1879. He then entered the Lowenbein's Sons' establishment, and in 1881 was admitted to partnership with his brothers in the firm He is affiliated with Girard Lodge, No 631, Free and Accepted Masons, in which he is a past master, and is a member of the Delta Beta Phi college fraternity. In 1881 he married, in Tivoli-on-the-Hudson, Miss Catherine Oberbaugh, and they are the parents of a son, Ralph.

CHARLES VAN BUREN.

The gentleman whose name forms the caption for this narrative enjoys the unique distinction of contributing in peculiar degree to the instruction and amusement of tens of thausands of people, native Americans and foreign tourists, through his skill in a peculiar field, that of manufacturer of wax figures, in which he is a master of unsurpassable ability.

He was born in Liverpool, Illinois, February 17, 1866, son of William Levi His father was twice married, his first wife being Martha Kill, who bore him a daughter, Louise M., now the wife of Frank W Wilson, residing in New York. By his second wife, Nancy, Mr. Levi had two children: One who died in infancy, and Charles, the immediate subject of this sketch The father died in October, 1872, the mother surviving him and dying about 1874.

Charles, above named, after the death of his parents, came under the care of his stepfather, Mr. Van Buren, a direct descendant of President Martin Van Buren, and he adopted that family name (Van Buren) as his own. Charles Van Buren had no school advantages, and he carved out his own career. At the age of twenty-one years he enlisted in the United States regular army, in the Fifteenth Regiment Infantry, Colonel E. A. Crofton commanding, and completed a full five years term of service on the western frontier, having made a most honorable military record, also receiving a medal of honor for life saving, and was honorably discharged at Fort Sheridan, near Chicago, Illinois. About 1897 he engaged in the study of waxworks figures in the Eden Musee, Chicago, Illinois, and developed a remarkable artistic and mechanical ability in the conception and execution thereof. In 1901, a master of his art, he located in the city of New York, at 262 Green street, where he has been busily occupied with his profession. A large number of his productions are among the exhibits in the celebrated Eden Musee in New York city, and he numbers among his patrons a large number of the leading department stores and other emporiums of fashion throughout the city and country. He is an enthusiast in his chosen field, and has made for himself a widespread reputation.

PEOPLE'S HOME CHURCH AND SETTLEMENT PARISH.

The excellent work now being conducted under the name of this institution was inaugurated under the auspices of the Federation of Churches and Christian Organizations in New York city, with the purpose of engaging in a movement to redeem the city through a co-operative movement. In planning the work for the Fourteenth Assembly District, four blocks were assigned to the People's Home Church and Settlement Parish—the region just north and northeast of Tompkins Square, five blocks east of Grace (Protestant Episcopal) Church, and near the East river. This work was formulated under the foregoing plan in 1900, but its foundation had been already well laid. In 1892 the Rev. Ernest L. Fox, then engaged in missionary work in the old

Asbury Church (Methodist Episcopal) on Washington Square, was appointed to the permanent charge of the work, and renamed the church "The People's Home Church," and, making his residence in the building, continued upon a larger scale his work of forming clubs, classes, boys' brigades, etc. In time he was enabled to acquire a tenement house adjoining, which was refitted to include an auditorium, gymnasium, with lockers and bath; eleven rooms for the residents, and eight rooms for library, reading room, parlor, kindergarten circles, nursery, clubs and classes. Besides the gymnasium classes, sewing, carpentry, clay modeling, basketry and cooking are taught; and in the literary classes Italians are taught in the English language. Through the Home Makers' Club mothers are trained to make better the home life, and in the Men's Club is maintained a "free forum" for hearing addresses and engaging in discussions upon questions of the day In the summer season provision is made for camp outings for mothers with small children, and for boys upon a colony farm The settlement work is conducted by the Rev. E. L. Fox, headworker and treasurer, who has as assistants: The Rev. A. S. Muirhead, assistant pastor and business manager; the Rev. Joseph Braun, German pastor; Miss J. B Fogg, director of work with boys; and Mrs. G. H. Diehl, chorister. There is also a corps of seventeen dispensary matrons. The People's Home Church is located on East Eleventh street, near Avenue B, Manhattan.

The Rev. Ernest L. Fox, founder and conductor of this beneficent work, is a man in the prime of life, admirably adapted by education and natural disposition for his self-appointed task, and possessing a boundless enthusiasm and undismayable optimism He was born December 31, 1857, in Oneida county, New York. He obtained his elementary education in a country school, subsequently attended a preparatory institution, and entered

Syracuse University, from which he was graduated in 1881. For four years following his graduation he was engaged in missionary work on the western frontier. In 1885 he took up theological studies in the Garrett Biblical Institute at Evanston, and subsequently spent two years in the study of similes and philosophy at Yale University. After leaving Yale he spent two years as pastor of the Methodist Episcopal Church in Waterville, New York, then coming to New York city to engage in the work previously outlined in this narrative He was ordained to the ministry in Nebraska, in 1885.

ST. PETER'S GERMAN EVANGELICAL LUTHERAN CHURCH.

This flourishing parish was organized on May 1, 1862, as a mission of Old St. Matthew's Lutheran church, now corner Broome and Elizabeth streets, and the first services were held in a hall over a feed store on Third avenue near Forty-ninth street. On May 27, 1864, the congregation purchased the property of St. Alban's Episcopal church in Fiftieth street, between Lexington and Third avenues, and in October, 1871, it sold this property to a building contractor, purchasing the Presbyterian church at the southwest corner of Forty-sixth street and Lexington avenue. Here the congregation remained until June 15, 1903. On account of the improvements being made by the New York Central railroad, the old church had to be vacated. Services were then held in the Methodist Episcopal church on Beekman Hill until December 12, 1904, when the basement of the new church building was so far completed that it could be occupied. The cornerstone of this church, which is at Lexington avenue and Fifty-fourth street, New York city, was laid with appropriate ceremonies, November 29, 1903, and the church was dedicated May 14, 1905. The building is of Indiana limestone, is of modified Gothic architecture, sixty by eighty feet, with spacious basement and auditorium. It is heated throughout with steam, and lighted by electricity, making it one of the most modern and imposing of the church edifices in the city. It has a seating capacity of seven hundred; the communicant membership is fourteen hundred; and the average Sunday school attendance is five hundred and fifty. Sunday school classes are held in German in the morning, and in English in the afternoon. There is an afternoon parochial school, which holds sessions four times a week. The church services are conducted in German, with the exception of the evening service on the first Sunday of each month, when the services are held in English. The choir consists of a hired quartette, and a chorus of mixed voices. The organist is Paul Ziegler.

In addition to the church property, the congregation owns the three adjoining buildings on the east—Nos. 130, 132 and 134 East Fifty-fourth street—the second being used for a parsonage, and the last for a parish house. It is the intention of the congregation to erect a new parish house on the site of these two buildings in the near future. They also own the buildings, Nos. 827 and 829 Lexington avenue, adjoining the church building on the south, which they are holding for the future needs of the parish. The value of the church is three hundred thousand dollars. The societies connected with the church are as follows: Ladies' Aid Society, founded in 1862, one hundred and eighteen members; Young Men's Association, incorporated, founded in 1875, two hundred members; Young Ladies' Society, founded in 1898, sixty-three members. Rev. Christian Hennicke, the founder of the congregation and the first pastor, served from May 1, 1862, until July 31, 1871, when ill health compelled him to relinquish his charge and remove to the northwest.

Rev Edward F. Moldenke, Ph D., D D, deceased, the second pastor of St. Peter's, was born in Insterburg, East Prussia, Germany, August 10, 1836. He was educated at the college in Lyk, and also at the universities of Koenigsberg and Halle, Germany. After having served his prescribed time as the principal of a public school in East Prussia from 1858 to 1861, he was sent by the German Mission Board to the United States, especially to Minnesota and Wisconsin, where he became a missionary pastor to the Lutherans of that section of the United States. He labored faithfully and successfully in that field for five years, and after having organized many congregations he founded in 1866 the Lutheran College at Watertown, Wisconsin, now called the Northwestern University. In the same year he returned to Europe and took charge of a large Polish congregation in Johannisburg, East Prussia, where he was obliged to learn the Polish language. He became dissatisfied with German church government and returned to America. He founded the Zion Evangelical Lutheran church, in New York, in 1869, which, in 1871, consolidated with St. Peter's, of which church he was the pastor from August 1, 1871, until his death, June 25, 1904. He was president of the general council of the Lutheran church of North America from 1895 to 1899, was editor of various church papers, and the author of several works on church government. How well he was liked by the congregation and how successful were his labors is attested by the fact that his catechumens have set a large and expensive window to his memory in the new church building, and the congregation has, in addition, erected a memorial bronze tablet.

Rev. Alfred B Moldenke, Ph. D., the third and present pastor was born in the city of New York, December 15, 1871. His early education was acquired in the Columbia grammar school, from which he was graduated in 1887. He entered Columbia University in September of the same year, and was graduated from that institution in June, 1891. He continued his studies until 1893, when he received the degree of Doctor of Philosophy. Later in that year he went to Europe and for three years studied in the universities of Halle and Berlin. Returning to America in 1896, he was ordained and became a member of the Lutheran Ministerium of the state of New York. During this year he was appointed associate pastor of St. Peter's, and upon the death of his father, the Rev. Edward F. Moldenke, he was unanimously elected his successor, July 1, 1904, and has since that time filled the office very acceptably. He is well liked by his congregation, and under his guidance and care the church looks forward to a future full of hope and promise. Dr. Moldenke is a clear and convincing preacher, gives careful thought to all the details of his work, and is very thorough. He is logical and energetic, and possessed of great executive ability. These characteristics, combined with his kindness of heart and charity, make him well fitted for the position he occupies.

REV. FREDERICK BREZINSKI.

Rev. Frederick Brezinski, former assistant pastor of St. John's Evangelical Lutheran church, is the son of Frederick and Catherine Brezinski, and was born in the province of East Prussia, Germany, November 2, 1872. He secured his education in his native land at the public schools, and under his father, who was a teacher there for thirty-six years. He entered the seminary at Brecklum, 1890, graduating in the spring of 1895, after which he came to this country and was ordained to the ministry, September 29, 1895 He had, however, in the month of June, of the same year, entered the ministry as pastor of the German Lutheran church at Turners Falls, Massachusetts. He served that people for six years and in June, 1901, was elected to be assistant pastor of St. John's of this city. His labors began here September 1, 1901, and ended August 31, 1906.

ST. MATTHEW'S EVANGELICAL LUTHERAN CHURCH.

St. Matthew's Evangelical Lutheran church at One Hundred and Fifty-sixth street is the oldest Lutheran church in the Bronx; it was founded in 1862, the congregation worshiping for two years in a hall. In 1864 a small frame building was erected on Courtland avenue, between One Hundred and Fifty-fourth and One Hundred and Fifty-fifth streets, in which services were held until the present church was erected. The first pastor was followed by Rev. Paul Lubkert, and the succeeding pastors were Rev Zenmer, Rev Suddein, Rev. Knortz, Rev. E. A. Behrends. The last named was instrumental in the erection of the church edifice. Succeeding him came Rev. Paul Schneider, who officiated one year and was followed by the present pastor, Rev. William T Junge. The present officers of this church are as follows: George Scholl, secretary; Adam Moell, financial secretary; John M. Weiss, treasurer; A. Schulte, president; A. L. Lee, organist; George Scholl, assistant Sunday school superintendent St. Matthew's has a seating capacity of about eight hundred. It is an imposing brick building with free-stone trimmings and its interior is handsomely decorated. The societies of this church are: St. Matthew's Ladies' Mutual Aid Society, Tabca Society for young ladies, Matthew's Young Men's Society, Confirmation League, Sunday School and Teachers' societies.

Rev. William T Junge was born in the northern part of Germany, May 29, 1872, and is the son of William and Catherine Junge. His early education was received in the land of his nativity, and when thirteen years of age he came to America and soon entered the Wagner College of Rochester, New York, where, after pursuing a course preparatory to entering upon his theological course, he graduated in 1892. He then entered the Theological Seminary of Philadelphia, where he took a three years' course in theology, graduating with honors, with the class of 1895. His ordination to the ministry took place June, 1895, at St. Peter's Evangelical Lutheran church, Brooklyn, and immediately afterwards he was appointed pastor of the Lutheran church at Kendall, New York, where he labored faithfully and efficiently for three and one-half years and was then appointed to the pastorate of the church at Newburg, New York, remaining for one year, and in 1899 was made pastor of St. Matthew's, his present charge.

EVANGELICAL LUTHERAN CHURCH OF OUR SAVIOUR.

The Evangelical Lutheran Church of Our Saviour, which is located at One Hundred and Seventy-ninth street and Audubon avenue, New York city, has for its present pastor Rev. William H. Feldmann, born in the city of New York

His early education was acquired in the public schools of his native city and he pursued his classical studies in Gettysburg College, from which he was graduated with honor in 1895. He studied theology in Gettysburg Seminary, and spent one year at the universities of Erlangen and Leipzig, being graduated in 1898. Upon his return to the United States he was ordained to the ministry at Asbury Park, New Jersey, September 28, 1898, and shortly afterward assumed his duties as pastor of his present parish. He is an earnest, zealous worker, of an unselfish, self-sacrificing disposition, and has the best interests of his congregation at heart. His sermons are eloquent and forceful and he has made many converts

Rev. William H Feldmann, pastor of the above mentioned church, was born in the city of New York.

ST. STEPHEN'S EVANGELICAL LUTHERAN CHURCH.

St. Stephen's Evangelical Lutheran church at Union avenue is a thriving religious community, which was founded in 1902 by the present pastor. The church edifice is a frame building of a cheerful and inviting exterior, and the interior is no less inviting and homelike. It has a seating capacity of about four hundred, and a membership roll of three hundred. The Sunday school which is connected with this church was commenced with seven children, and has now (1906) an average attendance of over three hundred. The church also conducts a day school and a kindergarten, which are exceedingly popular. The instruction is in both the English and the German languages. The church music is rendered by a mixed choir and a chorus of male voices. The services are entirely in German, as the congregation consists entirely of Germans or those of German descent. This church is a branch of St. Matthew's, and the parish has been brought to its present flourishing condition by the pastor, Rev. Paul Roesener. There are a number of societies connected with the church, which do their utmost to further its interests. The societies are: Ladies' Association, Young Ladies' Association, Young Men's Association, and Sunday School Teachers' Association.

Rev. Paul Roesener was born in Brandenburg, Germany. He received his early education in Erfurt and Breslau, making a specialty of philosophy and theology. He emigrated to America in 1875, and completed his theological education in Concordia Seminary, St Louis, Missouri. He was ordained at Little Rock, Arkansas, and his first pastorate was at Spring Creek, Harris county, Texas, where he officiated for three years He was then stationed in New Orleans for nine years, leaving there to accept a call to Altenburg, Missouri, where he ministered for twelve years, and during that time he was president of the western district of the Evangelical Lutheran synod of Missouri, Ohio and other states. While there he received the call to St. Stephen's church, which he accepted, and under his ministration it is growing in size and prosperity. He is a man who is thoroughly in earnest, and is so imbued with the true spirit of his work that he must of necessity leave his impress on all that he undertakes. He is greatly respected and loved by those under his guidance, and his counsel is sought in worldly troubles as well as spiritual ones.

GUSTAVUS ADOLPHUS SWEDISH LUTHERAN CHURCH.

Gustavus Adolphus Swedish Lutheran church is located on Twenty-second street, near Third avenue This parish was organized in September, 1865, by Rev. A. Andreen. Services were held in St. James' Evangelical Lutheran church on Sixteenth street Subsequently they purchased land and built a church on the site of the present edifice. The cornerstone of the new building was laid, and the house was dedicated the same year by Rev. Dr. Hussenquist. During the construction of the new church the congregation worshiped again in St. James. The value of the church and parsonage is placed at $127,000. It is built of stone and has a seating capacity of eight hundred and fifty. The number of members is twelve hundred; number of souls in the parish fifteen hundred. The two Sunday schools have an average attendance of three hundred. The societies connected with this congregation are: Two Sewing Societies, Young People's Society, Sick and Benefit Society, Aid Society Once each month a service is held in English, but all others are in German, three being held each week. The mixed choir furnishes excellent music The pastor has placed a new organ in the church, and organized a mission at Harlem, services being held at No. 168 East One Hundred and Forty-first street. The parish is now in a very flourishing condition. The first regular pastor of this parish was Rev. Axel Waetter, who remained three years, and was succeeded by Rev. J. Prihcell, who after a few years was succeeded by Rev. C. E. Lindberg, now the professor of theology in the seminary at Rock Island, Illinois He ministered to this church for eleven years, and in 1890 was succeeded by the present pastor, Rev. Mauritz Stolpe

Rev. Stolpe was born in Stockholm, Sweden, June 15, 1858, and there obtained his primary education. In 1879 he came to America, and the following year was ordained at Lawrence, Kansas, and appointed to preach at Marquette, that state. He remained there until 1885, which year he went to Ishpeming, Michigan, where he was pastor five years, and came to New York in 1890. He received the degrees of A. B. and A. M. from Bethany College, and that of Doctor of Divinity from Augustina College and Theological Seminary. In 1901 they conferred upon him the order of Wasa This church has been brought into much prominence by numerous celebrities. Madam Christine Neilson presented the church with one thousand dollars; the late Captain John Erickson, the famous inventor, was one of its trustees; in 1893 Right Rev. Bishop H. Gezvon Scheele, on a visit to America to the Lutheran churches, was a guest of this church while here, he being the first Lutheran bishop to visit the city. He also visited this country again in 1901, on a mission to President Roosevelt, when he was once more the guest of this church. In the autumn of 1905 this church celebrated its fortieth anniversary. The present officers of the church are: Trustees—M. E. Halbertson, chairman; C. A. Peterson, treasurer; P. S. Lundin, secretary. The deacons are—John Ohlin, S. Anderson, S. Ulberg, T. Johnson, A. Valentine, L. Matson, O. J. Olson, L. Brodie. The present deaconess is Ingred Anderson; organist, Professor J Rudvall; sexton, Nels Linborg.

SWEDISH EVANGELICAL LUTHERAN BETHLEHEM CHURCH, BROOKLYN

Swedish Evangelical Lutheran Bethlehem Church of Brooklyn, New York, was organized in 1874, by Rev. P. J. Sward, pastor, who held services in private houses on Hudson avenue, then in Olive Chapel, Bergen street, in the German Lutheran church on Schermerhorn street, also in a hall on the corner of Boerum place and Pacific street. In 1882 a small chapel was bought from the Second Presbyterian church, which served until December 15, 1895, when the church was dedicated. It has a seating capacity of fifteen hundred. It is a brick building, trimmed in stone; also has a chapel in basement seating seven hundred. There were, on January 1, 1907, one thousand and sixty-four communicants, with a total membership of one thousand five hundred and forty. The Sunday school is very large and prosperous. The Swedish department has an average membership of five hundred and fifty, the English two hundred and fifty-five. The Ladies' Sewing Society has a membership of seventy-five, Ladies' Missionary Society of fifty, the Lutheran League one hundred and fifty, Young Ladies' Society seventy, and the Aid Society one hundred and twenty-five. Young Women's Home, 202 Dean street, Brooklyn, opened May 1, 1906, gives a temporary home to young Scandinavian women who are without friends and employment who need rest and who desire employment in good homes.

Rev. Jacobson is a native of Sweden, born in Yllestad, March 17, 1863. He came to this country in 1869 with his parents, locating in Rockford, Illinois. He obtained his primary education in that city, and then took a classical and theological course in the Augustana College at Rock Island, Illinois, entering in 1878; he completed his classical and scientific course in 1885, receiving his degree of Bachelor of Arts and Bachelor of Science. He then spent one year at Wheaton College, Wheaton, Illinois, preparatory for the university work at Yale, which he entered in the autumn of 1886, pursuing studies which led to the degree of Doctor of Philosophy, which was awarded him June 26, 1889. His first pastorate was the Swedish Lutheran (Bethesda) church of New Haven, Connecticut; he also during that time held the position of lecturer on the history of philosophy in Yale graduate department. After two years thus busily engaged he came to Brooklyn, October, 1892.

The former pastors of the church have been: Rev. Dr. P. J. Sward, succeeded by Rev. E. A. Fogelstrom, and he by Rev. Albert Rodell. Assistant pastors: Rev. C. M. Esbjorn and C. M. Englund The organist, Professor A. W. Anderson, is a graduate of Boston Conservatory of Music, and the private graduate student of Mr. Felix Fox, Boston, Massachusetts.

HELLENIC ORTHODOX CHURCH OF THE HOLY TRINITY.

This parish was first organized in 1893, in a church building in West Fifty-third street, by Theodore and Antony Ralli (the latter now deceased), and services were held in this building until 1898, when the congregation removed to a church which they had rented on East Twenty-seventh street, and this was used as a place of worship until May 2, 1904, when the present church property at Nos. 151 and 153 East Seventy-second street was purchased for the sum of sixty-five thousand dollars. This was bought from Frederick N. Gilbert, and was originally used for a Protestant church. The parishioners of Holy Trinity have expended about twenty-five thousand dollars in remodeling it to present an appearance like the Acropolis at Athens, Greece. When completed it will be one of the finest church edifices in the city of New York. The altars are entirely of marble, imported especially from the Penteli mountains of Greece; all the work is in the hands of Greek artisans, the carving of the interior being done on the premises; this is said to be of a most imposing character, nothing of a similar kind existing in the United States. It has a seating capacity of about three thousand people, and is the only Greek Orthodox church in the city

The first rector was Rev. Paysios Ferentinos, who was followed in succession by Rev. Kalinikos Dervey; Rev. Agatheodoro Papageorgopulo; Rev. Rafael Joannides; Rev. Zissinos Typaldos. The last named was succeeded by Rev. Methodios Kourkoulis, who took charge of the parish November 1, 1904, and under his able ministration its membership is increasing and it is in a flourishing condition.

Rev. Methodios Kourkoulis was born in Metilin, Turkey, Asia Minor, October, 1864, and studied theology in Athens and in Germany. He was ordained priest at Lesbos in 1892, and for twelve years was engaged in missionary work in Asia Minor, Egypt, the Soudan, Smyrna, and the Holy Land. He was sent to America in 1904 to take charge of the spiritual welfare of the Orthodox Greeks in the city of New York. This work he has taken up with heart and soul, and is deservedly looked up to and his opinions regarded by his parishioners.

HENRY ELSWORTH MURGATROYD.

Henry E. Murgatroyd, a civil engineer and city surveyor, was born in New York city, September 19, 1859, son of William James and Esther (Middleton) Murgatroyd. He was educated in the public schools and completed a course in the University

Abram Delano Child

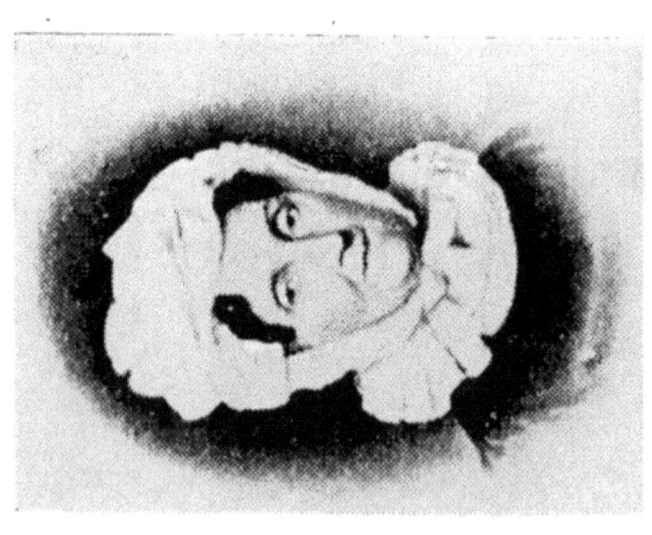

Fannie Aymar (Moffitt) Child

of New York city, graduating in 1886 with the degree of Bachelor of Arts and Civil Engineer. After his graduation he worked with the Dutch, South Shore and Atlantic Railroad Company; also in Michigan. Since 1888 he has been engaged in business for himself He has come to be known as an expert in his profession, and is a highly esteemed citizen. Mr. Murgatroyd is one of the deacons in the Ascension Baptist church and has served several years as Sunday school superintendent.

June 2, 1892, he was united in marriage to Sameletta L. Richards, daughter of Joseph and Nancy L. Richards. Two children have been the fruit of this union: Ruth and Elsworth.

DAYTON FAMILY.

This ancient family, the members of which, on both sides of the sea, have rendered distinguished service to the state, both as citizens and soldiers, numbered among its representatives Charles Willoughby Dayton, of New York, who has for many years borne a conspicuous part at the bar and in the political history of the city and state of New York.

The original home of the Daytons was the village of Deighton, in the parish of Deighton, in the east riding of Yorkshire, England, about four and a half miles southeast from the city of York. The name of the family, apparently derived from the place where they lived, was spelled in various ways, as Deighton, Dyghton or Deyson, but before they came to America had become stereotyped in its present form of Dayton.

(I) Robert de Deighton, with whom the authentic family record commences, was admitted as freeman in 1305. He was a yeoman, a title given to "gentlemen of small estate," and had four sons: Robert, of whom later; William, Nicholas and John.

(II) Robert de Deighton, eldest son of Robert de Deighton

(I), is known to have been a freeman in 1329. His sons were: John, of whom later; Walter, Golfudis and William

(III) John de Deighton, son of Robert de Deighton (2), was a freeman in 1349, and held the office of "collector of tolls or taxes." He had two sons: William, and Robert, of whom later.

(IV) Robert de Deighton, son of John de Deighton (3), was a freeman in 1372. He was the father of two sons: Willard, and John, of whom later.

(V) John de Deighton, son of Robert de Deighton (4), was a freeman in 1389 He held the honorable position of "Marshal," defined as "an officer standing highest in arms," "an officer who regulates combats in the lists," and "an officer who regulates ranks and order at a feast." He married Isabel, daughter of John de Duffield, a silk merchant of York, and his sons were: Golen, William, of whom later, and John.

(VI) William de Deighton, son of John de Deighton (5), was a freeman in 1419, and Drake's History of York shows that he was a man of wealth. His wife was Joan, daughter of Robert de Morton, a merchant. He died September 14, 1456, and was buried beside his wife, on the south side of York minster. He had one son, William de Deighton.

(VII) William de Deighton was the father of a son, John de Deighton.

(VIII) John de Deighton was the father of a son, Henry de Deighton.

(IX) Henry de Deighton, son of John de Deighton (8), was a freeman in 1504, and in 1522 was made city chamberlain of York In 1524 he became sheriff, served as alderman from 1525 to 1531, and in the latter year was made lord mayor of York. His second wife was Alice, widow of Robert Petty. He died in

September, 1540, and in his will directed that "he should be buried in All Saints, on North State Street."

(X) Robert Deighton, son of Henry de Deighton (9), was the first of the line to drop the *de*, which shows the race to be of Norman origin He was born in 1525, and was freeman in 1557 In 1550 he married Elizabeth, daughter of John Copeley and Margaret, his wife, daughter of Sir John S. Stapleton, of Wighill, York. Their son was William, of whom later.

(XI) William Deighton, son of Robert (10) and Elizabeth (Copeleyand) Deighton, was born in 1551, and was the first to leave the family seat, going to London, where he lived at St. Martin's-in-the-Fields. He married, August 9, 1584, Agnes, daughter of Ralph Green, and his sons were: William, Thomas, Ralph, of whom later; and Nicholas.

(XII) Ralph Dayton(as the name was then spelled), son of William (11) and Agnes (Green) Deighton, was born in 1598, at St. Martin's-in-the-Fields, London. In 1629 he married Agnes, daughter of Henry Pool. In 1636 he emigrated to Boston, thus becoming the founder of the American branch of the family. With him came his brothers, Thomas and Nicholas, and his two sons, Samuel and Robert. In 1639 he removed to New Haven, being one of the original settlers, and about 1648 he and his sons settled in Southampton, Long Island, the oldest English town in the state of New York. Ralph Dayton was among the company of Southampton men who settled the town of East Hampton, and on March 7, 1650, "it is ordered that Ralph Dayton is to go to Keniticutt, for to procure the evidence of our lands and for a boddie of our laws."

On December 1, 1657, we find "An Action of Trespass upon the Case, by Ralph Dayton, against John Cooper, defendant." The case was decided in favor of John Cooper, and "Samuel

Dayton, of ye North Sea, and Robert Dayton, of East Hampton," give bonds to prosecute the appeal to the court at Hartford.

Ralph Dayton, on coming to America, was a widower, and about 1649 he married Dorothy Brewster, by whom he had a son, Brewster Dayton. He was married for a third time to Mary, widow of James Haynes. His death is thus noticed:

"Sept. 22, 1650. At a Quarter Court the will of the deceased Ralph Dayton was brought into the Court, and approved of by ye Magistrates, and ye ten pounds that Robert Dayton owed to his father hee hath put into the estate."

This gives the approximate time of the death of founder of the Dayton family in America.

Of his two sons, Samuel and Robert, the latter belonged to the line now under consideration. Concerning Samuel the following details are recorded:

In 1653 Samuel Dayton was the owner of a lot in the "Saggaponack Division," and in 1654 he drew a lot in the Seaponack Division. In March, 1653, he was one of the members of a whaling squadron, and in September, 1653, he was engaged in a controversy with Thomas Vayle On June 20, 1657, he purchased from Edward Joanes (Johns) "three acres of land that was formerly Mr. Stanborough, with a house upon it," and on December 12, 1656, "John Howell hath bought of Medlin (Madeline) Dayton, ye wife of Samuel Dayton with his consent, 4 acres of ground in ye great plains, being next to ye four acres commonly called by the name of Harcres lot."

He was one of the nine men who, with their families, settled North Sea, a village about four miles north of the village of Southampton, and situated on Peconic bay, which in the earliest times was called "the North Sea" to distinguish it from the Atlantic ocean or "the South Sea."

(XIII) Robert Dayton, son of Ralph (12) and Agnes (Pool)

Cornelia Laura (Adams) Tomlinson

Charles Willoughby Dayton

Dayton, was born in England in 1630, and was a resident of East Hampton. In 1652 he married Elizabeth, daughter of John Woodruff, of Southampton, the ancestor of many families of the name in New Jersey and elsewhere. Robert Dayton died in East Hampton, October 16, 1712, aged eighty-four.

(XIV) Samuel Dayton, son of Robert (13) and Elizabeth (Woodruff) Dayton, was born in 1653, and was an extensive owner of real estate in Long Island and Connecticut. His wife was Wilhelmina and they were the parents of five sons, the youngest, Isaac, of whom later. Some of these remained in East Hampton, while others settled in the town of Brookhaven.

(XV) Isaac Dayton, son of Samuel (14) and Wilhelmina Dayton, was born in 1698, and leaving Long Island settled in Connecticut. He married Sarah, daughter of Daniel Brewster, of Brookhaven, Long Island, and granddaughter of the Rev. Nathaniel Brewster, of honored memory.

(XVI) Brewster Dayton, son of Isaac (15) and Sarah (Brewster) Dayton, was born on Long Island, at the home of his maternal grandfather, where much of his boyhood was passed In 1755 he removed to Connecticut and settled at Stratford, where he married Ruth Judson, in 1777. In the war of the Revolution he took an active and honorable part, serving in 1778 as a member of the coast guard and a private in the company of Captain Yates, in the regiment commanded by Colonel Enos, which was stationed on the Hudson river. His wife having died, he returned home at the expiration of his term of enlistment, and on December 25 married Elizabeth Willoughby, of England. By this marriage he became the father of two children: Elizabeth (or Pollie); and Charles Willoughby, of whom later. The third wife of Brewster Dayton was Pollie Gary.

(XVII) Charles Willoughby Dayton, son of Brewster (16)

and Elizabeth (Willoughby) Dayton, was born in 1795, in Stratford. His mother died at the time of his birth. The boy was brought up in the household of the Rev. Nathan Birdsey, and was given an opportunity for a college education, but when prepared to enter Yale he expressed a preference for a business career, whereupon he was supplied with money to establish himself as an importer of woolens in New York His business ability enabled him to amass a handsome competence, and his residence in New York was in Washington square, one of the most exclusive sections of the city There he entertained President Van Buren, Captain Maryatt, the famous novelist, and many other distinguished personages. In social life he held a high position. His horses and equipages were a feature in the world of fashion, and his appearance on horseback, often accompanied by his son Abram, attracted much admiration. Much of his time was spent in England. He is described as "unusually handsome, had a perfect English complexion, dark blue eyes, brown curly hair, a beautiful mouth and perfect teeth." He had literary talent, and verses written by him show poetic fire and spirit.

Mr. Dayton married, at the age of nineteen, in New York city, Jane Raveau, daughter of Abram and Frances (Moffitt) Child, the Childs being one of the well-known families of the metropolis. Mrs. Dayton died in the early years of their marriage, and her husband remained a widower. He died suddenly, January 30, 1861, leaving a pleasant and honorable memory, cherished by many friends.

(XVIII) Abram Child Dayton, son of Charles Willoughby (17) and Jane Raveau (Child) Dayton, was born March 2, 1818, in Dey street, New York, baptized in the Middle Dutch church on Nassau street, and at the age of seven sent to a school kept by Monsieur Coudert, one of Napoleon's officers. This school was situated near the Tombs building, and among his school-

Maria Annis (Tomlinson) Dayton

mates was the late Rev. Robert Howland, of the Church of the Heavenly Rest, and a boy nicknamed "Teuton," afterward the Confederate General Beauregard. A few years later he was sent to school in Dresden, Germany, and he afterward went to Berlin, but before leaving presented to the Museum at Dresden a complete set of American coins. He was well versed in the ancient and modern languages.

Having in his early days enjoyed all the advantages of wealth, adversity found him unprepared, but not unwilling to meet the struggle for existence. For several years he was engaged in literary work, and was for some time editor of "Porter's Spirit of the Times." Subsequently he became a member of the New York stock exchange. His best work was his book, "The Last Day of Knickerbocker Life in New York." This was published in 1896 by G. P. Putnam's Sons, and is a vivid, truthful and charming portraiture of a period of the city's life—from 1837 to 1876—which will always have historical and literary value. A monument worthy the man.

Mr. Dayton married, shortly after his return to the United States, Maria A., daughter of David Tomlinson, M. D., and Cornelia L. Adams, and their children were: Charles Willoughby, of whom later; William Adams, M D ; Harold Child, in railway supply business; and Laura Canfield Spencer, wife of Benjamin A. Fessenden Mr. Dayton "was one of the last gentlemen of the old school," and died August 3, 1877.

(XIX) Charles Willoughby Dayton, son of Abram Child (18) and Maria A. (Tomlinson) Dayton, was born October 3, 1846, in the present borough of Brooklyn, New York city, and shortly thereafter his parents removed to the present borough of Manhattan, where he was educated in the public schools and in 1861 entered the College of the City of New York Owing to the necessity of earning his living before completing his college course, he entered a law office and Columbia Law School, graduating in 1868, and at once commenced the practice of his profession He organized and was counsel for the Twelfth Ward Bank and the Empire City Savings Bank, and was director of the Seventh National Bank, the United States Life Insurance Company and the Fort Lee Ferry Company. He was a trustee of the Harlem Library, the Church of the Puritans, and one of the incorporators of the Post-Graduate Medical School.

Throughout his life, from early manhood, he has been active in politics, holding a high position in the councils of the Democratic party. In 1864 he supported the candidacy of General George B. McClellan for the presidency, and has been a consistent party man since that time. In 1881 he was elected to the legislature, serving on the judiciary committee, and has been identified with measures for municipal reform. He has served as delegate to several state Democratic conventions, and in 1884 was presidential elector and a secretary of the college, which cast the vote of New York state for Cleveland and Hendricks In 1888 he made a speech at Burlington, Iowa, which was printed and circulated by the National Democratic committee in the campaign of that year In 1892 he was president of the board for improvement of Park avenue, and in 1893 was delegate to the constitutional convention of the state of New York. On June 3, 1893, he was, without application or solicitation on his part, appointed by President Cleveland postmaster at New York city, the first Democrat to hold that office since John A Mix, in 1860 The "Springfield (Massachusetts) Republican," an opposition paper, said: "President Cleveland seems to have made a hit in his appointment of Charles W. Dayton as postmaster." Indeed, the entire press of the city of New York and the country was unanimous in its approval of

Laura Augusta (Newman) Dayton

Mr. Dayton's selection, and the senate confirmed it promptly and unanimously In 1894 he visited London and Paris to study the postal system in those cities. He introduced many improvements at the New York office, and upon his resignation, in 1897, was honored with a banquet given by fifteen hundred letter carriers, also receiving from President Cleveland the following letter:

"Westland, Princeton, New Jersey.
"May 24, 1897.
"Hon. Charles W. Dayton.
"My Dear Sir:—
"In reply to your letter written upon your retirement from the Postmastership of the City of New York, and expressing your appreciation of the honor conferred by your appointment, I beg to assure you that the faithful and efficient service you have rendered the Government and your fellow citizens during your term of office, entitles you to an acknowledgment of my personal obligation for the credit thus reflected upon the appointing power.

"Hoping that prosperity and contentment await you in all your future undertakings, I am,
"Very truly yours,
"GROVER CLEVELAND."

In the Postmaster's reception room there has been placed a bronze bust of Mr Dayton, paid for by the postal employes in subscriptions not exceeding fifty cents each. Below the bust is the following inscription:

CHARLES WILLOUGHBY DAYTON,
Postmaster
At New York, N Y.
Appointed by President Cleveland
June 3, 1893,
Erected February 1897
By the Employes of the New York
Post Office, who desire to perpetuate Mr Dayton's record for
Efficiency, Discipline, Justice
Courtesy and Kindness.

At the city convention of October 1, 1897, Mr. Dayton's name for mayor of Greater New York swept the delegation. The press of the day fully described the remarkable demonstration. Mr. Dayton was not acceptable to the "machine," and the preference of the convention was stifled by the nomination of Robert A. Van Wyck. This led to the nomination of Henry George for mayor by the "Jefferson Democracy." Mr. Dayton was urged by Mr. George and others to accept the nomination for comptroller as a protest against "boss rule," without endorsing the philosophical doctrines of Mr. George Mr. Dayton consented, and with Mr. George made a whirlwind campaign in which he supported the Democratic state ticket. The effort proved too great for Mr George, who was prostrated and died one week before the election. Mr. Dayton insisted upon keeping up the fight, though it had become hopeless of success. Henry George, Jr., was substituted in his father's place. Probably in no similar circumstances did such a significant result follow. Mr. George, Jr , polled about twenty-five thousand votes, while Mr. Dayton polled about forty thousand.

In 1901 Mr. Dayton was nominated for justice of the supreme court. The entire ticket was defeated by reason of attacks upon Robert A. Van Wyck and others upon it, although Mr. Dayton ran well ahead of his fellow candidates for that office, and the small difference of about three thousand votes would have elected him. In 1904 he was a delegate to the National Democratic convention at St. Louis.

In all these varied and responsible positions Mr. Dayton has commanded the respect and esteem, not only of his own party, but also of his political opponents and the public. Notwithstanding Mr. Dayton's political activity, he steadily maintained his professional career, as the records and reports of

C. C. Alexander Mr. F. Alexander

the courts will show, and in 1906 was again a candidate and was elected justice of the supreme court, his vote leading that of seven other candidates who were elected with him on that judicial ticket.

He is a member of the American Society of International Law, the New York City and State Bar Association, and was one of the vice-presidents of the New York State Bar Association. He belongs to the New England Society, the New York Historical Society, the Sons of the Revolution and the Masonic Order. He is connected with the National Democratic Club, the Harlem Democratic (which he organized), Players', and is one of the governors of the Manhattan Club.

Mr. Dayton married, in 1874, Laura A., only daughter of the late John B Newman, M. D , and Rebecca Sanford. They have three children: Charles Willoughby, John Newman and Laura Adams Mr Dayton resides at No. 13 Mount Morris Park West, having a farm at Jefferson Heights, West Somers, Westchester county, New York.

THE FAMILY OF ALEXANDER.

The Greek title of Alexander, the "Helper of Men," has long since become a family name, with many branches and very numerous representatives.

Among the families of that name in this country are the descendants of John Alexander, who was born in Scotland about 1700, and settled in Pennsylvania with his three sons, Hugh, James and John. The various branches of this family are the most numerous of the name in America The race in Scotland are very closely connected with the earls of Stirling Among them may be mentioned William Alexander, who made an unsuccessful effort to establish his legal title to the earlship, but who distinguished himself in a far greater manner as one of the bravest generals in the war of the Revolution.

From Hugh Alexander, mentioned above, was descended Captain Charles Alexander, one of the earliest officers in the American navy. At the very beginning of the Revolution the marine committee in the city of Baltimore in the month of November, 1775, equipped and sent from Baltimore two vessels—the sloop "Hornet" of ten guns and the schooner "Wasp" of eight guns—the latter boat commanded by Captain Charles Alexander. These two boats were ordered to join the fleet that was being assembled in the Delaware river under the command of Esic Hopkins They were the first vessels that ever put out to sea as regular cruisers under the new government.

The united fleet of Hopkins, in February, 1776, reached Abaco in the Bahamas and from there a descent was made on New Providence; the "Wasp" was prominent in the attack and the place was taken with large stores of powder and war material In this fleet was John Paul Jones as first lieutenant. The captured war material, including more than one hundred cannon, was used by Washington in his battles near Trenton. On the 9th of May the "Wasp," while cruising under command of Captain Charles Alexander, captured the enemy's bark "Betsey," a very valuable vessel, and it was a hotly contested fight On October 10, 1776, congress, by resolution, declared that the number of captains in the navy should be twenty-four, and Captain Charles Alexander was No 10 and John Paul Jones No. 18 in that list. On July 4, 1776, the English had formally in commission one hundred and twelve vessels of war, mounting three thousand seven hundred and fourteen guns, and of this force seventy-eight men of war, mounting two thousand and seventy-eight guns, were stationed on the American coast The Americans on the same date had twenty-five cruisers, mounting four hundred and twenty-two guns, but only six of these vessels were built for war purposes. After Fort Mifflin fell into the hands of the British the "Wasp," Captain Alexander, had a well contested struggle in company with other boats, with the British frigate "Roebuck," of forty-four guns, and the "Liverpool," of twenty guns; this was about May 1st. This encounter resulted in driving the enemy from the river During this affair the "Wasp," Captain Alexander, was active and conspicuous in cutting out a tender of the English ships from under their guns.

Captain Charles Alexander, whose exploits have been narrated, was the father of William Joseph Alexander, who was a merchant in New York, his place of business being where the "World Building" now stands on Park Row He had a son, William Alexander, born in 1802. He married Lucinda, daughter of Joseph Sarles, of an old New York family, and they were the parents of Charles C. and William J Alexander, who are the present representatives of the family. Their father, after a useful life, died in 1862. He had several brothers and sisters, but they separated and went to distant portions of the country and cannot now be traced

The two sons, Charles C. and William J Alexander, were born at their father's residence, No 551 Broome street, New York. At a later date he removed to No. 16 Watts street, where he made his home during the remainder of his life. The boys first attended a "dames school," kept by a French lady named Chadeauine, in Varick street, and here they learned "the seeds of learning, A, B, C." They next attended a private school kept by a man named Lawson, who was a Scotchman, "a short, bald-headed, lame man." His school was in the basement of the Scotch Presbyterian church on the corner of Grand and Mercer streets. Among the pupils was a boy named Clarke, afterwards a famous actor, as was his father before him. Others, John and David Duncan, who in later years were the proprietors of a fine grocery at Fourteenth street and Union Square. Also three sons of Joshua Brown, the largest dealer in wall paper of his time. His house in Canal street, near Broadway, cost him $12,000, and was afterwards sold for $50,000 to the American Express Company. With these were the sons of William Hicks, a jeweler in Maiden Lane, who made silver pencils After leaving school the two sons of William Alexander learned the trade of iron manufacturing with their father, and were instructed in all the details of the business, at No. 98 Grand street. At that time almost everything was done by hand, and they made all the various kinds of iron work that was then used in buildings. The business was extensive and gave employment to a large number of men The establishment to which they succeeded was originally carried on by Mr Paulus Hedl, a monument of whose skill may be seen in the iron stairs and railing in the City Hall The material made by the Alexanders entered a great many buildings in the lower part of the city. At that time there was but few other establishments of the kind. When Mr. William Alexander learned his trade there were with him as fellow apprentices J. B. and W. W. Cornell, George R. Jackson and Michael Gross, all of whom have made large fortunes from establishments of their own The two sons still continue the business, are extensively known, and hold an honorable position among the iron manufacturing interests of the city. But the day of hand labor has passed away, and steel frames, beams and girders are made by processes then utterly unknown

William Joseph Alexander, eldest son of William and Lucinda (Sarles) Alexander, was born at the family home, No 551 Broome street, New York, July 5, 1841. His education was acquired in the schools of his native city, and later he entered the employ of his father as an apprentice, and in due course of time became proficient in the iron working business. Upon the death of his father he entered into partnership with his brother, Charles C. Alexander, and together they have successfully continued this business for forty-four years. The business is one of the oldest in the city of New York, it having been established by his father, William Alexander, in 1836. William J. Alexander is a highly respected citizen, and the firm, of which he is the senior member, is well and favorably known for their strict integrity in all business matters. He has served as a school commissioner, discharging his duties creditably and efficiently He is a member of Bethel Lodge, No. 733, Free and Accepted Masons, and Zerubable Chapter, No. 157, Royal Arch Masons.

Mr Alexander was married in New York, July 24, 1881, to Hattie A. Connor, and to them have been born four children: William C., Grace Vera, Milton Joseph and Larine B. In religious views the family affiliates with the First Methodist Episcopal Church, Hasbrouck Heights, New Jersey, Mr. Alexander being one of its trustees.

Charles Curtis Alexander, second son of William and Lucinda (Sarles) Alexander, was born at the family home, No. 551 Broome street, New York, December 25, 1842. After completing his education in the schools of New York he engaged in the iron working business with his father, becoming thoroughly proficient therein, and continued in his father's employ up to the time of his death, when, in connection with his brother William J., they assumed control of the business and are still conducting it successfully. Mr. Alexander is a popular and progressive citizen, aiding to the best of his ability all measures which tend to better humanity. He has been connected with the General Society of Mechanics and Tradesmen for eighteen years, and is chairman of the purchasing committee for that library.

Mr. Alexander was married at No. 215 Thompson street, New York, September 8, 1870, to Mary Louise Bloodgood, daughter of Freeman and Matilda W. (Raynor) Bloodgood, and their children are as follows: Florence M., Marion B., died in childhood; Helen G., Louise B., Alice, deceased; and Dorothy, deceased.

It remains to add a brief notice of the maternal ancestry of the Messrs Alexander. Mr. Kearney, the great-grandfather, was a member of an ancient family living in Bedford, Westchester county. He was an officer in the American army under Washington during the Revolutionary war. While George Washington was president of the United States, on October 15, 1789, he left New York city, accompanied by his two secretaries and six servants, and visited the New England states, journeying on horseback and in coach, both he and his companions having very beautiful horses. During the progress of this journey he stayed over night at the home of Mrs Haviland, who kept an inn at Rye, and after the evening meal he took Eleanor Kearney, grandmother of the Alexander brothers, then only four years of age, on his knee and talked to her, saying, among other things, that she would be able to tell her children that she sat on the knee of General George Washington. The following morning, as he was preparing to continue his journey, his silver garter buckle came off and was sewn on by the mother of Eleanor Kearney. After the war Mr. Kearney engaged in farming in Rye, and the products of his farm were taken by him to New York, the market most frequented being the Old Bull's Head, situated at what is now Third avenue and Twenty-sixth street. The road was a very dangerous one, as during the entire Revolutionary war it was the debatable land separating the English army in the city and the Patriot army which was in Westchester county The main road crossed the Harlem river where the present Farmers' Bridge is, and the bridge was called by that name long before the Revolutionary war. There was a dense wood on the top of quite a hill on the Westchester side of the bridge approach, and it was near this spot that Mr. Kearney was last seen alive. He had sold his farm products in the city and was returning alone through the wooded place, when he was spoken to by a neighbor who was going in the opposite direction. Never was anything further learned about him. A neighboring farmer on his return journey through the same piece of woods was fired upon by some one in ambush and the bullet went through the man's hat, but by whipping up his horses into a gallop, he succeeded in escaping

Mrs. Kearney was a very pious woman and constantly prayed the Lord to reveal to her what had become of her husband. Quite a long time afterward she had a dream that seemed to her to be more than a dream, and in this dream she saw her husband lying dead in the bottom of a farm wagon, with a great gash across his throat. This dream was considered by Mrs. Kearney as a direct answer to her prayer.

Eleanor Kearney, daughter of Mr Kearney, was born in Cherry street, old Bedford village, August 23, 1785 In her seventeenth year (1802) she married Joseph Sarles (or Searles, as the name is sometimes spelled, and is presumably the correct form). They were the parents of Lucinda and Chlorinda Sarles (twins), born in 1813. They were born in the old house just north of what is now Katonah, and in the graveyard attached to the old Quaker meeting house, but a short distance away, Mr. Sarles was buried All that land is now under the surface of the Croton Reservoir caused by the building of the Cornell dams.

Lucinda Sarles came to New York and lived in Canal street,

nearly opposite Wooster street, and the house is standing there at the present time, and here on the 2nd of August, 1840, she was married to William Alexander.

THE FAMILY OF PHILLIPS, AND THE HEBREW COLONY.

The earliest arrivals of any of the Hebrew race in New Amsterdam were Jacob Aboof and Jacob Barsimson, who came in the ship "Pear Tree," July 8, 1654. They were soon followed by a larger party from Brazil, their object being to escape the persecutions of the Inquisition, which some Catholic writers of the present day attempt to delude themselves and the world with the belief that it was a mild and beneficent institution.

Among the prominent in the new arrivals were the descendants of Dr. Samuel Nunez, a court physician, and eminent in his profession in Lisbon, the capital of Portugal. He was imprisoned by the Inquisition, but was released when his medical skill was required, but upon condition that two of the spies of the Inquisition should live in his house. Under these galling circumstances he resolved to escape to a land of greater freedom. Being a man of wealth, he had an elegant mansion on the shore of the Tagus, and made an agreement with the captain of a British brigantine, who was invited with a party to dine at the house. The whole family, including the spies and invited guests, went on board the vessel, and while they were being regaled in the cabin the captain spread sail and escaped to open sea and thence to England The members of the family had concealed on their persons all their gold and valuables, but the property left behind was confiscated Among them was David Mendez Machado, a relative, whose elder brother had been burned by the Inquisition as a relapsed heretic. From England they came to America, and went to Georgia in 1733. David Mendez Machado

Synagogue, Nineteenth Street, New York

married Zipporah, daughter of Dr. Samuel Nunez, and came to New York, where he acted as "reader" in the synagogue, and was also licensed to slaughter cattle after the Jewish method. Among the more prominent at that time were David Gomez, born August 14, 1697, and died July 16, 1769, and Benjamin Pereira Mendez, who as "reader" was the successor of Machado.

David Mendez Machado and his wife Zipporah were the parents of two children: Sarah, who married Raphael J Moses, of Charleston; and Rebecca, born in Stone street, New York, November 17, 1746 She was married in Philadelphia, November 16, 1762, to Jonas Phillips, and the event was duly entered upon the records of Shearith Israel in New York city.

Jonas Phillips was born in Germany, 1736, his native place being Busick, or, according to some accounts, Frankfort-on-the-Main He was son of Aaron Phillips, and came to America, November, 1756. He settled first at Charleston, but came to New York, bringing a good recommendation from the former place. He was a freeman, and in business was a retailer and auctioneer, or "vendue master," as it was then termed During the Revolution he with most of the congregation joined the patriot cause. The result was that they found themselves compelled to place the scrolls of the law and the valuable portable property of the synagogue in a locked chest in the care of the rabbi, Rev. Gershom Mendez Seixas, and carried to Philadelphia. Jonas Phillips, who removed to that city, was licensed to trade there in 1778 He enlisted in Captain John Linton's company of militia, Colonel William Bradford's battalion, and was mustered into the service of the United States. After the war he returned to New York and engaged in business, but in 1789 went again to Philadelphia, and died there Shabat 6, 5663 (January 29, 1803). His remains were brought to New York and laid to rest in the Jewish cemetery on Oliver street. His widow survived for many years, and died in Philadelphia in 1831. They are the parents of twenty-one children, some of whom died young. Of the rest were Sarah, who married Michael Levy, father of Commodore Urich P Levy, United States navy; Benjamin I, whose son, James B. Phillips, was assistant district attorney of New York; Manuel, a prominent physician and assistant surgeon United States navy, 1809 to 1824; Joseph, a soldier in the War of 1812; Aaron J, famed as an actor; Zipporah, who married Manuel Noah, and was the mother of Mordecai M. Noah, famous as an author, politician and editor; and Naphtali.

Naphtali Phillips was the father of Isaac Phillips, who was at one time appraiser of the port of New York. He was born at his father's residence, corner of Rivington street and Bowery, June 16, 1812, and died August 4, 1889 In 1856 he married Miriam Trimble, a native of St. Johns, New Brunswick, Canada. She was born April 25, 1830, and died January 9, 1882. Her parents were Matthew and Jane (Crowe) Trimble. Isaac Phillips was also commissioner of education, grand master of the Masonic Order, editor of the *Union* and other papers in New York, one of the incorporators of Mount Sinai Hospital, and a well known member of the New York bar from 1870 to 1889.

Naphtali Phillips, the father, was born in 1773, and in 1797 he married, at Newport, Rhode Island, Rachel, daughter of Jochebed Levy and Moses Mendez Seixas.

A mention of a Jewish synagogue in New York is contained in a deed dated October 30, 1700, by which Jacob Melyn sells to Katharine Kerfbyl a house and lot bounded "south by Mill street, and east by the house and lot of John Harperdingh, now commonly called the Jews' Synagogue." How long it had been used for this purpose we do not know, but it was long enough to be well known as a synagogue, and is mentioned in Dutch church records, 1682.

On December 14, 1728, Cornelius Clopper sold to three or four prominent Jews a lot on the north side of the same street (now No 24-26 South William street), and upon this a synagogue was erected. In 1758 they purchased from Cornelius Clopper, Jr, a lot next east, and this with a small subsequent purchase extended their lot to what is now known as the "Goelet Lot" (No 18) Upon this place they worshipped the God of their father for a hundred years. In the rear of the synagogue was in later years a school house The increasing numbers rendered a change necessary, and in 1833 the lot and buildings were sold for $40,000, and in the great fire of 1835 the Jewish synagogue disappeared. The congregation, which had always borne the name of Shearith Israel, or the Remnant of Israel, then erected a new synagogue at No 58 Crosby street. On February 11, 1859, they purchased a lot on the north side of Nineteenth street, one hundred feet west of Fifth avenue, and upon it they erected the finest synagogue in the United States. The corner stone was laid on the 9th of Tamooz, 5619 (July 11, 1859), and the building was consecrated with imposing ceremonies on the 25th of Elool, 5620 (September 12, 1860). On May 26, 1898, the whole was sold for $135,000, and the congregation, after an existence of more than two hundred years, now worship in a still more elegant edifice on Central Park West.

Foremost among the officers of this synagogue is the name of N. Taylor Phillips (son of Isaac and Miriam Trimble Phillips), who was born at No. 324 West Twenty-second street, New York, December 5, 1868 He attended Columbia Grammar School, and entering Columbia University, graduated in 1886 with the degree of LL. B. At the age of twenty-one he was admitted to the bar of the Supreme Court of New York, and three years later was admitted to practice in the Supreme Court of the United States. He was at first connected with the law firm of Stanley, Clarke & Smith, and afterwards by himself until January 1, 1902, when he became deputy comptroller of New York city. In 1897 he was elected member of the legislature, and re-elected in 1898-1899 by the largest majorities ever received

Hon N Taylor Phillips

by a candidate from the Ninth (New York city) district While a member he served on committees on the judiciary, banks, public health, canals, labor and industries. In 1900 he was appointed member of the joint statutory revision commission of legislature to revise the statutes of the state, and which made report in 1901. On January 1, 1902, he was appointed first deputy comptroller of Greater New York by Comptroller Edward M. Grout, and reappointed in 1904 He was continued in office by Herman A. Metz, when he assumed the office of comptroller in 1906, and still retains the position As acting comptroller he is a member of the board of revision of assessments, and since January, 1904, has presided as chairman of that board Under his direction the law division of the department of finance was organized, and of that department he is still the leading head.

From 1889 to 1901 Mr. Phillips was a member of the General Committee of Tammany Hall, but resigned to assist in the organization of the Greater New York Democracy, of which he was one of the founders, and delivered an address at a mass meeting in Carnegie Hall, April, 1901, when it was organized This organization was one of the principal elements in the "Fusion movement" which elected Seth Low to the mayorality on the Reform ticket.

The military services of his ancestors have been mentioned, and it remains to add that Reuben Phillips (grandson of Jonas) served in the Civil war, and several grandsons were in the Spanish-American war

Since 1889 Mr Phillips has been clerk to the Synagogue of Shearith Israel. In this position he succeeded his father, Isaac Phillips, who in turn was the successor of his father, Naphtali Phillips, who served as trustee, clerk and president from 1803 to 1870 This position of clerk has now been held by the family for nearly a century.

Mr. Phillips is treasurer of the American Jewish Historical Society, also of the societies: Hebra Hased Va Amet of Congregation Shearith Israel, Columbia Industrial and Religious School for Jewish Girls. He is also director of the Federation of American Zionists, and is a member of all the Jewish charitable and educational institutions of New York, and of many nonsectarian institutions. He is chairman of the Tammany Hall General Committee of the Fifteenth Assembly District, New York city. He is also a member of the Bar Association, Democratic Club, chairman Board of Governors, Amsterdam Democratic Club, New York Historical Society, treasurer of American Scenic and Historic Preservation Society, of which Mr. J. Pierpont Morgan is honorary president; trustee of Hudson Fulton Commission, and member of executive committee. He is also member of Sons of the American Revolution, Kings County Democratic Club, Royal Arcanum, Loyal Association, Albion Lodge of Free Masons, University Settlement, honorary member of Hebrew Veterans War with Spain, Washington Continental Guard, Masonic Historical Society, and Brooklyn Yacht Club.

Mr. Phillips married, at Washington, D. C., March 9, 1892, Rosalie Solomons, daughter of Adolphus S. Solomon and Rachel Mendez Seixas Phillips, his wife, of the same ancestry as his own.

BLOODGOOD FAMILY.

The ancestor of this ancient family was Captain Frans Janson Bloetgoet, who was born in Holland in 1635, and died at Flushing, Long Island, November 29, 1676; his will was probated December 27, same year. He came to New Amsterdam in 1658, and settled at Flushing in January the following year From the very beginning he held a prominent position. He was secretary of the Colonies on the Delaware, Schepen of Flushing in 1673, and military officer in 1674. He died of wounds received in a skirmish with the Indians. He married Lysbeth Jans, of Gouda, Holland. Their children were: Geerthe, wife of John Marstern; Ariantie, wife of Hendrick Hageman; Isabella, wife of Ide Van Schaack; Judith, wife of Johanes Wynkoop; William, born 1667, married Mary Brinkerhoff; Neeltie, wife of Samuel Waldron; John, born 1672, married Mary Van

Valkersburgh; Lysbeth, who died unmarried. From these are descended all the families of Bloodgood so far as can be traced

The family of John Bloodgood, the second son of Captain Frans Jansen, removed to the region of the Upper Hudson, and representatives of them are to be found in Catskill, Greene county, New York, and in many other places.

William Bloodgood, eldest son of Captain Frans J. Bloetgoet, born 1667, left Flushing, Long Island, and went to Perth Amboy, Middlesex county, New Jersey. He was a tanner by trade, and he must have been the owner of considerable real estate, as there is a record of four pieces of property he purchased. In March, 1726, he married for his second wife Mary Gach, of Woodbridge, and their children were: Elizabeth, born February 12, 1728; Mary, born January 17, 1730; Moses, born July 24, 1734; Gage, born September 4, 1736; Aaron, born January 24, 1738, mentioned hereinafter; Joshua, born July 20, 1743, died April 10, 1811.

Aaron Bloodgood, second son of William Bloodgood, born January 24, 1738, followed the sea for a number of years, and finally settled at Perth Amboy, New Jersey, where he followed farming. He married, March 31, 1763, Abigail Carman, born June 14, 1741, and their children were: Margaret, born November 2, 1764, married Jonathan Freeman, and died December 11, 1806. Mary, born June 6, 1766. Samuel, born February 20, 1768, died April 16, 1854; William, born March 12, 1770, mentioned hereinafter; Joshua, born July 26, 1773; Aaron, born September 15, 1776. Aaron Bloodgood, father of these children, died February 26, 1813.

William Bloodgood, second son of Aaron Bloodgood, born March 12, 1770, died August 7, 1842. He settled on his father's farm at Perth Amboy, New Jersey, whereon he was born, and throughout his active years devoted his time and attention to the cultivation and improvement of the same He was a manly man, actuated in all he did by the highest principles and a broad humanitarian spirit, and his memory is hallowed by the love and regard which he engendered in the hearts of all who knew him He married Doziah Freeman, of Metuchen, New Jersey, born December 2, 1779, died February 5, 1880, who bore him the following children: Margaret, born June 21, 1800, married Elias Tirrell, no issue, died February 11, 1883. Matthias, born March 12, 1802, married Maria Ackerman, has three living children, died January 5, 1890. Aaron, born April 7, 1804, married Janane Harnard, and they have three living children; he died October 15, 1877. Martha, born December 11, 1805, died unmarried January 15, 1894 Catharine, born July 26, 1809, married Obadiah Ayers, no issue, died December 20, 1902. Elizabeth. born April 10, 1812, died unmarried April 3, 1893 William, born March 17, 1815, married Susan Kinbridge, of Woodbridge, New Jersey, and they have one living daughter; he died October 1, 1873. Rebecca, born December 11, 1817, became the wife of Nathan Tyrell; she died March 26, 1843. Freeman, born June 4, 1820, mentioned hereinafter.

The old homestead of this honored family, and on which William Bloodgood lived and died, consisted of one hundred and five acres of land which had been purchased by their ancestor. The ancient house, which was the home of all these generations, still stands, although in a dilapidated condition, and not likely to remain long as an human habitation. This house, an interesting relic of the past, stands on an old road that runs west from the Woodbridge road, and is about three-quarters of a mile from the junction. After the death of William Bloodgood this farm was divided into nine parts, the widow having the house with land adjoining. About a quarter of a mile east of the house is a cemetery, called the Alpine cemetery, and this is the resting place of the generations of this family.

Freeman Bloodgood, youngest son of William Bloodgood, was born in Perth Amboy township, New Jersey, June 4, 1820. He acquired such limited education as was obtainable during the winter months in the primitive schools of his early life, the summer months being spent in duties pertaining to the farm. On April 5, 1838, he abandoned farm work and went to New York and lived with his brother Matthias, at No. 101 Wooster street, and later at No. 140 Wooster street. Together they carried on the business of masonry and building until 1849, when Mr. Freeman Bloodgood began business on his own account. At this time New York was, to use the language of Washington Irving, "a little city, where everybody knew everybody." The monuments of his skill and ability as a builder are everywhere to be seen. Among these may be mentioned the Berkeley House, at Fifth avenue and Ninth street; the house of Hon Orlando B. Potter, at the corner of Astor Place and Lafayette place. He built for James E. White the first fireproof store in the city, on the southeast corner of Broadway and Franklin street. Also a large and conspicuous building on the east side of Greenwich street, between Harrison and Jay streets. He was also the builder of a large building on the corner of Bridge and State streets, on the ground where the new Custom House now stands. The first building erected by Mr. Bloodgood was No. 204 Chatham street (now Park Row), nearly opposite Division street. The next was No. 203 Fulton street. The erection of all these buildings was executed with careful exactness of detail, which rendered them monuments of his skill. Since 1899 Mr. Bloodgood has enjoyed pleasant and well earned retirement at his comfortable residence in Westfield, New Jersey.

He has been a member of the General Society of Mechanics'

and Tradesmen for over fifty years. For over thirty years a consistent member of the Baptist church, and withholds his support from no movement or measure which he believes will prove of public good. He is a gentleman of unfailing courtesy and kindness, and his sterling qualities have endeared him to all who have come in contact with him, and it is safe to say that no man in the community is held in more sincere regard.

Mr. Bloodgood married (first), in New York, October 22, 1845, Matilda W. Raynor, daughter of ———— and Eliza Ann (Stansbury) Raynor, who was born at Flushing, Long Island, 1821, died November 4, 1860. Three children were the issue of this union: Eliza Matilda, Mary Louisa, wife of Charles C. Alexander, and has three children: William Edgar, born October 20, 1853. Mr. Bloodgood married (second), June 1, 1864, Eliza Ann Curtis, born in Warminster, England, October 25, 1830, died October 25, 1900. Their children are: Martha C., born April 16, 1866, wife of Walter L. Day; Freeman, Jr., born March 3, 1868; Ezra S , born February 11, 1871.

William Edgar Bloodgood, only son of Freeman and Matilda W. (Raynor) Bloodgood, born October 20, 1853, acquired his education in the public schools of New York, after which he gained a thorough knowledge of the mason and building trade under the tuition of his father. He then turned his attention to architecture, made himself proficient in this branch, and is now engaged lucratively in this profession. He is a consistent member of the Baptist church at Montclair, New Jersey. He married, January 20, 1880, Ida Stillwell Bailey, who died October, 1885. Mr. Bloodgood married (second), March 20, 1889, Jeanette Low, and their children are: Ethel Raynor, born March 12, 1897, and Jeanette, born February 9, 1902.

Freeman Bloodgood, Jr., eldest son of Freeman and Eliza Ann (Curtis) Bloodgood, born March 3, 1868, was educated in

the public schools of New York, and afterwards acquired a practical and thorough knowledge of the mason and building business under his father's efficient tuition, and since 1899 has successfully conducted the business formerly carried on by his father He was married January 29, 1891, to Sarah A Ellis, a native of Wales, Great Britain, and their children are: Edward Ellis, born January 19, 1893. Miriam, born June 5, 1898. Elizabeth, born September 20, 1902

Ezra S. Bloodgood, youngest son of Freeman and Eliza Ann (Curtis) Bloodgood, born February 11, 1871, like his brother acquired a good public school education in New York city, and thereafter made himself proficient as a mason and builder under his father's tuition. He has followed this line of business continuously since early life, and since 1899 in connection with his brother Freeman has conducted the business formerly carried on so successfully for half a century by his father. He married Grace F. Smith, of Westfield, New Jersey, February 11, 1897, and they are the parents of one child, Earle A., born January 30, 1898.

NIELS POULSON

The small country of Denmark has furnished many citizens to the new world who have made their mark in the commercial, financial and industrial circles, and among the most prominent of these must be mentioned the name which heads this sketch.

Niels Poulson was born in Denmark, February 27, 1843, and in that country learned the trade of architect and builder. He came to this country in 1864 and was employed as a mason for about two years, becoming an expert in that line of work. At the end of this period he was engaged by the government as a draughtsman in the office of the supervising architect in Washington, District of Columbia, and resigned this position after two years, as he desired to locate in New York city and make a study of architectural iron work. He found employment with the Architectural Iron Works of New York, remained with them eight years, for seven years of this time having charge of the architectural and engineering department connected with the works. He started in business for himself on a very small scale in 1876, with a view of introducing a higher grade of work than had previously been prevalent. Mr. Charles M. Eger, who had been with Mr. Poulson as draughtsman at the Architectural Iron Works, came to him in a similar capacity, and about one year later was taken in as a partner and the firm name changed to Poulson & Eger. The firm of Poulson & Eger was incorporated under the name of Hecla Iron Works in 1897, Mr. Poulson now being president and Mr. Eger vice-president. The Hecla Iron Works, or, more correctly speaking Poulson & Eger, was the first concern to introduce electro-plating, galvano-plastic work, the Bower-Barff process and plastic patterns, and by economy in construction were able to make metal work compete in price with other materials in the construction of stairways, elevator enclosures, elevator cages, windows, doors, etc. The School of Mines, a few years ago, made a comparison between the iron work of Europe and America, and came to the conclusion that in work of this kind this country is far ahead of the rest of the world, and they were good enough to give this concern full credit for establishing in this country the present high class of work. Mr Poulson is the originator of many improvements in construction, few of which he has had patented, as he preferred to make them public property. He improved the methods of building fireproof stairs, elevator enclosures, elevator cages, book-stacks for libraries, etc. He furnished to the government, free of charge, modes of construction for the congressional library in Washington, which have proved so practical and successful that this style of construction is now universally adopted in all large libraries He has often acted in the capacity of consulting engineer and architect in connection with public improvements. He is a member of the following organizations: The Brooklyn Club, the Manufacturers' Association, the Brooklyn League, the Crescent Athletic Club, and the Bay Ridge Citizens' Association

Hecla Iron Works, located at No. 118 North Eleventh street, Brooklyn, New York, was incorporated in 1897 and has a capital stock of five hundred thousand dollars, and mortgage bonds of five hundred thousand dollars. It was founded by Niels Poulson and C. M. Eger, as previously stated, and the original nature of the business was architectural metal work. The present officers and members of the firm are: Niels Poulson, president; Charles M Eger, vice-president; Francis D. Jackson, second vice-president; Fernand S. Bellevue, treasurer; Robert A. McCord, secretary; Frederick W. Smith, in charge of the designing and construction departments; and Charles Dipple, superintendent. These names also constitute the board of directors. The company now manufacture all kinds of ornamental and architectural work in all metals, and has departments for designing, modeling, moulding, pattern making, grille working, electro-plating, etc. For many years Hecla Iron Works had practically no competitors in the higher grades of work, but since then many young men who learned the business with this firm have started for themselves or have been engaged by other concerns, until this high class work is now universally established. Hecla Iron Works was the pioneer in introducing better metals and better workmanship, and they have been well rewarded in their efforts to improve the business in which they engaged. The factory is located at North Tenth, Eleventh and Twelfth streets, from

Wythe avenue to Berry street, Brooklyn, New York, covering forty-one city lots, and when in full operation employs one thousand men The yearly business amounts to over one million dollars, and they have agencies in Boston, Baltimore and San Francisco.

WILLIAM FRANCIS ELLIS.

William Francis Ellis, widely and favorably known as an inventor, as well as for his great practical ability as a general machinist, is a descendant of an honored Colonial ancestry. The Ellis family is of English and Scotch extraction, and its members were among the earliest settlers of Vermont

John Ellis, paternal grandfather of William F Ellis, was a soldier in the patriot army during the Revolution. By his wife Sarah he had a son Alfred, born in Brattleboro, Vermont, who passed his entire life there as a farmer and machinist. He was a man of ability and high character, and was proferred various important public offices, which he persistently refused, preferring the duties and responsibilities of private citizenship. He married Elizabeth MacNash, a native of the same town with himself, a daughter of Moses MacNash, and of Scotch ancestry. Of this marriage were born two sons: Charles C, deceased; and William Francis.

William Francis Ellis was born in Brattleboro, Vermont, September 28, 1828, and was educated in the common schools of that place, then a mere village. After leaving school he was apprenticed to a machinist, and became so proficient in his chosen calling that on completing his term he secured employment in the United States Arsenal at Springfield, where he labored efficiently until he removed to Boston to take employment in the locomotive works About 1875 he located in New York city and engaged in the manufacture of book backing, stamping and trimming machinery, and for twenty-six years past has been estab-

E. J. Nevins

lished at his present location, 17 Center street His shops are unsurpassed for their equipment for their purpose, much of the machinery being of Mr. Ellis's own invention. His talent for machinery invention was evidenced in his early youth, and when only seventeen years old he produced an entirely practicable side-hill plow, while among his more recent inventions is a potato harvester which has found wide use.

Mr Ellis married, in New York, Miss Elizabeth McAffrey, of Brattleboro, Vermont, and of this marriage were born three children: John F., residing in St Louis, Missouri; Elizabeth, who is the wife of Cornelius W Bogart, residing in New York; and Anna Maria, who is the wife of Charles W. Dickerson. The mother of these children having died, Mr Ellis married (second) Miss Agnes Wheatley, a native of Brooklyn, New York. There are no children of this marriage. Mr. and Mrs. Ellis are both consistent members of St Thomas (Protestant Episcopal) Church, Brooklyn

ELIPHALET SMITH NEWINS.

Eliphalet Smith Newins, a highly respected citizen and a member of the old firm of Floyd & Newins, formerly of 177 South street, New York city, was born at Setauket in the town of Brookhaven, Suffolk county, New York, September 13, 1825, the only child of Eliphalet and Sarah Woodhull (Jayne) Newins, whose deaths occurred at Setauket, Long Island, August 30, 1825, and February 13, 1869, respectively. Eliphalet Newins (father) gained his livelihood by the tilling of the soil

Eliphalet S Newins received his elementary training in the schools of Setauket, and at the early age of thirteen began to depend upon his own resources to gain a livelihood. He came to New York city and at once secured employment with William Floyd, who was then engaged in the grocery trade at No 4

Goerck street, and continued the same for a period of six or seven years, during which time he succeeded by his industry and fidelity to duty in impressing upon his employer the importance of his usefulness and business capacity. At the expiration of the above period of time he was admitted to partnership with Mr. Floyd and for some time they conducted the business at the old stand, but subsequently, owing to the increasing demands of their trade, removed to more commodious quarters at No 15 James Slip, New York city Here they engaged in the wholesale grocery and provision trade, and by their persistent efforts built up a large and profitable business. Later they engaged in the shipping and marine trade, owning their own ships which they had built in conformity to their ideas, and for a number of years engaged in the coastwise and foreign trade, in which line of undertaking they achieved a marked degree of success. In order to secure better facilities for their constantly increasing trade they finally removed to No 177 South street, where they successfully continued the mercantile business up to within a short time of the death of Mr. Floyd, which occurred July 11, 1903 The firm of Floyd & Newins was widely and favorably known in commercial and marine circles, and everywhere was recognized as being synonymous with straightforward and honorable business methods. The confidence reposed in him by his fellowmen is evidenced by the fact that he was chosen a member of the board of trustees of the East River Savings Bank of New York city, one of the leading financial institutions of the metropolis. He is a member in good standing of Pacific Lodge, No 233, Free and Accepted Masons, of New York city

Mr. Newins married, October 19, 1852, Sarah C. Delamater, born November 6, 1832, daughter of William B. and Sarah (Felter) Delamater, the latter of whom was a native of Orange county, New York. One child was the issue of this marriage,

Charles Mortimer, born September 21, 1853, referred to hereinafter. The faithful wife and mother died July 3, 1885 Mr Newins married (second), March 30, 1887, Adelaide Z, daughter of Hamilton and Harriet Jane (Allen) Jayne, no issue.

Charles Mortimer Newins acquired his education under the private tuition of Professor Marshall and in public school No 40 in New York city At the age of seventeen he entered the office of Floyd & Newins and under the direction of his father learned the various details of the business, with which the latter had been so many years identified. He is a worthy representative of the name and family, and has proved himself a worthy son of a worthy sire. He is identified with Ridgewood Lodge, No. 710, Free and Accepted Masons, of which he is past master. Mr Newins married, at Keyport, New Jersey, October 19, 1876, Eleanor Meserole Luqueer, born July 13, 1856, daughter of Jacob and Catherine (Van Cott) Luqueer, and their children are: Floyd Smith, born August 9, 1877, died November 28, 1877. Grace Eleanor, born June 6, 1879, became the wife of Wilson W. Brown, of Brooklyn, New York, and has one child, Grace Eleanor Brown Lillian Van Cott, born August 3, 1881, became the wife of Charles B Van Leer, of Brooklyn, New York, and has one child, Charles Newins Van Leer, born March 22, 1902 Edward Mortimer, born February 22, 1883. Charles Meserole, born November 3, 1887.

JAMES J POWERS, JR.

James J Powers, Jr., who conducts a large and important real estate and insurance business at No. 109 West Twenty-ninth street, New York city, and who in the course of his business career has handled millions of dollars worth of property in this city, traces his paternal ancestry to Newfoundland, and his maternal to Ireland.

Joseph Powers, grandfather of James J. Powers, Jr., was a resident of Newfoundland, where he married Ann Burns, and had children: Matthew, Joseph John, and James J., Sr., of whom see forward.

James J. Powers, Sr., was born in Carbonear, Newfoundland, October 16, 1826. He left Newfoundland in 1846 and went to Boston, Massachusetts, and from thence to New York, where he remained for three years. During this time he learned the trade of shoemaking, and in 1849 returned to Newfoundland, taking up his residence at St Johns, where he worked at his acquired trade for a period of fifteen years He returned to New York in 1864 and again took up his trade of shoemaking in that city, subsequently engaging in the retail shoe business for a number of years, but he retired from active business life some years prior to his death, which occurred June 10, 1904, having amassed a competency He married, in St. John's, Newfoundland, Eliza Simms, born in St. Johns, February 28, 1831, daughter of Henry and Mary (Meagher) Simms. Henry Simms was born in the county of Waterford, Ireland, emigrated to Newfoundland, and taught in the schools there for the long period of fifty years He then removed to New York, where he resided for many years He married Mary Meagher, who was born in Newfoundland, went to Ireland with her father, when she was a child, was educated there, and then returned to Newfoundland, where she was married The children of Mr and Mrs Simms were: Eliza, who married Mr. Powers; Julia, deceased; Mary, deceased; William, deceased; Ellen, and Francis Mr. and Mrs James J. Powers, Sr., had children: 1. James J., Jr, see forward 2 Mary Ann, a Sister of Charity. 3 Ella, married Patrick H. Ryan, of Brooklyn, New York. 4 Margaret, married William J. Smith, of Brooklyn. 5 Julia. 6. Agnes, a Sister of Charity whose pious labors are with the New York Foundling

Institute   7. Joseph Henry, who resides in Brooklyn.   8. Henrietta.

James J. Powers, Jr., son of James J., Sr., and Eliza (Simms) Powers, was born in St. Johns, Newfoundland, October 13, 1856. He was eight years of age when his parents came to the United States, and his education, which was well begun in his native city, was completed in New York city in St. Bridget's Parochial School, at Avenue B and Eighth street. He left school with an excellent foundation for an active business career, and at once took employment as a clerk, and later, in 1874, in the same capacity was connected with the William Repenile estate, to which he rendered acceptable and trustworthy service for the long period of twelve years. For a number of years afterward he had charge of the property of Michael Coleman, and is now entrusted with the large interests of the Samuel Babcock estate, which were committed to him several years ago. For thirty years past he has been continuously engaged in a general real estate business, and during that time has handled some of the most valuable property in his section of the city, and much of which has been greatly improved as a result of his bringing it to the attention and into the possession of discerning men with means sufficient to enhance its value by liberal building operations. As an almost necessary incident to his real estate operations, he has at the same time carried on an insurance business which has expanded to large proportions. Throughout his career he has enjoyed an enviable reputation for progressiveness, wise discernment, and unsullied integrity, and he numbers among his clientele many of the foremost active business men of that great center of city business in which he is situated   Mr. Powers is a Catholic in religion, a communicant of St. Gabriel's church, and is an active member of the social and benevolent order of Knights of Columbus. In politics he is a Democrat. He married (first), in New York city, Josephine Partello, who died. He married (second) Amelia Miller. Both marriages were childless.

GEORGE FOX.

George Fox, until his death the head of the oldest boiler works in the city of New York, was a native of England. He was born in Dewsbury, son of Isaac and Sarah Fox, both natives of England, the former spending his entire life in that country.

George Fox was educated in his native land, and was there apprenticed to the trade of boiler making, in which he became proficient. In 1849 he came to the United States and located in the city of New York, working at his acquired trade as a journeyman until 1853. In this year he removed to Paterson, New Jersey, where he held the position of foreman for the Danford & Cooke Locomotive Works for a period of three years. He then returned to New York, and in 1856 established boiler works at No. 511 West Thirty-fourth street, which are still in operation at the present time, under the supervision of three of his children. This business is the oldest of its kind in the city, and has a well established reputation. Mr. Fox was a man who thoroughly understood not alone his business, but business conditions in general; ready to take advantage of every opportunity which presented itself and make the most of it, and this was in all probability the main cause of his remarkable success. He was quiet and unassuming in his manner, and held in high esteem by all. He was a member of Corinthian Lodge, No. 488, Free and Accepted Masons, and attended the Methodist Episcopal church.

Mr. Fox married, at Bradford, England, Martha Thorpe, and they had nine children: John, married Emeline Carr, had two children, Walter and Emily, and died in 1875, survived by his widow and two children William, died in infancy. George, born December 2, 1847, in Liverpool, England, came to America with his parents at the age of two years, was educated in the public schools of New York, learned the trade of boiler making in his father's business, and since the death of the latter has been a member of the firm of George Fox's Sons. He married, December 21, 1870, Jennie P Owen, daughter of Jasper and Susan Owen, and has three children: Edith J, Mabel E., Lillian S. He is a member of St. Paul's Methodist Episcopal church, in which he holds the office of steward. Benjamin, married Lavinia Flandreau; children: Benjamin, Mattie and George. Martha, wife of Robert H. Law; has three children: Marion F., Robert H, Jr., and Martha. Henry, deceased, married Rosania Schnieble; widow and two children, John and Frank, survive him. Elizabeth, died in childhood. Charles, died in childhood. Mary, died in childhood.

WILLIAM H TAYLOR.

William Taylor, father of William H. Taylor, was born in Virginia, and was a sailor. He married Sarah Marshall, born in Accomac county, Virginia, and a few years after his marriage he removed with his family to Staten Island. This was in 1860. Mr. and Mrs. Taylor were the parents of four children: Samuel E., William H, Southard, May J.

William H. Taylor, second son and second child of William and Sarah (Marshall) Taylor, was born August 11, 1850, in Accomac county, Virginia. He lived there until he was ten years of age, when, in the fall of 1860, his parents removed to Staten Island. It was in the public schools of Staten Island that he received his education. After leaving school he turned his attention to a seafaring life, which had always possessed great attractions for him. He followed the occupation of a sailor for several years, and then worked in an oil business for four years. On December 12, 1896, he took charge of school No. 20, as janitor, and has remained in that capacity up to the present time. The same earnestness of purpose which characterized Mr. Taylor as a boy at school, and which aided him to gain success there, has attached to him throughout his career He is painstaking, ambitious, and has great force of character.

Mr. Taylor married, February 10, 1871, M. Eleanor Kimball, born January 22, 1852, in Virginia, daughter of Benjamin Franklin and Catharine (Simonson) (Brooker) Kimball. Benjamin Franklin Kimball was born in the state of Maine, and was a boatman by occupation. He married Catharine (Simonson) Brooker, of Tompkinsville, Staten Island, widow of John Brooker, and a descendant of the Simonson and Degroot families, the former among the first settlers of Staten Island. Mr. and Mrs. Brooker were the parents of three children: John, Mary and William. Mr. and Mrs. Kimball had children: George Washington, M. Eleanor, Benjamin F., Oliver K. Mr. and Mrs. William H. Taylor are the parents of six children: Alice, Nora, Paul, Ella, Samuel E., Sadie O.

GILBERT L. DUPUY.

Gilbert L Dupuy, an enterprising and prosperous agriculturist of New Springville, Staten Island, residing and conducting operations on a farm which has been in the possession of the family since the first settlement in this country, in 1700 or thereabouts, is a descendant of a family of great prominence.

Nicholas Dupuy, great-grandfather of Gilbert L. Dupuy, was a Huguenot, and emigrated from his native land, France, to America, about the year 1716 His son, Nicholas Dupuy, Jr., grandfather of Gilbert L. Dupuy, married Catherine Decker, of Holland Dutch ancestry. Their son, Barnett Nichols Dupuy, father of Gilbert L. Dupuy, was a farmer by occupation, attended the Methodist church, cast his vote for the candidates of the Republican party, and served many years as trustee of public schools. He married Mary Jane Crocheron, a member of the Methodist church, and their children were: Nicholas, Gilbert L., Geraldine, Victor, Forestine, died when about two years of age; Forester, died at about the age of thirty-eight years.

Gilbert L. Dupuy was born in New Springville, Staten Island, obtained a common school education, and throughout the active years of his career has followed farming, with the exception of five years, when his attention was directed to the oyster business. He attends the Methodist Episcopal church, to the support of which he contributes liberally, and his political allegiance is given to the Republican party. Mr Dupuy married, March 19, 1879, Mary Dodge, daughter of James and Martha (Humphrey) Dodge, the former one of the city judges of Syracuse, New York, and the latter a descendant of a very prominent family. One child, Shirley Stuart Dupuy, born September 12, 1885, was the issue of this union.

PROFESSOR ABRAHAM JACKSON DU BOIS.

Professor Abraham J Du Bois, a well known instructor in the art of dancing, is a representative of the ancient family of Du Bois, of whom a more extended account is given in this work. The line of descent beginning with the first known ancestor is as follows: Jacques Du Bois, Peter, Johanes, John, Peter John, Peter and Abraham J. Du Bois.

Peter John Du Bois, grandfather of Professor Du Bois, married a Miss Van Wart, who was a sister of a revolutionary patriot, one of the three young men who captured Major Andre, of the British army. They were the parents of six children: Peter, referred to hereinafter; Benjamin; Stephen; Rachel, married Thomas Allaire, who was for many years connected with the Tradesman's Bank of New York city; Amanda, married George Decker; and Eliza, unmarried. The remains of Peter John Du Bois and his wife were interred in the old Dutch burying ground at Tarrytown on the Hudson.

Peter Du Bois, father of Professor Du Bois, was born in the vicinity of Tarrytown, Westchester county, New York, 1815. He was for many years engaged in the carriage manufacturing business in the city of New York, and was recognized in business circles as a man of honesty and integrity. By his marriage to Lucinda Wilson, a native of Cold Spring, Putnam county, New York, and a descendant of an old Holland family, one son was born, Abraham Jackson, whose name heads this sketch. Mr. Du Bois died at his home in New York city, 1869.

Abraham Jackson Du Bois was born in the city of New York, January 7, 1844. He was educated in the schools of his native city, and under the competent tuition of his father learned the trade of wagon-maker and followed the same for a number of years He abandoned this line of industry in order to devote his attention to the art of dancing and theatrical performance, in both of which professions he has proved himself a very successful and efficient instructor. Professor Du Bois was married in April, 1888, to Louise Junke, born March 20, 1869, daughter of James A. and Margaret (Carr) Junke, and they are the parents of one child, Abraham Jackson, Jr., born April 24, 1889

GUSTAVE ZIMMERMANN.

Gustave Zimmermann, well and favorably known in sporting circles, is regarded as one of the leading marksmen and rifle experts in this country, and has become recognized as such from the Atlantic to the Pacific coast and has also won favorable recognition as a rifle expert in many of the European countries.

He was born in the town of Endingen, in the Grand Duchy of Baden, Germany.

Gustave Zimmermann acquired his educational training in the schools of the fatherland. He was left an orphan at an early age and was placed in the care of a guardian. Upon attaining to years of discretion he decided to come to America, hoping here to find better opportunities for his skill and labor. Upon his arrival at Philadelphia, Pennsylvania, he at once came to Paterson, New Jersey, where he secured employment. Being ambitious to make for himself an honorable name and reputation, he applied himself assiduously to his work and faithfully looked after the interest of his employer. From Paterson he came to Westchester county, New York, where he became a resident and citizen. In 1880 his expert marksmanship became known to many of the leading marksmen and riflemen of this country, and in 1881 he was sent to Europe to compete in the international shooting match, in which he was awarded the highest prize for expert marksmanship. In the years of 1887-90-92-94-96-97-98-1900-01-02-03-05 Mr. Zimmermann took part in each of the international shooting matches, and has in his possession numerous valuable trophies which were awarded to him in various contests. He has also taken part in numerous contests in this country, at which he has always secured many awards. Mr. Zimmermann is a member of numerous rifle teams in this country, and is captain of the New York Independent Scheutzer of New York city. He is a member of the Free and Accepted Masons and numerous other social and fraternal organizations that have for their object the good and welfare of the community wherein he resides.

Mr. Zimmermann married, October 5, 1880, Mary Kaempf, daughter of Henry and Catharine (Denner) Kaempf, both of whom were natives of the Kingdom of Bavaria, Germany. Of this marriage there have been the following children: 1. George Theodore, born July 4, 1881, attended the schools of New York city until 1894, when he went to Germany and there attended the Academy of the City of Freiburg for two years, when he returned home and in 1896 attended Packard's Business College of New York city, graduating from the same, and has since that time been engaged in assisting his father in his numerous business interests 2. Catharine, born September 17, 1883 3. Amelia, born January 19, 1885.

FRANK SCHULZ.

Frank Schulz, manufacturer and repairer of all kinds of cutlery, whose plant is located at No. 4 Bleecker street, near Bowery, New York, was born in Schwetzingen, Baden, Germany, March 17, 1872, son of John and Caroline (Licar) Schulz, both natives of Schwetzingen, and now (1907) residents of Harlem, New York. John and Caroline Schulz came to America about the year 1895, previous to which time John Schulz worked at the cutlery business in his native land, and now successfully conducts the same line of trade in Harlem, New York.

Frank Schulz acquired an elementary education in his native land, and when thirteen years of age emigrated to the United States, locating in the city of New York, where he learned the cutlery business with Fred. Westpfal, at No. 192 Essex street, thoroughly mastering all the details of the same under his efficient tutorship, and after completing his apprenticeship with this firm worked for them as a journeyman until July, 1903, since which time he has been engaged in business on his own account. Mr. Schulz is an expert in his business, and now manufactures everything included in cutlery, embracing pen and pocket knives, cook and carving knives, concave razors, tailors' and barbers' shears, barbers' supplies, razor straps, knives, cutting blades and shirtmakers' knives, pocket book makers' and furriers' tools, etc., and also gives particular attention to grinding and repairing. He is a man of sterling integrity, and the success which has crowned his efforts is an eloquent testimonial to the truth of this fact, also to his rare business qualifications. He is a member of the Germanic Sick and Benefit Society.

DR. FREDERICK E. LAWRENCE.

Dr. Frederick E. Lawrence is a grandson of Frederick Lawrence, who was for many years a highly respected resident of the village of West Farms, Westchester county, New York. He was a man of affairs in the neighborhood and for a number of years was successfully engaged in the oyster planting business; he died at Bay Chester. He married Angeline Schofield, of Stamford, Connecticut, and had a family of two sons and three daughters, all of whom attained to years of maturity. The sons were William Frederick and Cornelius W., and the former married and removed to Michigan. He had a large family of sons and daughters. The second son, Cornelius W. Lawrence, was born January 24, 1836. He was educated in the schools of Westchester and upon attaining to manhood years engaged in navigating on the waters of Long Island Sound. He was for many years a licensed pilot and was regarded as a capable and able navigator. Captain Lawrence passed away at his home in City Island, November 23, 1902. He married, December 28, 1861, Georgiana Craft, born October 2, 1833, daughter of Edward and Temperance (Hall) Craft, both of whom were natives of Long Island. Of this marriage was born two children: 1 Frederick E., see forward. 2. Raymond C., born in City Island, October 24, 1872. He married, July 28, 1897, Florence Sadler, born July 21, 1874, daughter of Edward and Mary Ann (Victor) Sadler. Of this marriage he had born to him one child, Florence Ida Lawrence, born July 24, 1899.

Frederick E Lawrence, born in City Island, May 8, 1864, received his elementary training in the schools of City Island and under the private tuition of Professor Blenn, who was a graduate of Wilbraham University. At the age of twenty-eight years Frederick E. Lawrence took up the study of medicine. In 1891 he entered the New York University and graduated from that institution in 1895 He then entered Manhattan Hospital on Harts Island, where he remained for some time, and in 1898 began to practice his profession at City Island, attaining a marked degree of success Dr Lawrence is an active member of Pelham Lodge, No. 712, F. and A M.

Dr. Lawrence married, May 6, 1896, Margaret Cunningham, born November 13, 1870, daughter of Peter and Mary (Doyle) Cunningham, both of Liverpool, England, and is one of a family of four children, two of whom came to the United States, namely: Margaret (Mrs. Dr Lawrence) and Thomas, who took up his abode in New York city. The children of Dr and Mrs. Lawrence 1. Mary Margaret and Frederick C. (twins), born February 10, 1897; the latter died August 1, 1898. 2. Frederick C , born October 13, 1900 3. George, born June 12, 1903.

FAMILY OF BARTO.

The ancestor of this family appears to have been Francis Barteau. The name, however, has been changed into several different forms, as Bartow and Barto. Francis Barteau is said to have come from Paris, France, in advance of the general Huguenot emigration, which added to the population of this country one of its most important portions, a portion which has ever been a credit to the land of their adoption

Francis Barteau and wife Mary were living at Harlem,

New York, as early as 1676. From thence he removed to Flushing, where he was living in 1680 with his wife and nine children One of his sons, Francis, settled in Huntington, Long Island, and married Margaret, widow of James Morris. She was born in 1675 Another son, John, also settled in Huntington, and had wife Abigail.

There was a Francis Barteau who married Clemence Morris, in 1733, and went to Fire Place (now Brookhaven), in the town of Brookhaven, Long Island, in 1741 His descendants are still found there. This Francis Barteau, who was born in 1711, settled in Hempstead. He had children: Morris, see forward; Benjamin, died young; Francis, married Jemima Turner; and Stephen, who was killed in the Revolution.

Morris Barteau, born August 18, 1758, was killed in the French war, February 6, 1839 He married Hannah, daughter of Josiah Smith. She was born July 26, 1773, died October 18, 1816. Their children were: Jesse, born December 16, 1789, died December 16, 1832; Josiah Smith, born December 30, 1790; Philetus, see forward; Elkanah, born February 18, 1794; Mary, born January 5, 1796, died 1832; Israel, born October 21, 1797, died May 26, 1826; Reuben, born June 3, 1801, died in Wisconsin, 1867; Obadiah, born April 23, 1803; Jane, born January 23, 1805; Peter Coleman, born January 25, 1807; Sarah, born January 18, 1809; Hannah, born January 16, 1811; Julianna, born February 10, 1813, died young This branch of the family changed the name to Barto.

Philetus Barto, the third child, born October 5, 1792, died October 7, 1852. He married, March 11, 1813, Nancey, daughter of Jonah and Hannah Bishop. She was born September 18, 1795, died August 10, 1857. Their children were: Jonah, born January 26, 1814, died young; Luther and Phebe (twins), born February 14, 1816; Anna, born March 6, 1818; Susan, born September 21, 1821; Coleman, born October 25, 1823; Matthew and Phebe (twins), born February 21, 1826, died young; Jane M., born July 25, 1828, died December 1, 1864; Emma L., born September 8, 1831; Fanny E., born March 13, 1835; Charles Henry, see forward.

Charles Henry Barto, born November 20, 1837, married Sarah Jane, daughter of James Briggs, June 20, 1860. Their children were: Rev. Charles Elmore, see forward; Willie H., born November 20, 1868; Carrie Woodruff, born June 26, 1876.

Rev. Charles Elmore Barto was born at Northport, Long Island, October 5, 1862, and when one and one-half years of age removed to Brooklyn with his parents. After a preliminary training in the public schools he took a preparatory course in Trinity Church School, and in Hackettstown Institue, and graduated from Wesleyan University in 1890. He was ordained deacon by Bishop Foster at Bridgeport, Connecticut, 1888; ordained elder 1894 at Nostrand Avenue Methodist Episcopal church, Brooklyn. From 1890 until 1897 served in the pastorate of churches in Connecticut, at Beacon Falls, Cheshire, Clinton and Seymour. He then came to Queenboro, Long Island, and was for seven years connected with churches at Springfield and Astoria. While pastor in Springfield a new parsonage was built through his efforts, and at Astoria the church debt was extinguished. In April, 1903, he was appointed pastor of Willis Avenue Methodist Episcopal Church, borough of Bronx, the largest and most influential Protestant church in the borough of the Bronx, and since then $17,000 of the church debt has been paid. This church was founded in October, 1865, by laymen who held their first meeting in a grove near the Mott Haven railroad station. The church was soon organized, and services were held in the houses of the members. The first church edifice was a small wooden building erected in 1867.

Two years later a large frame church was built, which remained until the erection of the present edifice in 1897. The new church cost $70,000 exclusive of the ground. It is of elegant architecture. The auditorium seats nine hundred persons, while the Sunday school room contains facilities for seating twelve hundred scholars. It was built during the pastorate of Rev. William R. Barton, who was succeeded by Rev. Melville Y. Bovard, who was succeeded by Rev. Charles Elmore Barto, the present pastor. The church membership is six hundred and nine, and the average Sunday school attendance is four hundred. During the pastorate of Rev. Charles E. Barto more than two hundred members have been added to the church. Connected with the church are a Ladies' Society, Epworth League, Womans' Foreign Missionary Society, a Men's Guild and the Excelsior Club for young men. There has been also a flourishing Chinese Sunday school. The following are the present officers of the church: Class leaders—John Onderdonk, who is also president of the board of trustees, was one of the original founders of the church, and at the age of eighty-two is still active in the work; Richard B Eason, Thomas H. Eason. Local preachers —A. Frank Chamberlain, Harry C. Burrows. Trustees—John Onderdonk, A. J. Goodwin, Thomas Craig, Jr, A. C. Campbell, Daniel Kingsland, Lewis Lawrence, John B. Coombs, Thomas Davies, Richard B. Eason. Stewards—Edward P. Kingsland, John Young, William Cunningham, Charles Van Allen, E. Gordon Partridge, Ernest Chamberlain, John E. Cary, Richard Lawrence, James Nixon, Frank L. Pelo. Sunday school superintendent—Frank L Pelo.

Rev. Charles Elmore Barto married Nellie M., daughter of Silas W. and Irene Daniels, of Unionville, Connecticut, May 7, 1891 Their children are: Marjory Irene, born at Cheshire, Connecticut, February 14, 1892; Earl Briggs, born at Clinton,

Connecticut, June 14, 1893; Dorothy, born at Clinton, Connecticut, September 11, 1894; Elmore Gordon, born at Astoria, Long Island, January 24, 1903.

SHILO BAPTIST CHURCH.

Shilo Baptist Church, situated at No 6 Union avenue, New Rochelle, New York, whose present pastor is Rev. William H. Slater, though it cannot count many years in point of age, is in a most satisfactory and flourishing condition. This congregation was organized July 22, 1898, the first pastor being Rev. J. A. Sumner, who was succeeded by Rev. Burke, who ministered to the spiritual welfare of the congregation until October 6, 1900, when he was succeeded by the present pastor, Rev William H. Slater. Up to the present time (1906) divine services have been held in a hired hall, but a lot has been purchased in Winthrop avenue, and it is the intention of the members to erect a church building in the very near future The regular number of worshipers is about two hundred, of whom about one hundred are members in good standing, and the average Sunday school attendance is about sixty The associations connected with the church are: Ladies' Building Society, Juvenile Society, and the Willing Workers' Club.

Rev. William H Slater was born in Charles county, Maryland, May 16, 1866 He is a son of John H and Clora Slater, the latter deceased. He came to New York city in early boyhood and attended the public schools of this city. His classical and theological education was obtained under able private tuition He was ordained to the ministry in Newark, New Jersey, November 5, 1901, and the present is his first pastorate Since he has taken charge of this congregation the membership has increased rapidly and there is a spirit of emulation in the congregation which has helped greatly to place it upon its pres-

GENEALOGICAL AND FAMILY HISTORY 285

ent satisfactory footing Rev. Slater is president of the Baptist Ministers' Conference and is connected with the following associations: Boyer Lodge, No. 1, Free and Accepted Masons, being chaplain of this lodge; past noble father of the Grand United Order of Odd Fellows of America; past supreme officer of the Ancient Order of Sons and Daughters of Moses; Eastern Star Lodge; Alpha Chapter; past ruler of Grand United Order of Gallilean Fishermen

Rev. Slater married, September 17, 1889, in New York city, Rebecca Lewis, and they have had five children, four of whom died in childhood, the only one now living being Ethel P.

FOURTH CHURCH OF THE SEVENTH DAY ADVENTISTS.

The Fourth Church of the Seventh Day Adventists, which is located in the Miller building, Sixty-fifth street and Broadway, New York city, and which has held religious services there since the organization of the church, was called into existence by Elder James K Humphrey in December, 1902. The church has a membership of about fifty, and an average Sabbath school attendance of about thirty-five. Divine services are held every Saturday at half past nine and eleven in the forenoon; there are lectures on special Bible topics every Saturday evening, and two large Bible classes are held on Tuesday and Thursday evenings The associations connected with the church are: Young People's Society and Home Missionary Club.

Elder James K. Humphrey was born in Jamaica, British West Indies, May 7, 1877. He acquired his education, both classical and theological, in Jamaica, in a branch of the Regents Park College, of London, England. He also attended for one term the Seventh Day Adventist Academy in South Lancaster, and was found so efficient that he was put to work at once to lecture to both colored and white. He is an executive member of the Greater New York Conference, and officiates in the Second Church of the Seventh Day Adventists, in Brooklyn, New York, as well as in the Fourth Church of the Seventh Day Adventists. He was ordained in the Seventh Day Adventist denomination, September 29, 1906, before an imposing audience. There were several ministers present besides Bible workers. This denomination has its branches in all civilized and uncivilized countries, and the work of its missionaries is productive of much good. Elder Humphrey is an eloquent, fearless, convincing preacher, and is devoted to the interests of his church and its members. He is also very much beloved wherever he goes and speaks.

MESSIAH BAPTIST CHURCH.

The Messiah Baptist Church, situated in Ashburton Place, Yonkers, New York, has for its present pastor Rev. Henry Arthur Booker. This parish was organized in 1875, and for the first three years divine services were held in a hired hall in North Broadway. The present church property was purchased and presented to the congregation in 1888 by the late James B. Colgate. It is a frame structure of pleasing and attractive exterior, the interior being suitably and comfortably furnished, and has a seating capacity of three hundred and fifty persons. The membership roll contains one hundred and sixty names, and there is an average Sunday school attendance of eighty. The associations connected with the church are: Ladies' Home and Foreign Mission Society; Young People's Progressive Literary Society; and the Baptist Young People's Union. It also has a junior and senior choir.

Rev. Henry Arthur Booker, the present incumbent of the above named church, was born in Amelia county, Virginia,

April 15, 1868. His early education was acquired in the public schools of his native town, and he came to the city of New York in 1888. He studied for a time under the private tuition of Professor Scott, of Kissick's College, Brooklyn, New York, and then attended for some time the high school of Babylon, Long Island. Subsequently he studied theology under the preceptorship of Rev Dr. W. B. Primm, then pastor of First Baptist Church of Babylon. He was ordained to the ministry in March, 1897, in Bethany Baptist Church, Brooklyn, New York, and remained pastor of the Ebenezer Baptist church, Babylon, Long Island, working zealously until 1900. At that time he received a call to become pastor of the Messiah Baptist church, Yonkers, New York, where his excellent work has been productive of a vast amount of good. Since he has taken charge of this parish there has been a very perceptible increase in the membership and attendance, both at the Sunday school and church services, and the parish is in a very flourishing condition. Rev. Booker is a fluent and convincing preacher and carries the hearts of the audience with him throughout his discourse He is also the corresponding and field secretary of the New York Colored Baptist State Convention, which responsible position he fills with perfect satisfaction to that body and credit to the denomination.

FOURTH REFORMED DUTCH CHURCH.

The Fourth Reformed Dutch Church is one of those religious institutions which, beginning with a small number of worshipers, constantly and steadily advances to a larger attendance, as the good work done becomes more and more apparent. This church was organized in May, 1858, by a missionary of the American Foreign Christian Union, the congregation holding their first services in a private dwelling in Seventh avenue, between Twenty-seventh and Twenty-eighth streets. Here they remained for about one and a half years and then removed to Broadway, between Twenty-ninth and Thirtieth streets, where they held services in another private dwelling for another year and a half. They then removed to the school building of the Marble Collegiate Church on Twenty-ninth street, near Seventh avenue, where they remained for about six years, and then went to another private dwelling on Broadway, between Thirty-fourth and Thirty-fifth streets, remaining for about five years. In 1872 they erected a church building on Fortieth street, between Seventh and Eighth avenues, remaining there until 1903, when they removed to the present building, which was erected by the Marble Collegiate Church. The church is a brick edifice of pleasing exterior, and has a seating capacity of three hundred persons. The number of communicants is two hundred and fifty, and the average Sunday school attendance is one hundred and sixty. The church was dedicated December, 1903, the ceremonial being a very imposing and impressive one The services are held in both German and English to meet the needs of the class of which the congregation is composed. There has been but one pastor in this church since its organization

Rev. John H Oerter, D D., pastor of the Fourth Reformed Dutch Church, was born in Germany, October 15, 1831. He was educated in his native land, obtaining a thorough knowledge of the classics, and studying theology in the seminary of the Dutch Reformed Church and a seminary in New Brunswick, New Jersey. He was ordained in Warrenville, New Jersey, by the classis of Raritan, New Jersey, May, 1856, and appointed pastor of the German Church of Warrenville, continuing his ministrations in this congregation for two years He then received a call from the Fourth Reformed Dutch Church of New York, to which he responded, and has been the faithful and beloved

minister of that congregation, without intermission, until the present time (1906) Dr. Oerter celebrated the fiftieth anniversary of his ordination in May, 1906

He married, in Utica, New York, September, 1856, Frances T Dauer, and had five children, of whom two are now living: Samuel J, professor of music, organist of English Lutheran Church, and principal of private school in Utica; and Emma E, married Rev. Henry Nerger, and is organist of the church and a music teacher

ST. JOHN'S EVANGELICAL LUTHERAN CHURCH

St John's Evangelical Lutheran Church, which is located at 79-83 Christopher street, borough of Manhattan, New York, of which Rev. John J Young, D. D., is pastor at the present time (1906), is one of the most important bodies of that denomination. Before the advent of the white man upon Manhattan Island there seems to have been an Indian village where St. John's Church now stands. While the original settlers of Manhattan were members of the Dutch Reformed Church, there were, nevertheless, some Lutherans among them. This is evident from the fact that in 1649 there were enough Lutherans here to be called a "congregation." These enjoyed, however, few religious privileges as Lutherans At first they were permitted to have private services, but this permission was, however, withdrawn under Stuyvesant. The first Lutheran church was known by the name of Trinity It was erected in the year 1671 at the corner of Broadway and Rector street, the original building being a log house, which was later replaced by a substantial stone edifice, which was destroyed during the Revolutionary war. In 1805 the property was sold to the Trinity Episcopal Church Thus ended the once prosperous Dutch Lutheran

Church, known as Trinity, the first Lutheran church on Manhattan.

In the fall of 1855 meetings were held at the residence of Rev. A. H. M. Held in Allen street, the result of which was a new organization which received the name of "Die Deutsche Evangelisch Lutherische St. Johannes Gemeinde der Stadt New York." Rev. Held was elected pastor of the new congregation and the following members composed the first church council: John W. Addicks, H. Grote and H. Halbe, elders; T. Neander, A. G. A. Brunjes, John Rodenburg, J. Guth, G. Peyle, J. F. W. Decker, D. Knubel, W. Koster and C. H. Doscher, deacons; G. Albers, G. H. W. Neander, H. Schmidt, J. Heinsohn, W. Grabau, W. Tiemann, F. Stucke, W. Halbe and H. Metz, trustees. Mr. G. Albers was elected president, G. H. W. Nenader, secretary, and H. Schmidt, treasurer.

The first divine services of the newly organized congregation were held on the fourth Sunday in Advent, December 19, 1855, in Hope Chapel, Broadway. Rev. Dr. Pohlman, of Albany, New York, president of the New York Ministerium, officiated at this memorable meeting. After worshiping three months in Hope Chapel the congregation moved into the chapel of the New York University, Washington Square, which had been secured at one thousand dollars per year. At a council meeting held on October 14, 1858, a resolution was passed to hold a special meeting of the congregation on October 24, at which time it was proposed to purchase St. Matthew's Episcopal Church in Christopher street, between Bleecker and Fourth, Rev. Held presiding over the same. At a trustee meeting on November 19, the president was instructed to purchase the same for thirteen thousand dollars. Arrangements were at once made to dedicate the church on the fourth Sunday in Advent, December 19, 1858. Rev. C E F. Stohlmann, D. D., was invited to preach in the morning and Rev. Raegner in the evening. Bishop Manton Eastborn, of Boston, was also invited to take part. The unusual eloquence of Pastor Held drew large congregations to the church, which often taxed its utmost seating capacity, and he served the congregation as pastor until August 16, 1878, when he tendered his resignation, being then in the seventy-second year of his age. It appears that during Rev. Held's ministry the following pastors acted as assistants to him at various and generally brief periods: Revs. Meinke, Wirtz, Behrens, Buttner and H. D. Wraage.

In 1860, a little more than one year from the time that the present church property was acquired, steps were taken to open both a Parochial and Sunday school in connection with this church. A small dwelling in the rear of the present Sunday school building was purchased and the three floors converted into school rooms The Parochial school was named St. John's Academy, and it flourished under its first director, Peter W. Moeller, who also cared for the Sunday school In May, 1866, the Sunday School Teachers' Association was formed independent of the Parochial school, which finally closed in 1868. The Sunday school steadily increased in numbers and in 1904 there were sixty-nine teachers and seven hundred and twenty-five pupils. In 1868 the school had outgrown the old Academy building, and the following year it was taken down and another one provided, the new building being dedicated Thanksgiving Day, 1869. In 1885 the church council was again appealed to for more room; the project went forward and the present fine edifice was erected; two thousand three hundred and eighty-six dollars was raised by the sale of bricks by the children, which sum was added to the fund. The new house was dedicated Thanksgiving Day, 1886, and thus it will be seen that the school has had three buildings since first organized

On November 3, 1878, Rev A C Wedekind, D D, pastor of St James' Evangelical Lutheran Church, New York, was unanimously elected as Rev. Held's successor. He took charge of the congregation January 1, 1879. During his ministry many improvements were made in the church, and December 20, 1880, the twenty-fifth anniversary of the congregation was observed with appropriate services Failing health finally compelled him to resign on August 16, 1891 Rev G. F Behringer filled the pulpit from February, 1891, to October, 1892, as pastor ad interim, and Rev. C E. Weltner was assistant pastor and pastor ad interim from October, 1892, to September, 1893 These brethren did good work and their labors for the welfare of the congregation were highly appreciated.

The next one to assume the pastorate of the church was Rev G W. Enders, D D., of Christ's Church, York, Pennsylvania, who entered upon his duties October 1, 1892 By permission of the church council he appointed Rev Weltner as his assistant till he could move to New York and take full charge of the work. In the meantime some difficulties arose, which finally led the church council to declare, December 12, 1892, that the relations between Rev. Dr. Enders and the St John's Evangelical Lutheran Church were dissolved, and the congregation declared vacant. Messrs F. Van Axte and John G C. Taddiken were now sent to Richmond, Indiana, to see whether they could not induce Rev. John J. Young, D. D, pastor of St. Paul's Evangelical Lutheran Church, to come to New York, which he accordingly did He preached on April 9, 1893, was unanimously elected April 24, 1893, and entered upon his duties as pastor September 1, 1893. His first efforts were directed towards the liquidation of the debt resting upon the congregation, and through concerted effort this has been accomplished, and the church celebrated its fiftieth anniversary without one cent of debt. His ministry has been noted for quiet activity, harmonious progress and internal growth. In spite of the uptown movement and the great change that has taken place in that portion of the city during recent years, the church is on a firm footing and in a prosperous condition, both spiritually and financially. Rev. F. Brezinski, pastor of the Evangelical Lutheran Church, Turner's Falls, Massachusetts, entered upon his labors as assistant pastor September 1, 1901, and is still serving in that capacity. In addition to the Sunday school already mentioned there are connected with the church various organizations, namely: St. John's Social Union, organized in the year 1882; Young Ladies' Luther Alliance, organized in May, 1892; and the Woman's Home and Foreign Missionary Society, organized January 17, 1894.

Rev. John J Young, pastor of St John's Evangelical Lutheran Church, New York, was born in Rhenish Bavaria, Germany, September 13, 1846, son of John Michael and Eva Katherine (Kruker) Young. The death of his mother occurred April 6, 1851, in her native land, and in the spring of 1858 his father emigrated to this country, locating in Baltimore, Maryland, where he died June 3, 1895.

In 1862, the darkest period of the Civil war, John J. Young enlisted in the Union army as a teamster, was captured June 28, 1863, near Rockville, Maryland, but fortunately was paroled the following day. In the spring of 1864 he was transferred to the New York Engineers Corps and remained with them until the close of the war, being honorably discharged in June, 1865. At the date of his enlistment he had no English education, but he took up the study of the language, and at the time of his discharge could read, write and speak the English language quite well. Immediately after his discharge from the army he served an apprenticeship at the trade of baker, at the same time continuing his study of the language. In 1869 he entered the preparatory department of Gettysburg (Pennsylvania) College, and graduated from the collegiate and theological departments of that institution in 1877. His first charge as a pastor was the Granville charge, at Garrett, Maryland, where he remained until 1882. He was then transferred to Richmond, Indiana, as pastor of St. Paul's Evangelical Lutheran Church, where he remained until 1893, at which date he was appointed pastor of St John's Evangelical Lutheran Church, New York city, the duties of which he is acceptably filling at the present time.

Rev. John J. Young married, June 6, 1878, Louisa E. Messersmith, of Baltimore, Maryland, of German parentage. Their children are: Cora E., Eva C., and Paul Milton, a student at the Gettyburg College, the same which his father attended.

ANDERSON MEMORIAL REFORMED CHURCH.

The Anderson Memorial Reformed Church of Belmont, corner of Monroe avenue and Columbine street (or, as the new street names have it, Cambreleng avenue and East One Hundred and Eighty-third street), grew out of the Sabbath school work taken up at that point by the Reformed Church at Fordham. At first the children were brought in stages from Belmont to the Fordham Reformed Church. This was in 1886, and the following year cottage services were held during the winter. The first of these meetings was held at Mr. Vredenberg's house. The stages continued to run from 1886 to 1892, at a cost of two hundred and fifty dollars per year, John Claflin, son of H. B. Claflin, paying for one stage, and the other being paid for by the school and some benevolent persons. William Prime, a colored man, furnished the stages and carried the children to and from Fordham during the entire time they were used.

GENEALOGICAL AND FAMILY HISTORY

May 29, 1889, George Edgar Anderson, brother of Rev. William F. Anderson, pastor of the Reformed Church at Fordham, died. He was the moving spirit in the Sunday school and its superintendent. It was to perpetuate his name, as much as anything else, that a church was located at Belmont. His brother, the pastor of Fordham Church, secured the promise of three thousand dollars from the Domestic Mission Board of the Reformed Church, and beside this was able, by subscription, to raise four thousand seven hundred dollars. A lot was purchased for about half the sum raised, at the corner of Monroe avenue and Columbine street, in the autumn of 1891. At the same time preaching services were held in a new store building on Kingsbridge Road, near Third avenue, the first being held October, 1891, with one hundred present. The next January the congregation moved from the little store room to the large ground floor of Mr. Henecke's new store building, at the corner of Adams Place and Kingsbridge Road, for which they paid twenty-five dollars per month rent. Here upon the first Sabbath in January, 1892, they held their first Sabbath school, an afternoon school and an evening service being held from January, 1892, to Christmas Sunday, 1892, when the school and the people moved into their new chapel, built upon the rear of the lots purchased the year before. During this time the congregation had been in the charge of Rev. Benjamin F. Guille, of the Union Theological Seminary. May 28, 1892, contracts were signed by Rev. William F. Anderson and the builder, John H. Metzler, for the erection of a chapel to cost $4,500, and to be completed in October, 1892. The corner-stone was laid August 6, 1892, by Dr. Bourne. The builders did not complete the chapel until late in the winter, and the first service was held December 25, 1892. January 29, 1893, there were received into the church over forty members, and they at once organized what they voted to term the "Memorial Reformed Church of Belmont." They celebrated their first communion there March 19, 1893. Rev. William F. Anderson, the founder, died July 24, 1893, which sad event at first cast a deep gloom over the work of the church, but, recalling all of his words of advice, the membership went resolutely forward. At the date of entering the new building and the organization of the church, Rev. John Giffin was the minister in charge, although never formally installed. This engagement terminated December 21, 1893, and he was followed by Rev. A. D. D. Frazer, who, after about one year, resigned to go to China as a missionary. April, 1895, Rev. Joseph Gaston became pastor, serving until October 11, 1896. Then came C. S. Watson, a student, and Rev. W. D Perry, who served as supply until September, 1898, when Rev. James Boyd Hunter became the pastor of the church and as such still continues. The little Sunday school has grown from forty-two to over three hundred pupils; the original membership of the church has grown from forty-five to about two hundred.

For the past ten years the great obstacle to the growth of the church has been the grading of the streets in the neighborhood. This has entailed great hardships upon the residents, since the vicinity is composed of rock, requiring heavy blasting. All who could moved away, while the majority of those who remained have been impoverished by the enormous assessments levied by the city to pay for the street improvements. The church has had its heavy share of these assessments to pay, and has had a constant struggle to obtain assistance from benevolent-minded friends. It is a pleasant statement to make that these assessments on the church and parsonage are nearly all provided for.

WEST FARMS REFORMED DUTCH CHURCH.

West Farms Reformed Dutch Church was organized February 13, 1839, by the members of the Reformed church at West Farms, and of their original number five came from the Fordham Reformed Church. Their first pastor was Rev. George Bourne. Ground was purchased on the Boston road and the corner stone of a church laid September 11, 1839, and the superstructure was dedicated June 17 following. The total membership was then but thirty-three. The first pastor remained until 1842; November 14th of that year he was succeeded by Rev. Barnabas B. Collins, who ministered until April 8, 1845, and following him came Rev. John Simonson, who in 1852 was succeeded by Rev. P. H. Burghardt. He remained until 1855 and was succeeded by Rev. P. Van Wyke. In 1867 he gave way to Rev. Evert Van Slyke, who remained until 1871, and was followed by Rev. John Simonson, who remained pastor until 1881. The next pastor was Rev. Harlan Page Blair, who was succeeded by Rev. Joseph Bolton, who was succeeded by Rev. L. Curry Andrews. In 1896 he was followed by Rev. Joseph D. Peters, who in 1898 was succeeded by Herman C. Weber, who remained until the present pastor came in 1902. The seating capacity of this church is four hundred and fifty. A new church-house, or chapel, is in course of construction at this date It is situated on the corner of Prospect avenue and Fairmount place. Later it is designed to erect a church edifice proper at that point. The present membership is fifty-five. Two Sunday schools are maintained, with two hundred and nineteen enrolled. This is the second oldest Reformed church in the Bronx.

Rev. Mr. Hart was born in Neshanic, New Jersey, and educated at Rutgers College and New Brunswick Theological Seminary. He was ordained and installed June 26, 1902

GRACE EVANGELICAL LUTHERAN CHURCH.

Grace Evangelical Lutheran Church at 123 West Seventy-first street, New York city, as a parish was founded in 1886, by Rev J Miller. Services were held in a hall at the corner of Ninth avenue and Fiftieth street for two weeks, then held at a hall at Seventh avenue and Forty-ninth street for about one year and at two other places, Tenth avenue and Sixtieth street and at 108 Amsterdam avenue, up to March, 1890. While services were being conducted at the hall at 108 Amsterdam avenue, the church was served by the following pastors: J. C. Graepp, Rev. Goessling, Dr J. A. W. Hass. In the early part of 1890 the present edifice was purchased from St. Andrews Methodist Episcopal Church at a cost of $30,000. It was dedicated March 21, 1890. In December, 1895, Dr. Hass was succeeded by Rev. John A. Weyl. The church building is of stone and brick and easily seats five hundred persons. The auxiliary societies to the church are: The Ladies' Aid Society, Grace Guild, Luther League, the Dorcas Society and the Sunday school. During the last two years handsome memorial windows were presented by members of the church. Many improvements have been made by Rev. Weyl in and about the church property. The church membership has been doubled and the church debt has been reduced by one-half, entirely by freewill offerings.

The pastor, Rev. J. A. Weyl, was born in Kingstown, New York, where he acquired his education at the academy, then took a preparatory course at Wagner College, Rochester, New York, graduating with the class of 1890. He then attended the Lutheran Seminary at Philadelphia, from which he graduated in 1893. Immediately after he left college, he took charge of the church at Liverpool, New York, having been ordained at Canajoharie, June 18, 1893. There he remained until he was appointed to his present pastorate. He is a member of the Board of Directors of Wagner College, and of the Board of Foreign Missions of the Lutheran General Council.

ST MARK'S EVANGELICAL LUTHERAN CHURCH.

St. Mark's Evangelical Lutheran Church, located at Nos. 323 to 327 East Sixth street, New York city, has a congregation composed almost entirely of Germans. The parish was organized in December, 1847, by Rev A. H. M. Held, and the first services were held in a hall on Houston street. Afterward they were held in the Church of the Redemption, in Sixth street, between Second and Third avenues. The building now occupied by this congregation was erected in 1848 by the parishioners of St. Matthew's Church, and was dedicated June 4, 1848. It was leased by the congregation of St. Mark's Evangelical Lutheran Church in the same year, and in 1857 purchased by them for eight thousand dollars. Since that time services have been held continuously in this building. In 1887 an addition was made to the church building proper, giving better facilities for meeting purposes. In 1889 a parsonage was purchased at No. 64 East Seventh street. In 1893 a new organ was purchased. The fiftieth anniversary of the founding of this parish was celebrated in December, 1897, at which time the entire interior of the church was beautifully renovated. Until recently the services were conducted entirely in German, but during the last five years, the second, fourth and fifth Sunday evenings have been set aside for services in English. The building has a seating capacity of about eight hundred, and the membership is between five and six hundred. There is a parochial school connected with the church, which at one time numbered about three hundred pupils

It had been the custom of this church to have a yearly

excursion for the benefit of the Sunday school pupils and their friends On June 15, 1904, this excursion started as usual, with thousands of happy faces and light hearts, having chartered the steamboat "General Slocum" to carry them to the grove which was their destination. The ill-fated vessel had proceeded but a short distance when fire was discovered on board. The origin of this will, possibly, never be discovered, nor whether the captain displayed good judgment or not in not beaching the boat at once; the result was one of the most frightful catastrophes ever recorded. More than a thousand persons perished, the greater number being children. Previous to this disaster the attendance at the Sunday school connected with St. Mark's Church had been nearly six hundred; this terrible calamity reduced it to about two hundred and fifty. In the basement of the church there are afternoon classes for instruction in sewing, and also for religious instruction in the German language. The church is entirely free from debt. It has on a number of occasions lent its aid in founding other congregations. The societies connected with the church are as follows: The Ladies' Aid Society, which has done an immense amount of good in assisting poor German families, especially in the practical way of showing them how they may best help themselves; the Young People's Luther League; and a Missionary Society.

Rev. A M. H. Held, the founder of the parish, was born in 1806, in Holstein, Germany, where he was educated. He emigrated to America in 1847, was licensed to preach, and became assistant to Rev. D. Stohlman at St. Matthew's. In 1848 he was ordained and called upon immediately to found the parish of St. Mark's, in which he labored until 1855, when he resigned and founded St. John's church in Christopher street. He was succeeded in St. Mark's by Rev Herman Raegener, born in 1822, in Brunswick, Germany. He was educated in Germany and came to America in 1855, and was for a short time in charge of St. John's church in Newark, New Jersey. He became pastor of St. Mark's in 1856 and was ordained soon afterward. He remained with this congregation until 1882, when failing health compelled him to resign ministerial service He was succeeded by the present pastor.

Rev George C. F. Haas was born in 1854, in Philadelphia, Pennsylvania, and acquired his education in parochial schools and the University of Pennsylvania, from which he graduated in 1876. He studied theology in the Lutheran Theological Seminary at Philadelphia, Pennsylvania, and graduated from that institution in 1880. He was ordained at Lancaster, Pennsylvania, the same year and immediately came to New York and officiated as assistant pastor of St Mark's church, and after two years became sole pastor Under his able leadership the congregation is a thoroughly united one, and he is greatly beloved by all its members.

GERMAN EVANGELICAL LUTHERAN TRINITY CHURCH, U. A. C.

In 1839 a number of German Lutheran families, who had left the "Fatherland" on account of religious persecution, settled in the lower east side of Manhattan Island, the district formerly known as "Little Germany." After arriving in the country of religious liberty, they gathered at the respective homes of members and read a sermon, sang hymns and served God. This was the beginning of the German Evangelical Lutheran Trinity church, U. A C., of the city of New York. At times a sermon was preached to them by some visiting pastor, a German Lutheran. The number of members increasing, services were held in a hall at the junction of Houston and Second streets. In 1842 the congregation sent a call to the Rev.

Theodore Brohm, at Perry county, Missouri, where he lived among the Saxon immigrants, who settled there in 1839. This was the first pastor of the congregation; he arrived in 1843, in which year a congregation was organized called German Evangelical Lutheran Trinity, U. A. C. The congregation at that time numbered eleven voting members and some one hundred souls. Services were held in Second street, later in Stanton and lastly in Columbia street

As the congregation increased in membership, they desired a church house, and funds were raised for that purpose. A lot twenty-five by one hundred feet was purchased in Ninth street, near Avenue C, a modest house of worship was erected and in 1850 the first church was dedicated. The congregation being in a German neighborhood gained rapidly and soon was in a very flourishing condition

In 1858 the Rev. Brohm was called to St Louis, Missouri, and the Rev F. W. Föhlinger took charge. It soon developed that the church was too small for the number of people attending and the congregation looked for larger quarters. A church at Ninth street and Avenue B, belonging to a Methodist congregation, being in the market, was purchased together with the parsonage at seventeen thousand and five hundred dollars and dedicated in 1863. This is the church in which the congregation still worships

The Rev. Foehlinger being obliged to resign on account of ill health, Rev. Fred Koenig was called from Cincinnati, Ohio, and he came to New York in 1872, and labored faithfully until November, 1892, when he went to sleep in Jesus, mourned by the entire congregation In 1891 the congregation, seeing his failing health, called as assistant the Rev. Otto Graesser, who at the death of the Rev Koenig was called and took charge, continuing until the present day, the fourth pastor since the organization of the congregation. The congregation still takes a very active part in all church life and matters, and though the neighborhood has materially changed, is still in the old locality, holding its own and hopes to continue there for many years to come. It is the oldest congregation in the East allied with the German synod of Missouri, Ohio and other states, the largest Lutheran body in the world. The congregation has during the whole time since its organization, used the German language exclusively in its services, and the official language of all societies is German.

Trinity church has since 1843 also maintained a parochial school, in which religion, German and English as well as all the other branches of knowledge are taught by competent teachers. Hundreds of good citizens have annually gone through this school. Within the congregation there is a large Ladies' Society over fifty years old, a Young Men's Society organized in 1883, a Young Ladies' Society, a Young People's Society and a church choir, who all labor for the benefit of the congregation. A large Sunday school meets twice on Sunday at nine in the morning and two in the afternoon, being organized in 1863.

So "Ninth Street church," as it is generally called, looks back upon a long and successful history, and after sixty-three years of diligent labor in the cause of God, still upholds the banner of sound Lutheranism, is still a city and a beacon upon the hill and preaches the Gospel to many inhabitants of our cosmopolitan city.

Rev. Otto Graesser was born of German parents in the city of Buffalo, New York, December 7, 1864. At six years of age he entered the parochial school in his native city, remaining until confirmed, and at thirteen and one-half years entered public school, No. 12, from which he graduated in 1881. In

October of the same year he took up the classical course at Concordia College at Ft. Wayne, Indiana, and graduated therefrom in June, 1887 In September, 1887, he entered Concordia Seminary of the German Lutherans at Missouri synod, St. Louis, Missouri, and in 1890 graduated therefrom and accepted a call as assistant pastor of the German Evangelical Lutheran Trinity church, Ninth street and Avenue B, New York. In 1892 he took full charge of the congregation, as his predecessor had been called home, and is still in charge of said congregation.

ST. PAUL'S EVANGELICAL LUTHERAN CHURCH.

This now flourishing church, located at One Hundred and Eighty-first street, attached to the synod of Missouri, has grown out of a mission organized May 1, 1898, by the Rev. John Heck. At first services were held in private halls. Mr. Heck gathered a congregation and ministered with zeal and success until 1902, when he was succeeded by the Rev. Gustav Bohm, who remained until 1904, when, July 31, the present pastor, the Rev. Otto Herman Restin, was installed, and the church was established upon an entirely substantial foundation.

After services had been held in halls until 1903, the congregation rented a church edifice from a body of Episcopalians, and this Mr. Restin procured by purchase in the first year of his pastorate, at an outlay of $5,500. It is a neat frame building, with a seating capacity of about one hundred and fifty. The church numbers about three hundred communicant members, the average Sunday school attendance is about one hundred and fifteen, and there is a large class of pupils who assemble on Wednesdays and Fridays for instruction in the German language A Ladies' Aid Society and a Young Men's Society are efficient aids to church work

The pastor, the Rev. Otto Herman Restin, was born in

Prussian Germany, 1857. After taking a thorough classic course in the gymnasium, he came to the United States in 1880, and took up theological studies in Concordia College, Springfield, Illinois, from which institution he graduated in 1888, at the age of twenty-three years. He was ordained to the ministry at Phillips, Wisconsin, and immediately engaged in missionary work. In 1888 he was called to the pastorate of Trinity church in that place, and during his ministry there built up a flourishing parish and procured the erection of a substantial church edifice. In 1890 he moved to Ashland, Wisconsin, where he exerted himself most usefully and successfully, in the course of five years largely augmenting the church membership, also erecting a new church edifice, purchasing a parsonage and establishing a parochial school. In 1894 he accepted a call to the Church of the Holy Ghost at Bergholtz, Niagara county, New York, where he labored devotedly for a period of nine years. He then came to New York city, where for more than a year he' served at the Lutheran Emigrant Mission, at 8 State street, under the care of the synod of Missouri, and was called therefrom to the pastorate of St. Paul's church, as before narrated In the latter part of May he was recalled to the Lutheran Emigrant Mission and on June 1st he took up that work. In 1905 he was appointed emigrant missionary of the synod of Missouri, Ohio and other states as successor of the late Rev. S Reyl Mr. Restin is in the prime of life, entirely devoted to his sacred calling, and is giving most faithful performance to a work which is as important as it is exacting

WASHINGTON HEIGHTS EVANGELICAL LUTHERAN CHURCH.

Washington Heights Evangelical Lutheran Church, situated in West One Hundred and Fifty-third street, New York city, whose present pastor is Rev. Ernest A. Tappert, was organized as a mission in 1890 The early services were held in a hall hired for the purpose at the corner of One Hundred and Fifty-sixth street and Amsterdam avenue, and they were in charge of Rev. l. Ehrhart and Rev. Gustave Tappert, pastor and assistant pastor, respectively, of St. Paul's Evangelical Lutheran church in One Hundred and Twenty-third street. Much credit is also due to Messrs. Henry Gieshen and Herman J. Haendle, both deceased, through whose efforts the first Sunday school was established.

Rev Ernest A. Tappert took charge of the parish in August, 1895, the congregation having at that time but six members, and it is largely owing to his earnest and zealous labors that the church is now in its present flourishing condition. Three lots were purchased in June of the following year in West One Hundred and Fifty-third street, and the cornerstone of the present building was laid November 14, 1897, and the church dedicated March 6, 1898 It is not yet completed, but when finished will be an imposing brick edifice with free stone front, three stories in height, covering seventy-five feet by one hundred feet of ground, and with a seating capacity of about one thousand persons. The interior will be handsomely and suitably decorated. A commodious parsonage was built adjoining the church in 1904. The services are held entirely in the German language. The membership roll at the present time (1906) contains upward of five hundred names, and there are two Sunday schools having an average attendance of two hundred and fifty scholars. There is also a mixed choir of twenty-four voices. The organizations connected with the church are: Ladies' Aid Society, Young Ladies' Society, Young Men's Society, Sewing School, German Parochial School.

Rev. Ernest A. Tappert, the present incumbent of the above mentioned church, was born in the province of Hanover,

Germany, October 8, 1874. His entire education, including his theological studies, was acquired in the educational institutions of his native land. He came to the United States in July, 1895, and was ordained to the ministry in St. Paul's Evangelical Lutheran church in West One Hundred and Fiftieth street by Rev. C. Brenecke, Ph. D. He has been indefatigable in his efforts for the welfare of the church in his charge and his parishoners, and the fact that he possesses in the fullest measure the love and esteem of those for whom he labors is proof of their appreciation He is an eloquent and convincing preacher, and his own exemplary life is the best object lesson he could give those who look up to him.

He married, July 7, 1896, in Meriden, Connecticut, Else Veers, a native of Schleswig Holstein, Germany, and they have children: Elizabeth Anna Alwine, born April 25, 1897; Wilfried Karl Heinrich, April 11, 1899; Friedjof Detlef, December 18, 1900; Ingeborg Magdalena Dorothea, May 3, 1903.

CHURCH OF SAN SALVATORE.

The Church of San Salvatore, located at No. 359 Broome street, New York city, is in the very heart of the Italian community and is easily accessible to the Italians in the down town section of the city for many miles around. The services are entirely in the Italian language, the assistant vicar, Rev. Abraham Cincotti, being a native of Italy, and the needs and habits of the people are specially considered in every particular. The work of this church is under the auspices of the New York City Episcopal Mission, Rev. Edward E. H. Knapp being the vicar, and as above stated, Rev. Abraham Cincotti his assistant. A parish house is connected with the church, which furnishes a home for the various societies, etc., which are dependent upon it. Especial attention is paid to the work of these societies, instruction being given the old in the Italian language and to the young in English.

The congregation was organized about 1880, services being held in Grace chapel by Rev. William Stauter, who was the first rector. He was succeeded by Rev. A. Pace, who was the incumbent for a number of years, services being held in a church situated at southwest corner of Bleecker and Mulberry streets. Later they removed to Bleecker street, the former edifice having been torn down by the city to widen the present Lafayette street. The cornerstone of the actual building was laid in 1900 and it was dedicated in 1902 by Right Reverend Bishop Potter. Rev. Dr. Nelson was the successor of Rev. A. Pace, served three years and was succeeded by Rev. John Henry Watson, who ministered to the needs of the congregation until 1904, giving place to the present incumbent, Rev. Edward H. Knapp. The church has a seating capacity of eight hundred, and the average attendance at the Sunday school is about two hundred. There are three services on Sunday, holy communion and sermon with morning prayer at 11, Sunday school at 9, evening service at 7:30, and each Friday in lent at 7:30 p. m. The Italian work is entirely under the personal supervision of the assistant vicar, Rev. Cincotti, who preaches in both services in his native tongue. The membership roll contains three hundred names, and the parish is in a most flourishing condition. Organizations connected with the church are as follows: San Salvatore Mutual Aid Society, with a membership of ninety; clubs for boys, junior and senior; Girls' Friendly Society; Boys' Surplice Choir, forty members; Sewing and Cooking classes; a gymnasium for boys and girls, and a Bible class.

Rev. Abraham Cincotti was born in Italy, 1874, acquired his education there, and was ordained to the ministry at the age of twenty-two years. For a time he taught Latin, and in 1899 came to America and for a number of years was engaged in mission work in various parts of the state of New Jersey. He became associated with the work of the Church of San Salvatore, November, 1903, and since that time has been an active worker in its interests. He enjoys great popularity among the members of his congregation, and his quiet, ready sympathy has made him justly beloved.

ST PAUL'S EVANGELICAL LUTHERAN CHURCH.

This parish was organized in 1864. In the course of the same year the erection of a church building was begun The corner-stone was laid September 3, 1864, and the church was completed and dedicated April 30, 1865 The present church was built on the site of the old one, and is of very attractive exterior. It is of blue-white Florentine marble, Gothic in architecture, and the entire framework is of iron. It is built on a lot seventy-five by one hundred feet in extent; the interior height of the church is eighty feet; it has two towers, each one hundred and twenty feet high. The seating capacity is seven hundred and fifty persons; the communicant members are seven hundred and fifty; average German Sunday school attendance is four hundred and fifty; average English Sunday school attendance is three hundred and twenty-five The morning services are conducted in German and those of the evening in English. The societies connected with the church are: Church Council, twenty-four members; Ladies' Aid Society, numbering about seventy-six members; Senior Luther League, fifty-five members; Junior Luther League, seventy members; Martin Luther Society or Men's Club, about fifty members; Tabea Society for Misses. thirty-five members. The deaconess of the church, who renders much valuable assistance, is Sister Rosa Dittrich. The first regular pastor of the church, Rev. Büttner, served about one year. After the first church building was finished, the first pastor was Rev. Julius Ehrhart, who ministered to the spiritual needs of the congregation for fully thirty years, and was then succeeded by Rev. Dr. John A. W. Haas (now president of Muehlenberg College, Allentown, Pennsylvania), who remained in charge until June, 1904.

Rev. Frederick H. Bosch was born in Brooklyn, New York, August 8, 1870. Is a son of Henry and Dorette (Dreyer) Bosch. He acquired his early education in parish and public schools, and graduated from public school No. 25 in 1885. For the next three years he was engaged in a commercial business in New York. He entered the Wagner Memorial Lutheran College, Rochester, New York, in 1888, and graduated in 1892; then entered the Lutheran Seminary at Mount Airy, from which he graduated in 1895. He was ordained to the ministry in Brooklyn, New York, June 23, 1895, and on July 1st assumed charge of St. John's Lutheran church, Prospect avenue, South Brooklyn, where he labored zealously for nine years. During 1899, through his efforts, a new church was built for his congregation, and the membership of the church largely increased. He was called to pastor of St Paul's Evangelical Lutheran Church in April, 1904, but did not begin his active ministration there until August of the same year. He is an eloquent and forcible speaker, a brilliant scholar, and is more than ordinarily endowed with all of the essentials that are necessary to fit him for his chosen profession.

CHURCH OF ATONEMENT.

The Church of Atonement, Evangelical Lutheran in denomination, located at Edgecombe avenue and West One Hundred and Fortieth street, Rev. Frederick H. Knubel, pastor, is an outgrowth of St. John's Church, Christopher street, New York. The parish was incorporated January 21, 1897, by the present pastor, and services were held for a year at No. 2603 Eighth avenue. On May 10, 1897, the ground for the church was purchased, and the corner-stone of the building was laid October 31, 1897. In April, 1898, the first story of the building was completed and used for services. The upper part of the building was completed in April, 1904, and on April 3, Easter Sunday, the building was dedicated. It is made of Indiana lime-stone and brick, is Gothic in architecture, and has a seating capacity of seven hundred and fifty. The communicant membership is four hundred and seventy-five, the average Sunday school attendance is five hundred and fifty, and religious instruction is given to the children four afternoons of each week. The societies connected with the church are: Ladies' Aid, Senior and Junior Luther Leagues, Young People's Association, and Sunday School Association. The deaconess of the church is Sister Jennie L. Christ.

The pastor, the Rev. Frederick H. Knubel, was born in New York, May 22, 1870, son of Frederick and Anna (Knubel) Knubel His preliminary education was acquired in grammar school No. 3, from which he was graduated in 1883, after which he pursued a two years' course in the College of the City of New York. He then gave his attention to mercantile pursuits and continued along that line for a period of four years. In 1889 he began his studies for the ministry in the Pennsylvania College, from which he was graduated in the class of 1893. He then entered the Theological Seminary at Gettysburg, Pennsylvania, graduating therefrom in 1896, and for one and a half years thereafter continued his studies in Leipsic University. He was ordained in October, 1896, in St. John's church, New York, and at once entered upon the duties of founding his present parish He has been a devoted and conscientious worker, is well beloved by his people, and in addition to the care bestowed upon their spiritual needs, leads their thoughts to higher ideals on many subjects, and in this way makes of them better and nobler citizens.

CHRIST EVANGELICAL LUTHERAN CHURCH.

This parish was formed by the present pastor, the Rev. Herman Van Hollen, in March, 1897, and its history is inseparably connected with the narrative of his own life.

Mr. Van Hollen is of German ancestry, born in the province of Hanover, December 1, 1852. He received a most thorough classical education in the gymnasium, and took theological courses in the universities of Hanover and Saxony. March 22, 1878, being then in his twenty-seventh year, he was ordained to the ministry in the city of Hanover, and was at once appointed to the pastorate of the Deaconnesses' church, in connection with the institution of the same name, and served acceptably as such until 1896, covering the long period of eighteen years, only severing his connection with it to answer the call of the Apostolic Association to go to the United States to found a parish in that section of New York city where is now located the Christ Evangelical Lutheran Church After encountering opposition which would have proven unsurmountable by one of less determination and not entirely consecrated to his mission, he established his church upon a substantial foundation in 1897, and was happy in the dedication of the sacred edifice on March 27 of the same year. It is a brick edifice, neatly furnished, with a seating capacity of about four hundred. The work of the church is in larger degree among a poor class of the German population. A flourishing Sunday school is conducted for children, using only the German language, and another for those who use the language of the country A Ladies' Aid Society, working under the direction of the pastor, is doing excellent work in ameliorating the condition of the sick and distressingly poor. Owing to a lack of accommodation for the Young People's Association and the Sunday schools, an addition, ten feet wide by seventy-five feet deep, was built on the east side of the church in the spring of 1906, thereby giving ample accommodation to the increase in this branch of the church.

Mr. Van Hollen is credited with another excellent work, the establishment of the Association for the Relief of Indigent Germans in the Public Institutions of the City and State of New York, and of which he has been chaplain from its institution. This truly commendable organization has for its purposes: 1. To provide spiritual aid and regular church service for the German inmates of the public, penal, correctional and charitable institutions of the city and state of New York. 2. To ameliorate the condition of the German inmates of said institutions by material and moral aid. 3. To assist German inmates of such institutions after their discharge therefrom. 4. To provide suitable work and employment for them. 5. To exercise a supervision over the families of the German inmates of the said institutions, and to assist such families in case of extreme necessity These purposes have been most efficiently discharged, and the work of the association is recognized as placing it in the front rank of philanthropic institutions in the great metropolis, in character, if not in extent. To the church and association Mr. Van Hollen devotes his entire ability, and the people among whom he labors with such unselfish assiduity regard him as their chief and most devoted friend His residence is at 552 West Fiftieth street, between Tenth and Eleventh avenues, Manhattan.

Mr. Van Hollen married, in Hanover, Germany, June 29, 1890, Matilda Lomberg, and to this union was born seven children, three of whom died in childhood, and the four surviving are: William, a student for the ministry, now at Wagner College, Rochester, New York; Marica, Carl, Lydia.

EVANGELICAL LUTHERAN CHURCH OF THE ADVENT.

The Evangelical Lutheran Church of the Advent, situated at the northeast corner of Broadway and Ninety-third street, is a building finished in recent years. This parish was founded in 1896 by the present pastor, and is an offshoot of the old church of the Holy Trinity, now at the corner of Sixty-fifth street and Central Park West, of which Mr. Krotel was formerly pastor. The Church of the Holy Trinity was organized by him in 1868, and many of its members were formerly members of St. James, which was the oldest and up to that time the only English Lutheran church in the city of New York. From 1896 until the completion of the new church edifice services were held in halls The corner-stone of the new building was laid in 1900, and the church was consecrated in 1901. It is of brick with limestone trimmings, and the style of architecture is Gothic. It has a seating capacity of five hundred, and there are over three hundred communicant members. Two hundred and forty scholars attend the Sunday school. The services are conducted entirely in the English language. The societies are as follows: Ladies' Aid Society, Young People's Society, Missionary Society, Kindergarten and Sewing School.

Rev. G. F. Krotel, D. D., LL. D., who resides at No. 65 Convent avenue, this city, was born in the kingdom of Wurtemberg, Germany, in 1826. He came to this country when but four years old, with his parents, and they located in Philadelphia, Pennsylvania, where he acquired his education and studied for the ministry. He graduated from the University of Pennsylvania in 1846, and entered the ministry at Easton, Pennsylvania, in 1848.

His first pastorate was in Philadelphia, and afterwards he was located at Lebanon and Lancaster, returning to take charge of a congregation at Philadelphia. In 1864 he became one of the founders of the Theological Seminary at Philadelphia and a member of its first faculty. He is at present (1906) president of the board of the seminary. He has been president of the Evangelical Lutheran Ministerium of Pennsylvania, the oldest Lutheran Synod in America, and of the New York Ministerium, and has also served three terms as president of the General Council. In 1868 he came to New York to organize Holy Trinity Church, of which he had charge until 1895, when he organized the Evangelical Lutheran Church of the Advent, of which he is pastor at the present time During his pastorate of Holy Trinity church, that congregation established the Church of the Epiphany, now located in East One Hundred and Twenty-eighth street. In 1889 he was elected to the St. John's professorship in the Philadelphia Seminary, but, at the request of his people, declined. For the past ten years he has been editor-in-chief of *The Lutheran,* the official organ of the General Council of the Lutheran church.

THE EVANGELICAL LUTHERAN CHURCH OF THE HOLY TRINITY.

The Evangelical Lutheran Church of the Holy Trinity, Central Park West and Sixty-fifth street, was organized in 1868 by G. F Krotel, D. D. Soon after its formation a church building was purchased on Twenty-first street, between Fifth and Sixth avenues, known as Dr Bethune's Dutch Reformed Church, and in this building services were held until 1902. Dr. Krotel was for a quarter of a century the faithful pastor of this flock, and Sebastian Sommer, now deceased, was the organist, and Charles M. Adler, also deceased, the sexton for the same period of time. In 1896, Dr. Krotel was succeeded by Rev. C Armand

Miller, D. D., the present pastor. In February, 1902, the old church was sold, land for a new church purchased and a building at once commenced November 9, 1902, the corner stone was laid, and May 15, 1904, the new building was dedicated with appropriate ceremonies. During the construction of the church, services were held in the West Side Branch of the Young Men's Christian Association.

The present building is an imposing structure, built of Indiana limestone, the foundation being of granite. Its architecture is of the early Gothic type and the interior presents a very attractive appearance. The seating capacity is seven hundred. The membership of the church is seven hundred, with an average of two hundred and seventy-five in the Sunday school The church societies are the Ladies' Aid, Woman's Missionary Society, Luther League, Young Ladies' School, Young Women's Missionary Society, and Trinity Brotherhood. In 1902 a comfortable parsonage was provided adjoining the church. In connection with the church is a Mission Sunday school, held at Christ Lutheran church on West Fiftieth street by members from Holy Trinity Sister Rose Barbour, the Deaconess of Holy Trinity, is of great service as a helpmate to the pastor, giving her entire time to teaching week day classes for religious education and caring for the sick and poor of the parish. Visitors are much impressed with the attractive interior of this church, and it is said to be one of the finest of the many fine ones in New York city. It has a beautiful marble altar, given by the Young Ladies' Social Society of the congregation at a cost of $1,400. It also has a marble baptismal font, a very powerful and handsome organ, costing $10,000, and is beautifully illuminated by a fine system of electric lights. Prominent among the founders of Holy Trinity was Peter Moller, who founded the Wartburg Orphans' Farm School at Mt. Vernon

Rev. C Armand Miller, the present pastor of this church, was born in Shepherdstown, West Virginia, 1864, receiving his primary schooling at Staunton, Virginia, graduating from Roanoke College, Salem, Virginia, 1887, with the degree of Bachelor of Arts, and in 1892 received the degree of Master of Arts from the same college. In 1889 he graduated from the Lutheran Theological Seminary of Philadelphia. In 1903 he received the degree of Bachelor of Divinity from the Lutheran Theological Seminary of Chicago, and that of Doctor of Divinity from Roanoke College in 1904. He was ordained to the ministry in 1889 by the Southwest Virginia Synod His first pastorate was at College church, Salem, Virginia, where he labored faithfully for eight years, and in April, 1896, took charge of Holy Trinity as its pastor, since which time he has greatly endeared himself to his people. Dr. Miller is a member of the Southern Society, Virginians, and Quill Club. He is a member of the Board of Directors of the New York Federation of Churches. He is the author of popular works entitled: "The Way of the Cross" and "The Perfect Prayer."

ST. PAUL'S EVANGELICAL LUTHERAN CHURCH.

This parish was organized in 1881 by Rev. Hugo Richter, the first services being held in a private dwelling in One Hundred and Fiftieth street. About one year later a small frame church building was erected, with a Sunday school room in the rear, and services were held on these premises until 1898, at which time the church was sold to a Polish Roman Catholic congregation, and from May, 1898, until October of the same year, services were held in the homes of Messrs Schloman and Behrens on Prospect avenue The ground for the new church was purchased in 1897, and in March, 1898, excavation for the foundation of the church was commenced In July of the same year the cornerstone of the building was laid with appropriate ceremonies by the present pastor, and the church was dedicated October 23, 1898. At the same time the parsonage in the rear of the church was erected. The church frontage is of stone, and the side walls of brick. At present (1906) but one story has been completed, and it has a seating capacity of five hundred people. The communicants number five hundred. The Sunday school is in the rear of the church building, and there is an average attendance of five hundred in the German Sunday school, and of one hundred in the English. The services are conducted mainly in the German language. The pastors who have at various times had charge of the affairs of the church are as follows: Rev. Hugo Victor, from 1882 to 1892; Rev. Herman Rippe, 1892 to 1893; Rev. H. Reumann, 1893 to 1895; and then the present pastor. The church societies are: Ladies' Aid Society and Young Men and Young Ladies' Society.

Rev. Gustave H Tappert was born in Hameln, in the province of Hanover, Germany, February 10, 1872. His early education was acquired in the schools of his native town He studied theology in Kropp Seminary, Schleswig-Holstein, Germany. He came to America in 1892, and was ordained in Canajoharie, New York, June 11, 1893. From 1892 until 1895 he served as assistant pastor of St Paul's church, One Hundred and Twenty-third street, and since August of that year has ministered to his present parish, the name of which heads this sketch. During the eleven years of his pastorate, the congregation has been steadily increasing in numbers and prosperity, and Rev. Tappert enjoys the respect and love of the entire community.

EVANGELICAL LUTHERAN CHURCH OF THE EPIPHANY.

This parish was founded in 1880 by Rev. Dr. Krotel, the services being held for six years in what was then known as Parepa Hall, a building at the northeast corner of Third avenue and Eighty-sixth street, and which is now used for commercial purposes. The attendance steadily increased, and finally, through the efforts of the Christian Band, this congregation removed to Harlem and held services in the upper part of the old court house on One Hundred and Twenty-fifth street. About two years later they were able to purchase the present church and parsonage at 70-72 East One Hundred and Twenty-eighth street, together with a dwelling on the eastern side of the church from a Unitarian congregation. The church edifice is of brick of pleasing exterior, and has a seating capacity of three hundred. The number of members is two hundred and seventy, and the average Sunday school attendance is one hundred and seventy The societies connected with the church are: Ladies' Aid Society, Luther League, and the Epiphany Brotherhood, composed of the young men of the parish. A kindergarten is also conducted. The services are conducted entirely in English. The church is in excellent standing, and has a slowly but surely increasing membership and attendance The first pastor was Rev. D H. Geissinger, D. D , who ministered from 1880 until 1882. He was succeeded by F. F Buermeyer, D. D , who conducted services until 1891 Then came Rev J. W. Knapp, Ph. D., who filled the pastorate until 1902, when he was succeeded by the present incumbent

Rev. F. B Clausen was born in New York city, February 25, 1880. He was left an orphan when a very young child, and was reared at the Wartburg Orphan Farm School in Mount Vernon, New York. His preliminary education was acquired there, and he then attended Wagner College, in Rochester, New York, graduating as valedictorian of his class in the class of 1900; the Mount Airy Lutheran Theological Seminary, in Philadelphia, Pennslyvania, graduating with honors in 1903. He was ordained in St Mark's Lutheran church the same year During 1902 he occupied the pulpit of the Epiphany church, and immediately after his ordination was appointed pastor of the same, a position in which his services are highly appreciated. He is greatly beloved by his congregation, and is earnest in his endeavors to raise the spiritual tone of those in his charge.

EMANUEL EVANGELICAL LUTHERAN CHURCH.

This parish was organized at Easter, 1901, by the present pastor, the earlier services being held in a storage room at the corner of One Hundred and Thirty-fifth street and Brook avenue for about six months. They were then held in a hall at No. 628 East One Hundred and Thirty-sixth street until Easter of 1903. Ground for a new church was purchased in June, 1902, at One Hundred and Thirty-seventh street and Brown place. The lots cost fifteen thousand dollars, and the buildings will cost upwards of seventy thousand dollars. Building operations were commenced in October, 1902, and the corner-stone was laid in November of the same year The church was dedicated May 22, 1904, with appropriate ceremonies, the dedicatory sermon being preached by Rev. Dr. Hartman, secretary of the Board of Home Missions, of Baltimore, Maryland; the presentation address was by Rev. J. B Riemensnyder, president of the New York and New Jersey Synod; and addresses were made by various other Lutheran ministers. The church building is of marble, and at present (1906) is finished as far as the basement and first story are concerned. Work on the other portions of the building is being pushed as rapidly as possible. It has a seating capacity of three hundred, but can accommodate three hundred and seventy-five. The communicant members number two hundred and ninety-six, and there are four hundred and fifty names on the Sunday school roll. The services are conducted in the English language, and the organist is Fred Goering. The organizations connected with the church are as follows: Ladies' Aid Society, numbering about sixty-five members; Young People's Social Union, upward of one hundred members; Luther League, forty; Dramatic Club, forty-five.

Rev A. Arthur King, the present pastor of Emanuel Evangelical Lutheran church, was born in Easton, Pennsylvania, February 18, 1868. His early education was received in the Moravian school, Nazareth Hall, Nazareth, Pennsylvania, and this was supplemented by a course in Pennsylvania College, Gettysburg, Pennsylvania, from which he was graduated in 1891. He studied theology in the same college, and completed his course in 1894. Was ordained minister at the East Pennsylvania Synod, in session at Allentown, Pennsylvania, in the same year. His first appointment was as pastor of the First Lutheran church, in Glen Garden, New Jersey, where he labored actively and faithfully for seven years, and then received his call to the present parish, where he has become justly beloved and popular with all in the congregation. He is a forceful and convincing preacher, and his kind heart and sympathetic manner open all hearts to him. Under his guidance the parish is in a very flourishing condition.

BEREAN BAPTIST CHURCH.

Berean Baptist Church, whose present pastor is Rev Leonard J Brown, is located in Bergen street, Brooklyn, New York. This congregation was organized in 1851, Rev. Daniel Riece being the first pastor, and the services being held in a church building in Prospect place, near Utica avenue. The church became the property of the congregation about 1870, and they continued to worship in this building until it was destroyed by fire in 1892. For about one year following this disaster the services were held in Hawer's Hall in Bergen street. Five lots were purchased in 1893 and the present church edifice erected upon them. The corner stone was laid with appropriate ceremonies the following year by Rev. W. T. Dixon, D. D., and addresses were made, suitable to the occasion, by Rev. Dixon, Rev. D. C. Eddy and others, all eminent divines of the Long Island Baptist Association. The structure is of brick with brown stone trimmings, has a seating capacity of five hundred persons, a membership roll of over two hundred, and an average Sunday school attendance of two hundred and fifty. The organizations connected with the church are: Women's Christian Temperance Union, Willing Workers, Missionary Society, Young People's Union, and Progressive Relief Society. When Rev. Brown took charge of this congregation the membership had dwindled to such a low figure that it was practically out of existence. It is due solely to his indefatigable efforts, his personal labor in every field of the work, that it has been brought to its present flourishing condition. It was he who purchased land for the site of the present church, after the destruction of the former one by fire, and the new building was erected at a cost of twenty-five thousand dollars. From a membership of five souls at the beginning of his pastorate, the roll has been increased by over two hundred.

Rev. Brown was born in Amelia county, Virginia, 1851. During 1868 and 1869 he was an attendant at a country school, and in the following year came to Brooklyn, New York. His energy and enterprise were most remarkable, and it is due to his own strenuous efforts that he acquired a classical and theological education, attending schools and enjoying the advantages of private tuition. He was ordained in March, 1892, at the Concord Baptist church by delegates from all the churches of the Long Island Baptist Association, but had been regularly licensed to preach for two years previously. For fourteen years prior to this time he had been the superintendent of Concord church Sabbath school, and now for fifteen years has been the honored pastor of the Berean Baptist church. His simple, unaffected manner and sympathetic helpfulness in time of trouble have endeared him to the hearts of his congregation, and his most excellent sermons and exemplary life have been productive of the greatest amount of good. The edifice in which they worship is almost free from debt.

SEVENTH PRESBYTERIAN CHURCH OF JESUS CHRIST.

The Seventh Presbyterian Church of Jesus Christ was organized March 27, 1818, by Rev. Elihu W. Baldwin, D. D., in the home of William Badoe, and the first house of worship was located on Sheriff street, near Broome. In 1826 the cornerstone of the present church was laid and the church was dedicated May 6, 1827. It is the oldest Presbyterian building in New York city. It is built of brick, and has a seating capacity of one thousand. Dr. Baldwin was followed by Dr. E. W. Halfield, in 1835. During his ministry one thousand five hundred and fifty-six persons were added on confession. Rev. T Ralston Smith ministered to the congregation from 1856 until 1866, and was followed by Rev. Henry T. Hunter, D. D., who supplied the church two years. From 1868 to 1885 the Rev. Mr. Belland and Rev. Mr. Day officiated as pastors. In 1885 Rev. John T. Wilds was ordained and installed as pastor, and has continued longer in the pastorate of the church than any other. In 1895 Rev.

T. C. Hock became his associate The present membership is between three and four hundred. Two Sunday schools (one in German) are held each Lord's Day in the lecture room. The average Sunday school attendance is about three hundred and twenty-five. The pastor spends two hours each week with the young people preparatory to confirmation. The church is endowed and free from debt.

ELTON AVENUE METHODIST EPISCOPAL (GERMAN) CHURCH.

Rev. John Mueller, the present pastor of the Elton Avenue Methodist Episcopal (German) Church, was born in Germany, February 11, 1859 His preliminary and classical education was acquired in the institutions of learning in Saxony, Germany, and he began his theological studies under private tuition. He came to the United States in 1887 and completed his theological studies in the German Wallace Seminary in Berea, Ohio. After that he obtained an appointment in Brookville and Batesville, Indiana, where he was a zealous worker for a period of two years He was ordained to the ministry in Allegheny, Pennsylvania, in 1892, and then was appointed to a pastorate in Indianapolis, Indiana, remaining there four years, and in 1896 was called to take charge in Ironton, Ohio, where he remained until 1900 He was then transferred to the East German Conference and by them appointed to the Second German Methodist Episcopal Church, No 348 West Fortieth street, New York city, where he labored until April, 1906, when he was transferred to Elton Avenue Methodist Episcopal Church, Elton avenue and One Hundred and Fifty-eighth street. He is imbued with the true spirit of his work, and this together with his convincing, eloquent and forceful sermons, has endeared him to the hearts of his congregation.

CHARLES WAKEFIELD TARBOX.

Charles Wakefield Tarbox, who has been prominent in real estate circles during the past thirty years, and an important factor in the councils of the Democratic party in whose interests he has been an active worker, is a descendant of Miles Standish through the intermarriage of the Tarbox and Standish families, and on the maternal side, is a direct descendant of the Davenports, who were among the earliest settlers in Connecticut One of his direct ancestors on the paternal side was John Tarbox, who settled in Lynn, Massachusetts, about 1605; another was John Green, a resident of Quidnessett, Rhode Island; and still another, General Nathaniel Greene, whose fame was acquired during the War of the Revolution. One of the earliest direct ancestors of Mr. Tarbox on the maternal side was Paul Davenport, who settled in Connecticut, and whose brother, John Davenport, founded the Colony of New Haven. Among the other ancestors of Mr. Tarbox were Samuel Adams, who acquired fame during the troublous period of the Revolution, John and John Quincy Adams, second and sixth president of the United States, respectively.

Hiram Tarbox, son of Fones Whitford and Sarah (Spencer) Tarbox, was born in West Greenwich, Rhode Island, June 15, 1817. His boyhood days were spent in Connecticut and at the age of seventeen years he went to Lisbon, in that state, taking up his residence there with his uncle Hiram, for whom he had been named, and there learned the trade of watch-making. He removed from Connecticut to New York in 1844 and was for many years engaged in the manufacture of watches in Maiden Lane in that city, in connection with his uncle, who also had a watch factory in Geneva, Switzerland, and was subsequently connected with Tiffany, of New York. Mr. Tarbox had a natural genius for mechanics, and invented some of the most intricate and delicate tools in use in the watch-making trade. He introduced many improvements along this line, his first invention being perfected when he was but sixteen years of age. He perfected his last invention when he was almost eighty-seven years old, but his untimely death rendered it impossible to patent this At the first World's Fair, held in the Crystal Palace in Forty-second street, he exhibited many of these inventions, which were totally destroyed by the fire which laid low this building in 1856 He was engaged in the watch-making business alone until 1850, when he associated himself with John H Giffen, with factory and office at the northeast corner of Broadway and John street, the present site of the Chatam National Bank This business was merged into that of the Waltham Watch Company, whose great operations were made possible by Mr. Tarbox, who originated the machine process of watch movement construction He then engaged in the manufacture of watch cases and chronometers and continued to conduct this until his retirement from active business life about 1890.

Mr Tarbox was a man of great energy and executive ability, two qualities which are not often found united in one person to such an extent as in his case. He was one of the prime factors in making Upper New York what it has become. He, with about fifty men of similar mind, purchased a large farm in Upper Morrisania in 1848, and later had the name changed to Tremont. Through the instrumentality of Mr. Tarbox the National Government established a postoffice at this place and he was appointed to the position of postmaster in September, 1861, by Hon. Salmon P. Chase, then secretary of the treasury under Abraham Lincoln. Thirteen years later this section was annexed to the city and county of New York, and the postoffice became a branch office with Mr. Tarbox as its superintendent.

Altogether he was at the head of this department for a period of twenty-two years. He was one of the founders of the Republican party in that section of the city, and furnished the lot on which their meetings were held when the party first assumed its commanding position during the stirring times of the Civil war. He helped organize a fire department, a free library, a stage line, and was one of the organizers of the Morrisania and Harlem Steamboat Company and one of the officers of that corporation. He selected a site near the New York and Harlem Railroad depot for his home, and on this he lived for more than fifty years, in all that time constantly spending large sums in the improvement of his property and the vicinity. This property was that purchased from Gouverneur Morris in 1848. Mr. Tarbox was one of the charter members of the West Farms Baptist Church and for years, and up to the time of his death, was one of its deacons. Personally he was a man of genial and courteous manner and was as much beloved in his own home as he was admired and esteemed by all his friends and acquaintances. Man of influence as he was, many of the troubles and trials of his fellow citizens were brought to his personal attention, and his charity, kindness of heart, and readiness to lend a helping hand wherever it was in his power to do so will not soon be forgotten by the recipients of his bounty. His acts of charity were many and always performed in an unostentatious manner. With his death, which occurred in July, 1904, the last of the pioneers of the fifties in Tremont has passed away.

He married, 1839, while living at Parkersville, Connecticut, Mary Davenport Clark, born at South Canterbury, Connecticut, July 30, 1818, died September 15, 1897, daughter of Seth and Abigail (Davenport) Clark, of Connecticut. The Davenport-Clark homestead in Connecticut, which is now almost three hundred years old, is at present in the possession of a son of Mr. Tarbox Mr. and Mrs. Tarbox had children: 1. Mary C., well known in educational circles 2 Hiram Thomas, who has a fine Civil war record, and has been a noted structional engineer for the past thirty years, is a resident of Boston, Massachusetts. He was engaged in the construction of the Eads bridge, at St Louis, Missouri, the most noted bridge of its class and day. 3. Sarah E., widow of Joseph H. Lee, was before her marriage also identified with educational interests. 4. Charles Wakefield Tarbox.

Charles Wakefield Tarbox, second son and fourth and youngest child of Hiram and Mary Davenport (Clark) Tarbox, was born in New York city, June 8, 1850. His education was acquired in the public schools of the city of his birth and he was graduated from them. Upon its completion he entered upon a business career with the firm determination to owe everything to his own abilities and unaided efforts, and this spirit is the keynote to his entire character. He took up the study of engineering alone, mastered all its difficulties, and made it a stepping stone to success. He was a born inventor, having evidently inherited the genius of his father in this direction, and since the age of sixteen years has perfected and patented many devices. Up to the present time upward of one hundred and fifty electrical, mechanical and other appliances have been devised and patented by him He commenced the manufacture of stationery in 1874, locating his business in Bleecker street, New York city, and continued this for about six years. He then turned his attention to real estate matters, thinking there was a great future in that direction for a practical business man, and since that time has been very profitably engaged in that line of business He has figured largely as city appraiser in condemnation proceedings He has one office at No. 261 Broadway, and another at No 4160 Park avenue, borough of the Bronx He is a director on the Provident Savings & Loan Investment Company of this city and has been connected with several other financial institutions He is a member of the New York City Democratic Club, and although he has been prominent in supporting the political views of his party, has never held public office, though frequently tendered nomination He is a member of the Schnorer Club of Morrisania and of the Fordham Club of New York.

Mr. Tarbox married, June 12, 1889, Margaret Behrens, daughter of Henry J and Margaret (Lattimer) Behrens, and they have one child: Elsa Davenport Tarbox

www.ingramcontent.com/pod-product-compliance
Lightning Source LLC
Chambersburg PA
CBHW071152300426
44113CB00009B/1173

www.ingramcontent.com/pod-product-compliance
Lightning Source LLC
Chambersburg PA
CBHW071151300426
44113CB00009B/1164